THE GHOSTS OF
THE PAST

THE GHOSTS OF THE PAST

Latin Literature,
the Dead,
and Rome's Transition
to a Principate

BASIL DUFALLO

THE OHIO STATE UNIVERSITY PRESS
Columbus

Library of Congress Cataloging-in-Publication Data
Dufallo, Basil.
  The ghosts of the past : Latin literature, the dead, and Rome's transition
to a principate / Basil Dufallo.
    p. cm.
  Includes bibliographical references and index.
  ISBN-13: 978-0-8142-1044-4 (cloth : alk. paper)
  ISBN-10: 0-8142-1044-9 (cloth : alk. paper)
  ISBN-13: 978-0-8142-9124-5 (cd-rom)
  ISBN-10: 0-8142-9124-4 (cd-rom)
  1. Latin literature—History and criticism. 2. Dead in literature. I. Title.
  PA6029.D43D84 2007
  870.9'3548—dc22
2006018337

Paper (ISBN: 978-0-8142-5626-8)
Cover design by Janna Thompson-Chordas.
Text design by Jennifer Shoffey Forsythe.
Typeset in Adobe Minion

FOR C. A. S. AND W. S. D.

CONTENTS

LIST OF ABBREVIATIONS

For abbreviations of ancient authors and works I have followed the lists in *The Oxford Latin Dictionary*, edited by P. G. W. Glare, and Liddell, Scott, and Jones's *A Greek-English Lexicon.*

AC	*L'antiquité classique*
AJA	*American Journal of Archaeology*
AJP	*American Journal of Philology*
ANRW	*Aufstieg und Niedergang der römischen Welt*
BICS	*Bulletin of the Institute of Classical Studies*
CA	*Classical Antiquity*
CIL	*Corpus Inscriptionum Latinarum*
CJ	*Classical Journal*
CP	*Classical Philology*
CQ	*Classical Quarterly*
CW	*Classical World*
FGrH	F. Jacoby, *Die Fragmente der griechischen Historiker*
HSCP	*Harvard Studies in Classical Philology*
ILLRP	A. Degrassi, *Inscriptiones latinae liberae rei publicae*
ILS	H. Dessau, *Inscriptiones latinae selectae*
JRS	*Journal of Roman Studies*
LCM	*Liverpool Classical Monthly*
MAAR	*Memoirs of the American Academy in Rome*
MDAI(R)	*Mitteilungen des Deutschen Archäologischen Instituts, Römische Abteilung*
MH	*Museum Helveticum*
NAWG	*Nachrichten der Akademie der Wissenschaften in Göttingen*
OLD	*Oxford Latin Dictionary*
ORF	E. Malcovati, *Oratorum Romanorum fragmenta liberae rei publicae*
PCPS	*Proceedings of the Cambridge Philological Society*
QUCC	*Quaderni urbinati di cultura classica*

RCCM	*Rivista di cultura classica e medioevale*
REL	*Revue des études latines*
RevNum	*Revue numismatique*
RhM	*Rheinsiches Museum für Philologie*
SC	*Syllecta Classica*
SIFC	*Studi Italiani di filologia classica*
SO	*Symbolae Osloenses*
TAPA	*Transactions of the American Philological Association*
ZPE	*Zeitschrift für Papyrologie und Epigrafik*

ACKNOWLEDGMENTS

ALTHOUGH this book is much changed from its original form as a dissertation, I owe many, many thanks to those who oversaw its inception: Katherine King, Bob Gurval, Carole Newlands, Sam Weber, and especially Tom Habinek, whose encouragement and guidance at key moments throughout the entire process have been essential. I have also benefited much from the generosity of Tony Corbeill, who offered comments on the dissertation manuscript, and Jay Reed, who read drafts of individual chapters during the process of revision. William Batstone and the anonymous readers for The Ohio State University Press contributed greatly to whatever the final text possesses of cohesiveness and readability. Special thanks to my editor, Eugene O'Connor, for his careful, practical criticism, as well as to Chad Schroeder.

Part of chapter 1 was first published in *TAPA* 131 (2001): 119–142 and part of chapter 4 in *Helios* 30 (2003): 163–79. My thanks to Steve Oberhelman for permission to reprint the latter. Early thoughts on what became the basis of chapter 2 appeared in C. Auvray-Assayas, ed., *Images romaines,* Actes de la table ronde organisée à l'École normale supérieure (24–26 octobre 1996), Études de Littérature Ancienne, Tome 9 (Paris, 1998) 207–19. I thank Lucie Marignac for permission to reproduce this.

I am grateful to the Walter D. Foss Endowment at The College of Wooster for its support of valuable research time at the Institute of Classical Studies, London.

Finally, I wish to thank my wife, Catherine Sanok, not only for the many hours of time she spent reading and discussing drafts, but also, more profoundly, for her confidence and love. As she knows, this book is in some way a record of our deep intellectual kinship and ongoing conversations.

The Dead as the Living

Nunc age, Dardaniam prolem quae deinde sequatur
gloria, qui maneant Itala de gente nepotes,
inlustris animas nostrumque in nomen ituras,
expediam dictis, et te tua fata docebo.

Come now, I will set forth in words what glory follows the Dardanian line,
what descendants of the Italian race await, distinguished spirits soon
to take up our name, and I will reveal to you your fate.
—Vergil, *Aeneid* 6.756–59

T HERE IS hardly a purpler patch in Vergil's *Aeneid* than the underworld "Review of Heroes" that closes Book 6. It is so much a classic, however, that we may forget what is so strange about it: not only the perspectival play that W. H. Auden labeled "hindsight as foresight," but also, specifically, the fact that the dead here imitate the aristocratic funeral procession designed by the living. Trying to imagine a modern writer's depiction of a state funeral set in heaven (or hell) enforces the point. On reflection, this aspect of Vergil's ghostly procession prompts a more general question about the "Golden Age" Latin literature of the first century BCE. Why do the dead in these texts act so much like the living? Elsewhere in the *Aeneid,* we see ghosts handing down Troy's sacred objects and engaging in philosophical discussion; we are asked to imagine them taking an interest in love affairs and city-founding. In other authors of the period, we find dead ancestors reproaching their living descendants for aberrant sexual conduct, dead statesmen returning to take part in contemporary politics, dead wives and mistresses addressing courtroom-style speeches to their surviving partners. We cannot ascribe such scenarios simply to the Romans' well-known obsession with ancestry and the emulation of illustrious Romans of the past, *imitatio maiorum.* Indeed, at issue here is not only imitation of ancestors but also something we might paradoxically term *imitatio posteriorum:* the

1

dead's "imitation of those who come after." This peculiarly Roman fantasy never manifests itself to the same extent in later Latin literature and there is no precedent for it in Greek literature, where, conversely, the activities of the dead are usually imagined in far less elaborate terms.

In this book I explain the Roman dead's literary life by developing a view of Latin literature's interaction with Roman culture. The evocation of the dead, I argue, is a means for Roman authors of the late Republic and early Principate to engage strategically with Roman cultural performances centered on the dead and their world—not only the aristocratic funeral reimagined in *Aeneid* 6 but also a number of others. The technique has a changing political purpose specific to Rome's transition from Republic to Principate, hence its prominence in the authors of the first century BCE. Republican literature, that is, draws upon this cultural context for the ends of political competition among the clan-based Roman elite, while the literature of the new Principate seeks to restage the republican practices so as to recuperate them for Augustan society, in which the earlier type of intra-elite competition was no longer feasible.[1]

I have derived my understanding of literature's interaction with cultural performance from modern performance theory. Two concepts above all are key to my discussion. First, *orature,* a term itself borrowed by Joseph Roach from the Kenyan novelist and director Ngugi wa Thiong'o. For Roach, orature signifies the interdependence of the oral and the literary by foregrounding the degree to which the two have produced one another interactively over time. Since all ancient literary texts were commonly voiced by their readers, whether alone or before an audience, the idea of viewing literature as a script for performance—and hence a record of it as well—is already at home in Roman studies. But orature follows cultural forms such as "gesture, song, dance, processions, storytelling, proverbs, gossip, customs, rites, and rituals" from body and voice to text and back again, without positing the former as originary or the latter as a mere artificial reproduction of it. The oral is, in all but truly preliterate societies, "produced alongside or within mediated literacies of various kinds and degrees" and the literary is always already refashioning it, reframing it, to the extent that its traces in literature "may be usefully studied under the rubric of performance."[2] Literature tends to imply orature: the performance that either occasions is, for Roach, "surrogation," in the sense that "performance stands in for an elusive entity that it is not but that it must vainly aspire both to embody and to replace."[3] As the word "vainly" here intimates, Roach views this as a fundamentally anxious activity, dogged by emotions "ranging from mildly incontinent sentimentalism to raging paranoia,"[4] and riven by its simultaneous grounding in the corporeal and the incorporeal, the present and the past, the self and the other. Yet it is precisely by going beyond conventional categories that Roach's concept of orature facilitates the reading of Latin literary texts, with their curious blend of ambition and nostalgia, universality and local knowledge. This implementation of patterns drawn from the wider field of cultural activity is what interests me here.

The interdependence of orature and literature is a focal point in Roach's study of circum-Atlantic culture with special reference to London and New Orleans, sites linked by their common colonial history in the late seventeenth and eighteenth centuries. But the example of orature Roach uses to illustrate its historical importance—one chosen from the contemporaneous events of the American Revolution—resonates closely with my own emphasis, in the opening chapters of this study, on Ciceronian oratorical texts that both recreate or imagine an original performance and refer to a broad context of performance traditions, some far outside the official civic culture sponsored by the Roman elite. The American Declaration of Independence, Roach notes, was in fact a text meant to be declaimed: a script for oratorical performance.[5] Jefferson himself, moreover, characterized its elocutionary force as comparable to that of the expressive speech associated with Native Americans and Africans, performances that would seem, at first, vastly removed from the primal utterance of the nascent American colonial power. For Roach, "that the chant of the Declaration of Independence" thus "calls on the spirits of Jefferson's Anglo-Saxon ancestors to authorize his claims" renders it comparable in turn to still other seemingly disparate performance events, such as a freedom ritual of the Haitian Revolution, an act of political empowerment accomplished through both voodoo incantations and more familiar kinds of prayer: spoken words, which the revolutionaries "then took the trouble to write down."[6] Examining Cicero's published orations, we will see him summoning ancestral figures through techniques that point similarly to the magical and the arcane while advancing judicio-political agendas of the most established and recognizable sort.

My second key concept is Richard Schechner's *restored behavior,* a view of performance that, while it informs and is to some degree subsumed by Roach's own views, nevertheless sets forth performance's surrogative nature with an emphasis especially appropriate to the period of the early Augustan Principate, the focus of my last two chapters. For Schechner, performance "has at its core a ritual action,"[7] a restoration of behavior, which may manifest itself in various fashions and to various degrees, depending on the type of mimesis involved. At a basic level, a performer engages in an imaginative extension (and so, in a limited sense, a restoration) of his or her own particular self: "I" becomes "someone else." At an extreme, performance may pretend to the exact duplication of historical situations or events, with the understanding that the performers are *doing* something in their world by bringing aspects of the past alive. The reproduction not only of the event itself but also of a type of action, of tradition or cultural history, becomes as important as the verisimilitude of the represented acts.[8] Performance, in Schechner's view, is not strictly reproductive of past actions but is nevertheless strongly predicated on some understanding, conscious or unconscious, of repeated, customary, or habitual *types* of actions—behaviors—which it transforms according to the concerns of performer and audience. What is ultimately at stake in all such rituals is identity, whether of the performers, their audience, or an entire community.[9]

A notion of cultural restoration is essential to the rise of the Augustan Principate, the chief historical event underlying the poetry of Propertius and Vergil I treat in chapters 4 and 5. It may be that the evidence does not permit us to speak of the "restoration of the Republic" unless in terms of the attempted moral restoration that left such a strong impression on Augustus' contemporaries.[10] Together with moral renewal, however, Augustus encouraged a flowering of literature and the arts ("high culture" in the form of poems, historical treatises, paintings, sculpture, architecture, etc.), while carefully monitoring less specialized types of cultural activity (assemblies, trials, funerals, and the like) for signs of their conformity to the new ethos. Augustan literature responds to the idea of sweeping change in both morality and cultural practice and uses its own imaginary universe to model such change, as Vergil does in his version of ancestral funeral ritual. Sensitivity to the performance of Augustan poetry as restored behavior can thus deepen our appreciation of its ties to the wider culture. Augustan authors, that is, tap into something basic to performance—its ritual refashioning of culture itself—and exploit it as an intrinsic part of their creative endeavor.

This book close-reads one republican and two Augustan authors for the mimicry of cultural performance explaining the dead's characteristically Roman behavior in their work. Although the actual performances of the Romans are, of course, entirely lost to us, we are well-informed enough about their fundamentals for historical reconstruction to serve as the basis of such an approach.[11] The aristocratic funeral procession to which Vergil alludes in *Aeneid*, Book 6 made a deep and lasting impression on Roman viewers.[12] Before the body walked actors wearing wax masks (*imagines*) of the deceased's illustrious ancestors. The actors were chosen for their physical resemblance to the actual personages they portrayed, and were accompanied by props evocative of political achievement, such as the *fasces*. Music and dancing accompanied the procession, and could take the form of parodic behavior by dancers dressed as satyrs. Hired mourners were also in attendance, magnifying the mourning of the family, which would officially last until the ninth day after the funeral. Young men were especially encouraged to watch the proceedings, so as to be fired by ambition to imitate the achievements of the noble dead, but the admiration for distinguished Romans of the past was something in which all present could share.

Having reached the forum, the procession stopped and the masked actors, together with the corpse, formed an audience at the *rostra* (speaker's platform), which a member of the family, preferably a son of the deceased, ascended to deliver the *laudatio funebris* (funeral oration). The *laudatio*, unadorned in style, included lists of offices and achievements, not only of the person being buried but the earlier family members as well. Upon completion of the *laudatio*, the body was taken to the gravesite, typically in a family burial ground along one of the main roads leading out of the city, and the final rituals of interment were carried out. The grave was marked with an inscription meant to be recited aloud. On the ninth day the family returned to the gravesite to mark the completion of full mourning.

By the late Republic, theatrical games would regularly accompany a large funeral. Some of the plays put on at such events were probably historical dramas (*fabulae praetextae*) depicting the achievements of the deceased or famous ancestors, since the *praetexta* could bring the full resources of the stage to the funeral's emphasis on *res gestae* and the actors' performances in the *pompa funebris*.[13] But Latin comedies as well as tragedies modeled on the mythological theater of the great Greek dramatists Aeschylus, Sophocles, and especially Euripides were also popular among Roman audiences. The staging of Hellenic tragedy in particular, whether at funerals or on other occasions, has a strong claim to be regarded as a practice "centered on the dead," since, with its frequent use of ghosts and harrowing Furies, it offered a vivid, if troubling, way for audiences to imagine the interaction of the dead and the living, whatever the actual beliefs of any particular audience member.[14] Cicero makes it clear that the Furies repeatedly turned up as characters in the plays of his day (*Rosc. Am.* 67; *Pis.* 46) and our fragments of Roman mime and tragedy preserve ghost-scenes as well.

The republican aristocratic funeral developed into the funerals held for dead emperors, which, in spite of their importance as cultural events, occurred outside the time-frame of this book. Julius Caesar's funeral and posthumous glorification, however, which occurred within this time-frame, were key to this transition. Although the surviving accounts present a confusing picture, we can be relatively certain of some basic components. M. Antonius acted as Caesar's *laudator* (probably to underscore his claim to be Caesar's heir), delivered an unconventional funeral oration, and led ritual laments. A man acted the part of Caesar himself and a movable wax effigy of Caesar's wounded body was displayed for the benefit of the crowd. The ceremony ended in the unplanned cremation of the body in the Forum. After Caesar's funeral he became the object of ostentatious religious observances on the part of Antonius, Octavian (the future Augustus), and a figure known to historians as Pseudo-Marius. These events and their timing are central to my argument in chapter 3 and I will recount them in detail there.

The aristocratic funeral with its associated events was a public spectacle of the highest order. More private and less spectacular was the actual cult of the *di Manes* (spirits of the dead), for which families gathered at the grave and in the home to feast, offer prayers, and perform other religious observances. The principal festivals of the dead were the *Parentalia* (February 13–21), which centered on the grave and culminated in the *Feralia* on February 21, and the *Lemuria* (May 9, 11, and 13), which involved the cleansing of ancestral ghosts from the home. As much as they were family matters, these, like other major rites, were traditionally seen as crucial to the well-being of the state. As state-sponsored cult, the *Parentalia* addressed the dead in their role as benefactors of the community and so aligned them implicitly with Romulus as a mythic prototype. The *Lemuria* was intended in part to obviate communal problems caused by restless ghosts. In his etiological poem on the Roman calendar, the *Fasti*, Ovid derives the name of this festival from "Remus": it was instituted, he says, in honor of Romulus' dead brother and first known as *Remuria* (5.479–80).

In spite of Ovid's etiology (which is probably his invention), there was no festival officially designed to cleanse Romans of the primal guilt of Remus' murder. Nevertheless, the practice of invoking Remus to explain Rome's history of civil conflict became ingrained in Roman society, and it is prominent in Latin literature following the period of civil wars that brought Augustus to power. It must, however, be more than simply literary in origin, since the emergence of Remus as a figure in Roman myth is most plausibly dated further back even that of Latin literature itself in the third century BCE, and can be associated with conflicts between Romans from a similarly early date.[15] Thus literary references to and depictions of Remus, like those we will study below, are properly treated as part of a wider—and older—cultural field that had become essential to Roman identity by the time the literary record begins.

The primary means of addressing the communal problem of murder was the murder trial, as carried out in the Forum in standing courts devoted to the purpose. Here spectacle again played a large part, and regard for the facts and the finer points of law often took second place. The relatives of parties involved might appear in full mourning garb. The speeches for the accusation and the defense were designed to thrill, terrify, and entertain both the judges and the crowds that would gather for such occasions as much as to present a reasoned argument. Orators would often "call up the dead" to speak for themselves and in general tried to construct a fair verdict as what was due to the victim. Important trials attracted great attention and could inspire riots and civic mayhem. Such events lived on in the popular memory long after verdicts had been passed down and punishments exacted.

Outside the officially sanctioned realm of state-sponsored cult and legal procedure existed a thriving world of magic in which the dead were likewise central figures. The dead might be invoked in curses, whose words were often scratched on tablets and deposited in graves, or they might be consulted in necromancy, particularly at sites such as Lake Avernus, thought to be openings to the underworld. Along with the practice of magic itself, moreover, grew up a series of invective tropes used to stigmatize it, and this often makes it difficult to judge what constitutes the trace of a real ritual and what is purely an imaginative construct. Indeed, accusations of illicit rites involving the dead can be regarded as just as much of a cultural performance as the rites themselves. They often served the needs of politicians and their factions or found their way into invective poetry with a political edge. But magical rituals (or at least the fear of them) represented enough of a threat to warrant legislation during the period in question.

Philosophical discussions took account of the dead, not only in the *consolatio* (consolation) addressed to the bereaved but also in the theorization of the soul's posthumous existence. While one of the two most popular philosophical schools at Rome, Epicureanism, denied the soul's existence after death, the other, Stoicism, at least entertained the possibility of a celestial realm in which souls subsisted. Such notions might inspire imagined journeys to the world of the dead, like that represented in Cicero's "Dream of Scipio," and visions of the dead in otherworldly locales, which had an old tradition extending back to Plato, the Presocratics, and Homer, allowed for the idealization of philosophical dialogue itself. An otherworldly setting, that is, could provide an ideal backdrop for discussion of arcane matters because the dead could be thought to possess knowledge inaccessible to the living.

The means by which Roman authors integrated such practices into literature are manifold, but I will emphasize one technique above all that accounts for the dead's "imitation" of the living in literary fantasy: *prosopopoeia* or *fictio personae,* the "mask-making" by which ancient authors spoke in the voice of nonpersonal things and the dead, whether through direct speech or the descriptive introduction of a personified thing.[16] Roman rhetoricians identified *mortuos ab inferis excitare* (calling up the dead from the underworld)—a subtype of oratorical *prosopopoeia*—as an effective trope for stirring up strong emotions in the audience of a legal or political speech, but it is related intrinsically to the much older and broader phenomenon of adopting the persona of a ghost in poetic performance. *Prosopopoeia* allows Roman authors to have the dead speak and act in a manner suggestive of the practices outlined above. Indeed, the very act of "summoning" the dead or "bringing on stage" a Roman from the past can itself recall performances such as magic and drama. Quintilian illustrates the other descriptive sort of literary *prosopopoeia* with Vergil's *Fama*, the personification of rumor that stalks Dido's Carthage in the *Aeneid* (Quint. *Inst.* 9.2.36). In the texts under discussion, I will be especially interested in the *Furiae*, mythical avengers of murder victims and embodiments of the dead's curse upon the living, the madness (*furor*) that drives the guilty to their destruction. *Prosopopoeia*, of course, cannot account for every passage that will be important to my study—literary laments, eulogies, and prayers, for example, have their place as well. It underpins, however, the primary instances of the phenomenon with which I am concerned.

The first three chapters treat Ciceronian oratory. Chapter 1 focuses on Cicero's manipulation of the topos *mortuos excitare* in the *Pro Caelio* and the *Pro Milone*. The topos' very name, "calling up the dead," indicates a connection in the Roman imagination between oratory and magic. Although he denied the efficacy of magic himself, Cicero nevertheless understood the figurative magic of evoking the dead in a speech to offer considerable advantages to an orator and his client. The *prosopopoeia* of Appius Claudius Caecus in the *Pro Caelio* exploits the visualization of the dead to assimilate oratorical performance to a series of other, elite-sponsored performances, including funeral ritual, historical drama, and moralizing *carmina* (songs), meant to display the illustrious past with which Cicero seeks to be identified. The technique helps Cicero repackage scurrilous gossip about the notorious Clodia: connotations of elite performance, that is, authorize the rumors that Cicero purveys in Appius' persona. While instrumental in Caelius' defense, the shaming of Clodia also furthers Cicero's attack, in the same speech, on his political enemy, P. Clodius Pulcher. The *Pro Milone*, conversely, directs the connotations of magic inherent in the topos toward the stigmatization of the very figure, the dead Clodius, it is used to evoke. Through the opposition it creates between superstitious views of the afterlife and their more enlightened philosophical counterparts, this kind of magic helps Cicero relegate a dead enemy to the past rather than simply bring him alive.

Chapter 2 argues that Cicero's oratorical references to the Furies represent an appropriation of mythological tragedy for the purposes of characteristically late-republican political competition and thus represent a counterpart to his politically motivated use of *mortuos excitare*. As the embodiments of the dead's curse upon the living, the Furies were associated with tragic narratives of murder, madness, and vendetta-style violence, together with powerful emotions of fear, guilt, and religious awe. Cicero turns these associations to his advantage by allowing the motif not only to inform the imagery and characterization of his speeches in a deep and subtle fashion but also to lend coherence to the presentation of pressing civic issues on diverse occasions. The Furies help Cicero frame discussions of the aftermath of civil war, the recurrence of violence across generations, the exile of leaders, the return of tyranny, and the mismanagement of Rome's empire. In view of this dual function of the motif, the chapter begins with a detailed analysis of Cicero's early speech *Pro Sex. Roscio Amerino*, before turning, in briefer fashion, to a series of later orations.

In Chapter 3 I argue that the *Second Philippic*, a text written and circulated—but never delivered—during the final months of Cicero's life, characterizes oratory's traditional evocations of the dead as a preferable alternative to Julius Caesar's emergent cult. As he attacks his enemy, Antonius, on political grounds, Cicero also makes the literary representation of oratory into a means of resistance to changes in Roman culture portending the monopolization of power by a sole emperor. The ambivalent *laudatio* of Julius Caesar near the end of the *Second Philippic* constructs this cultural dichotomy directly, but its full rhetorical force emerges only by tracing Cicero's ongoing opposition of oratory to Antonius' behavior toward the dead in general. At earlier moments in the speech, Cicero decries Antonius' attempts to profit from Caesar's death, his selfish consumption of the dead Pompeius' possessions, and his failure to mourn those who had died in the recent civil war. The later *Philippics*, which were delivered in something close to their written form, confirm the centrality of this opposition within Cicero's idea of Roman culture.

Propertius' Elegies 4.7 and 4.11, spoken by the ghosts of Cynthia and Cornelia, respectively, are the focus of chapter 4. Although often studied from the perspective of the poetic tradition, these poems, I argue, adapt the republican oratorical trope of *mortuos excitare*. And we understand Propertius' technique best by thinking of his poetry as restored behavior in the Schechnerian sense. While orators like Cicero had evoked the dead in actual trials so as to have them speak for themselves, here an Augustan poet calls up the dead in the circumstances of imagined trials. Propertius' poems, however, illustrate the new political purpose behind the evocation of the dead in Augustan literature. For Propertius' elegiac use of a republican rhetorical technique represents an appeal to the concerns of his Augustan audience, whose interest in assimilating republican cultural institutions to the changed political circumstances of the Principate is attested in other areas. Elegies 4.7 and 4.11 reflect, in however ambiguous and humorous a fashion, the Augustan "restoration" of the *res publica* and the Princeps' suppression of the ruinous political competition that overshadowed Cicero's career. Further, I explain the uniqueness of Elegies 4.7 and 4.11 (no other Latin poems depict dead women delivering elaborate speeches of this kind) by showing how they also restore Propertius' particular set of poetic postures vis-à-vis the dead in elegy as distinct from those of his republican predecessor, Catullus, and Augustan contemporaries Tibullus and Ovid. The poems suggest a heightened sensitivity, fostered by the traumatic experience of civil war, to the problems and importance of commemorative performance itself.

Propertius' restaging of familiar republican performance finds a far grander analogue in Vergil's *Aeneid* 1–6, the focus of chapter 5. In spite of the ambivalence toward Augustus that scholars have often discerned in the epic, its evocations of the dead suggest Vergil's ambition to craft the central Augustan literary and cultural text. Here the evocation of Rome's curse, the corrupt murder trial, the stigmatization of magic, the rituals of the *Parentalia*, the idealization of philosophical dialogue, and, finally, the aristocratic funeral procession, all reemerge in forms at least outwardly compatible with Augustan society. While Vergilian epic rivals the republican oratory of Cicero for the sheer scope and variety of such techniques, the two authors' works underscore the central contrast of this book. With republican politics becoming a mere memory, Vergil grounds the *Aeneid* in the visible, bodily expression of what it means to be a Roman citizen under Augustus. He offers a mythic precedent for Augustan culture as it was lived by its participants.

Finally, an additional note about precedents and posterity. In some way, all *prosopopoeia* of the dead in Latin literature owes a debt to one of the founding acts of Roman literary production, Ennius' evocation of Homer at the opening of the *Annales*. Ennius reports a dream in which Homer's soul appeared and informed him that it had entered Ennius' body. Our fragments preserve words from Homer's speech, including his recollection of having first become a peacock, a detail inspired in some fashion by the philosophy of Pythagoras.[17] Insofar as the *Annales* bear the traces of characteristically republican political quarrels between the aristocratic clans from which Ennius drew his patrons,[18] the poet's bravado piece of literary self-promotion is also a political act, comparable to a passage such as Cicero's evocation of Appius Claudius Caecus in the *Pro Caelio*. Just as Ennius, drawing on philosophical tradition, makes himself the new Homer, worthy to sing the praises of a M. Fulvius Nobilior or M. Porcius Cato and elevate them above their political opponents, Cicero, drawing on a series of elite-sponsored performance genres, fashions himself as a new Appius, a figure of both political authority and literary renown, and a fitting defender of the young M. Caelius in the face of the decadent Clodii. Indeed, ideas of literary and familial ancestry must have been closely linked from the first in the republican imagination, since Latin literature itself emerged in part as a vehicle for aristocratic self-promotion focusing especially on military and political achievements worthy of the ancestors. The notion, however, of poetic inspiration through the ghosts of literary forefathers carried over easily into the circumstances of Augustan cultural experimentation. We will see Propertius calling for inspiration from the spirits of Callimachus and Philetas, Hellenistic poets embodying his aesthetic ideals, and Vergil's evocation of Hector, who confers the legacy of Troy upon the dreaming Aeneas, clearly bears some relation to the Ennian passage as well. While Ennius' dream makes us aware of how much we may have lost in terms of precedents, it also justifies this book's emphasis on *prosopopoeia* of the dead as a central Roman cultural gambit.[19]

Post-Augustan authors frequently evoke the dead in what might seem, at first glance, merely a continuation of Augustan techniques. Lucan, Seneca, and Statius, for example, revel in lurid portrayals of murdered ghosts and their Furies, and many such passages allude to similar moments in earlier literature. As I argue in the conclusion, however, "Silver Age" literature does not so much depict the dead's "imitation" of the living as the living's imitation of the dead: not the emulation of illustrious ancestors valued so highly in all periods of Roman history, but mimesis of the dead *as* the dead, an unsettling fantasy tied to growing anxieties over the imperial abuse of power. In Ovid's poetry we discern the transition from one attitude to the other taking place. Moving from Ovid's *Metamorphoses* to the *Fasti* to the poems from exile, we watch the Roman literary imagination coming to regard the dead past as a set of reified institutions through which to assess the imperial present.

CHAPTER ONE

Oratory and Magic in Republican Rome

A NYONE FAMILIAR WITH Ciceronian oratory is aware of the dead's central part in it. The *Pro Caelio*'s famous portrayal of Appius Claudius Caecus upbraiding his descendant, Clodia, for her scandalous sexual conduct is only the best-known passage of Cicero's speeches to make the dead participate somehow in the world of the living. In these texts we also find murder victims demanding recompense from provincial governors, dead war heroes attending to the senatorial debates over honors due to them, even dead political leaders intervening bodily in civic events. Familiar or not, this component of Cicero's literary imagination possesses the surprising quality of being unprecedented. We might have expected that in an area touching upon one of the most fundamental tenets of Roman society—the necessity of right relation between the living and the dead—Cicero would have stuck carefully to time-tested methods of persuasion. The Greek orators provided models for speaking of the dead in judicial and deliberative speeches, but Cicero goes far beyond them.[1] If we had more republican oratory, Cicero's style might seem less unusual in this regard, but the Latin rhetorical treatises suggest otherwise. *Prosopopoeia* of the dead was a recognized trope thought to be appropriate for passages of great *pathos* such as the conclusions of speeches.[2] It was envisioned, however, primarily as a way to introduce pathetic appeals on behalf of those involved in legal or political disputes.[3]

In Cicero's speeches, by contrast, the dead display a far greater range of behavior, language, and emotion. They resemble the living more closely, insofar as what they say and do recalls characteristic patterns of speech and action. Nothing that Cicero found in Greek oratory or ancient rhetorical theory could have led him to such creative mimicry of the wider culture. Rather than purely conventional techniques, Cicero's efforts represent a distinctive response to his historical moment. In these opening three chapters, I argue that they are a means of co-opting, through imaginative adaptation, a series of Roman cultural performances centered on the dead and their world. Cicero employs this strategy not only for the narrow persuasive goals of any particular speech, but also in service of the fierce, and ultimately ruinous, political competition that marked the late Republic.

Because there was no theoretical discussion of such methods in antiquity, Cicero's tactics require us to turn to modern theory that resituates literature within the broad field of cultural activity. Joseph Roach's concept of orature (outlined in the introduction) posits oral and literary genres coexisting in a mutually informing bond, a symbiosis that places them usefully together under the rubric of performance. Roach's views, even at first glance, fit well with oratorical texts like Cicero's, since these works, published and meant to be appreciated as literature (*litterae*), nevertheless imply oral performance in such immediate ways. On the one hand, the texts purport to record actual speeches (and even orations we know never to have been delivered, such as the second *actio* of the speeches *In Verrem* or the *Second Philippic,* maintain a semblance of oral delivery), while on the other hand, appreciation of them on the part of Cicero's Roman contemporaries involved performance as well.[4] When the possessor of a papyrus roll containing, say, the *Pro Scauro,* wanted to savor the delights of Ciceronian eloquence, he read the text—or had it read—aloud, attempting to recreate the original speech. But the appropriateness of Roach's theory in Cicero's case runs still deeper, since the variety of traits displayed by Cicero's dead reflects literary oratory's close ties to a diverse range of other performance traditions, adapted to suit Cicero's political ends. Addressing various aspects of Roman performance culture together with a number of Ciceronian orations, each of the following three chapters articulates this connection in a somewhat different fashion.

This chapter discusses Cicero's manipulation of the rhetorical topos *mortuos ab inferis excitare* in the *Pro Caelio* and the *Pro Milone.* In its very name, the topos reveals a connection in the Roman imagination between the techniques of oratory and those of magic.[5] For all the distrust with which necromantic magic was regarded by advocates of traditional religion or of philosophies that denied the existence of the soul after death (such as the Epicureanism of Lucretius), it nevertheless enjoyed a tenacious hold on the Roman mind.[6] Cicero himself rejected necromancy and decried others' interest in it (*Tusc.* 1.37; *Div.* 1.132; *Vat.* 14), but understood the figurative magic of calling up the dead in a speech to offer advantages beyond anything that the rhetoricians envisioned.

On the one hand, as we learn from the *Pro Caelio*, the visualization of the dead in the traditional topos inspired Cicero to assimilate oratorical performance not only to magic itself but also to a series of other, elite-sponsored performances meant to display the illustrious past with which Cicero sought to be identified. Speaking and acting as one of the dead here becomes a way to recall the aristocratic funeral with its procession of *imagines maiorum* and *laudatio funebris;* the mime, tragedy, and historical drama that brought the dead to the theatrical stage; the *carmina* that shared both their purpose and aspects of their presentation with the funeral *laudationes;* and even, in a self-referential fashion, the established uses of the topos *mortuos excitare* itself. In the *Pro Caelio,* such artful exploitation of Roman oratory's cultural context has a specific rhetorical purpose: it allows Cicero to guide the audience's perception of the scurrilous gossip about Clodia and Caelius that he presents in the persona of Appius. By arrogating to himself the cultural authority of elite genres, Cicero makes use of the informal, marginal information network of gossip to advance both a judicial cause and a political battle with his arch-enemy, P. Clodius Pulcher.

On the other hand, as the *Pro Milone* reveals, exploiting the connotations of magic in the topos *mortuos excitare* could be a way to stigmatize the very figure whom it was used to evoke. This kind of magic helps Cicero consign the dead Clodius to the past rather than simply bring him alive. In the *Pro Milone,* Cicero imagines a nightmare scenario in which Clodius, whose armed gangs had menaced Rome after their leader's death, is allowed to return to life. Cicero takes pains to set a vivid image of Clodius before the eyes of his audience and even to depict Clodius' corpse as an agent of destruction, burning the senate house with flames from its own funeral pyre. Such visions not only help Cicero underscore his claim that Rome is better off with Clodius dead, but also associate Clodius and the Clodians with notions of magic and a traditional underworld, while Cicero links his client, Milo, to philosophical views of an afterlife that the Roman elite would have regarded as more enlightened. Drawing on competing views of corporeal and noncorporeal existence after death, Cicero attempts to relegate the plebeian Clodius to oblivion, but insists that his killer, Milo, deserves a glorious immortality.

Cicero's *Pro Caelio* and *Pro Milone* introduce us to opposing aspects of the literary phenomenon and style of performance that forms the core of this book. The *Pro Caelio*'s embrace of the magical potential for visualization inherent in oratory finds its counterpart in the *Pro Milone*'s turn toward nightmarish fantasy and the stigmatization of its mythical sources in favor of philosophy. Republican politics both occasion and determine the complex set of cultural allusions, preferences, and anxieties that Cicero brings to the evocation of the dead in literary oratory.

Rumor and Gossip as Legitimate Means of Attack

In 56 BCE the young aristocrat M. Caelius Rufus found himself the target of a legal attack by L. Sempronius Atratinus, the son of another, previous legal adversary. The formal charges were various, but one concerned an alleged attempt to poison the notorious Clodia, with whom Caelius was said to have had an affair.[7]

Reading the *Pro Caelio*'s account of a libidinous Clodia's vengeful obsession with the good-looking Caelius, we are perhaps always at risk of behaving like those Romans who followed the common talk (*hominum sermo*) about the most scandalous aspects of Caelius' case: believing, that is, in what is said because it accords with Clodia's reputation (cf. Cic. *Cael.* 69). Aware of the pitfalls of credulity, scholars have long been anxious about whether the affair actually happened and was in fact a subject of gossip among Cicero's contemporaries.[8] We are right to wonder, since our doubt may not only determine our view of the speech as persuasion but also help us interrogate Roman misogyny as promulgated through judicial oratory and other types of public performance.[9] A Roman *quaestio* was of course supposed to elicit and divulge true information about a past event; the speeches, however, for both the prosecution and the defense could be expected to take full advantage of sexual stereotypes and might well involve distortion of the facts.

But our uncertainty about whether or not the affair represented new and reliable information for Caelius' jurors has prevented us from appreciating all that the text of the *Pro Caelio* can tell us about the connections between literature and culture in late-republican society. As many have recognized, it is through the famous *prosopopoeia* whereby he "calls up" the venerable Roman censor Appius Claudius Caecus that Cicero first reveals the key to his defense, namely, the premise that the charges of *aurum et venenum* (gold and poison) leveled against Caelius arise not from any criminal activity on Caelius' part, but rather from the failed love-affair between Caelius and Clodia.[10] Recent criticism of the Appius passage has centered on the rhetorical significance of Appius' antiquated morality and the comic or stock invective elements of his denunciation of Clodia.[11] Yet, whatever the status of the love affair, the introduction by Cicero's Appius of gossip about Clodia allows Cicero to benefit from the informal and marginal information network of gossip within the formal information system of Roman judicial procedure.[12]

Cicero benefits from gossip by transforming it. Helped only partially by the teachings of ancient rhetorical theory with regard to *rumores,* Cicero backs up his defense of Caelius' character by describing the latter's existence in the closely monitored elite world of male public life. It is from the perspective of this world, epitomized by the figure of Appius Claudius Caecus, that Cicero launches his attack on the far less public and more vulnerable Clodia. Taking on the persona of Appius, Cicero magnifies Clodia's threat to Rome by allowing the audience to hear the ill-report about Clodia through the dead Appius' ears. To guide, moreover, the audience's perception of the material he presents through Appius, Cicero adapts conventions of elite-sponsored public performance. Mime and comedy (emphasized by previous scholars) allow Cicero to represent Clodia's situation as ridiculous and to stigmatize the inflammatory rhetoric of Caelius' accusers. But comic allusion alone would do little to make a Roman audience take the gossip about Clodia seriously. Cicero's suggestion of other kinds of Roman performance designed to transmit what could be taken as authoritative information about aristocratic houses and their members, are at least as important. Sponsored and vouched for by the elite, performances like these had the advantage of being able to *show* rather than merely *tell* Roman audiences about Rome's illustrious past and Rome's relationship to that past.[13]

Cicero's Appius shows us that eliciting solidarity with the dead was effective both as a rhetorical technique and a means of political self-advancement. For the persona of Appius helps Cicero stigmatize not only Clodia herself but also her brother and his own political archrival, Clodius. Cicero's triumph over Clodia implicates Clodius by association, and Cicero also juxtaposes an actorly portrayal of Clodius (36) with that of Appius, whose stature in comparison to Clodia helps to set in relief the moral laxity he then imputes to Clodius. Cicero seeks both to magnify his own image and to damage that of a political competitor through aligning himself and his client with the most august civic traditions, embodied by Appius. The *Pro Caelio* is very much a part of the political infighting of the late-republican elite, and the cultural implications that Cicero attaches to "calling up the dead" are essential to his political machinations here.

To understand how Cicero's *prosopopoeia* of Appius Claudius Caecus helps him manipulate the gossip about Clodia and Caelius to his own legal and political advantage, it is first necessary to examine Cicero's larger strategy with respect to gossip in the speech as a whole. With scandalous gossip a key element in the attacks on Caelius as well as in Cicero's own speech, this strategy is twofold: on the one hand, to delegitimize outright the stories about his client, and, on the other, to refocus opprobrium onto Clodia, the gossip about whom he seeks to repackage and make use of. These two operations are to some degree temporally distinct, since defusing the gossip about Caelius is among the first tasks Cicero takes up in the speech. A famous distinction between *accusatio* (formal accusation) and *maledictio* (slander) occupies a prominent place early in the *Pro Caelio's praemunitio.*[14] Outlining the difference between proper courtroom procedure and the tactics of his opponents, Cicero here insists that *accusatio* demands a charge, the definition of facts, the close consideration of a man's character, and the support of argumentation and witnesses. *Maledictio,* on the other hand, has no other purpose than to insult (6). Cicero later specifies that Caelius' prosecutors have spoken at length of lust, love affairs, wild parties and the like (35), all material, Cicero implies, that is designed to capture the attention of a curious audience rather than build a solid case. Such techniques, he suggests, are not only misleading but dangerous, since at the most general and unmoderated level of discourse lurks *sermo,* which can proceed from arbitrary sources and attach to people simply by association, as Cicero suggests it has in the case of Caelius himself (18).

Cicero notes that the atmosphere of Caelius' trial has been tainted by the verbal license of the prosecutors and declares his own adherence to the rules of evidence-based procedure.[15] He claims to observe, for example, the discomfort of his youthful opponent Atratinus with *male dicendi licentia* (freedom of slander) and *libertas verborum* (licence with words) and expresses his mock-sympathetic wish that some more experienced orator had been asked to introduce such material (7–8). Clodia herself is portrayed as both a subject and a purveyor of uninhibited speech—she is *nota* (notorious), she delights in *libertas sermonum* (31, 49)—but Cicero insists that he will say nothing unless for the sake of refuting charges (31). In this way, Cicero claims, he will not be felt to engage in the promotion of hostility (32). Matching matter with matter, cause with cause, reason with reason, he will stick to *argumenta* (arguments) and *signa* (proofs) (22). As a corollary to this delimitation of his own comportment, Cicero declares that of the various charges leveled against Caelius, only those pertaining to the gold and the poison are legitimate *crimina;* all the rest is slander (30).

Ancient rhetorical theory would have offered Cicero guidelines for stigmatizing and rejecting informal speech in this way, and Cicero is particularly close to theory when he dismisses what is said about Caelius as mere slander.[16] Following theory's directives, Cicero characterizes loose talk as both a basis of false charges, something capable of moving otherwise impartial parties to believe these charges, thereby eroding the very fabric of the judicial system. Rome itself, Cicero asserts, is already a *maledica civitas* (a slanderous state) (38), where citizens can be put at judicial peril on the basis of unsubstantiated incriminations.

But the handbooks, which offered arguments for and against the use of *rumores* in separate circumstances, could be only partially helpful to Cicero once he had decided, in effect, to accept some rumors (those on Clodia) and reject others (those on Caelius). Cicero's discussion of Caelius' participation in Roman political life, for example, shifts attention away from gossip to Caelius' public persona, with the result that the sexual gossip about Caelius is discussed as, on the one hand, that which is said baselessly about any prominent, good-looking young man and, on the other hand, stories of youthful peccadilloes of the sort that are soon outgrown under the tutelage of upstanding public men. Cicero begins this process early in the *praemunitio*, when he suggests that Caelius is being slandered simply for being handsome (6). He goes on to recall that in his own youth, the public's perception that one was, like Caelius, a *vir inter viros* (man among men) ensured the stability of one's *fama* and a reputation for *pudicitia* (chaste behavior). Assiduous attention to public comportment was the only way a young man could make certain that *nemo loquebatur* (no one was talking) (11). Cicero points to Caelius' public association with particular upstanding men, such as Caelius' own father and Cicero himself (9), and uses this as the basis of his retort to the charge of Caelius' having been an acquaintance of the conspirator Catiline (10–15).[17] Cicero insists, in other words, that Caelius has lived in the most closely monitored arena of elite male political activity and ought to be assessed according to its rules rather than according to the vagaries of gossip over trivial matters. An emphasis on public life also helps his attack on Clodia because, as a woman, she possesses virtually no public persona other than that ascribed to her by word of mouth. Any ill report about Clodia is particularly shocking given the illustrious family of her birth. She is thus far more vulnerable than Caelius to judicial manipulation of gossip about her.[18]

Cicero's *prosopopoeia* of Appius Claudius Caecus initiates his attack on Clodia. It both draws attention to the world of Roman public life and emphasizes Clodia's *gens* and *fama:*

Sed tamen ex ipsa quaeram prius utrum me secum severe et graviter et prisce agere malit, an remisse et leniter et urbane. Si illo austero more ac modo, aliquis mihi ab inferis excitandus est ex barbatis illis, non hac barbula qua ista delectatur sed illa horrida quam in statuis antiquis atque imaginibus videmus, qui obiurget mulierem et qui pro me loquatur ne mihi ista forte suscenseat. Exsistat igitur ex hac ista familia aliquis ac potissimum Caecus ille; minimum enim dolorem capiet qui istam non videbit. Qui profecto, si exstiterit, sic aget ac sic loquetur: "Mulier, quid tibi cum Caelio, quid cum homine adulescentulo, quid cum alieno? Cur aut tam familiaris fuisti ut aurum commodares, aut tam inimica ut venenum timeres? Non patrem tuum videras, non patruum, non avum, non proavum, non abavum, non atavum audieras consules fuisse; non denique modo te Q. Metelli matrimonium tenuisse sciebas, clarissimi ac fortissimi viri patriaeque amantissimi, qui simul ac pedem limine extulerat, omnis prope civis virtute, gloria, dignitate superabat? Cum ex amplissimo genere in familiam clarissimam nupsisses, cur tibi Caelius tam coniunctus fuit? cognatus, adfinis, viri tui familiaris? Nihil eorum. Quid igitur fuit nisi quaedam temeritas ac libido? Nonne te, si nostrae imagines viriles non commovebant, ne progenies quidem mea, Q. illa Claudia, aemulam domesticae laudis in gloria muliebri esse admonebat, non virgo illa Vestalis Claudia quae patrem complexa triumphantem ab inimico tribuno plebei de curru detrahi passa non est? Cur te fraterna vitia potius quam bona paterna et avita et usque a nobis cum in viris tum etiam in feminis repetita moverunt? Ideone ego pacem Pyrrhi diremi ut tu amorum turpissimorum cotidie foedera ferires, ideo aquam adduxi ut ea tu inceste uterere, ideo viam munivi ut eam tu alienis viris comitata celebrares?"

But I would first inquire of the woman herself whether she would prefer me to deal with her in a stern, solemn, antique manner or in a light-hearted, playful, modern way. If in the austere manner, I must conjure up from the underworld one of those bearded men—not wearing a little beard like the one she delights in, but that unkempt beard which we see on antique statues and masks—a man who will upbraid the woman and will speak in my place so that she does not happen to become angry at me. Let there rise up someone from this very family—and best of all the famous Caecus. For he will be the least pained since he will not see her. If he arises he will act and speak like this: "Woman, what business do you have with Caelius, what business with a young man, with a stranger? Why were you either so familiar with him that you would lend him money or so inimical to him that you would fear poison? Had you not seen that your father was a consul, and heard that your uncle, grandfather, great-grandfather, great-great grandfather, and great-great-great grandfather were consuls? Were you not, finally, aware, that you had lately been married to Q. Metellus, a man most illustrious and brave and patriotic; who, the moment he set foot out of doors, outdid nearly all other citizens in valor, glory, and esteem? Since you had married from a most distinguished clan into a most illustrious household, why was Caelius so intimate with you? Was he related directly or by marriage, or a close acquaintance of your husband? He was nothing of the kind. What, therefore, was the reason if not a certain impetuosity and lust? But I ask, if the masks of our male line did not move you, did not even Q. Claudia, my own descendant, compel you to emulate the achievements of our clan in the renown that is appropriate to a woman? Or the famous Claudia, the Vestal Virgin, who, embracing her father when he was riding in his triumphal procession, prevented him from being dragged from the chariot by his enemy, a tribune of the plebs? Why did the vices of your brother influence you rather than the good traits of your father and grandfather, qualities found since my own time in both our men and particularly our women? Was it for this that I dissolved the peace treaty with Pyrrhus: so that you might daily strike amorous bargains of the most shameful sort? Was it for this that I built an aqueduct to bring water to Rome: so that you might use it for unchaste purposes? Was it for this that I built a road: so that you might frequent it accompanied by strange men?" (Cic. *Cael.* 33–34)

Though in effect a public shaming of Clodia, the passage nonetheless suggests a private scene of reproof in which Appius has been moved to indignation by what he has heard of his descendant. This suggestion of a private scene helps make Appius especially trenchant as a way for Cicero to benefit from gossip in the circumstances of judicial procedure. Appius' candid *response* to Clodia distances Cicero from the act of promulgating gossip about her, while Cicero nevertheless proceeds to do just that.

Appius' lack of ceremony is especially important in this regard. Having been "called up" from the underworld (cf. 33: *ab inferis excitandus est*), Appius does not state how he has come to know of Clodia's situation, but gruffly asks her, *Mulier, quid tibi cum Caelio, quid cum homine adulescentulo, quid cum alieno?* (Woman, what business do you have with Caelius, what business with a young man, with a stranger?) (33). The mixture of a colloquial, even conversational, tone into the high-flown rhetoric of Appius' diatribe may illustrate, as Geffcken asserts, the "comic principle of incongruity,"[19] but it also serves to transport Appius momentarily out of his public role as censor into a more private context in which he plays the role of an indignant *paterfamilias* anxious about his family's good name in the community at large. Yet, again, for all that Cicero suggests a private scene, he has Appius respond to the story being told about Clodia in court. Why, Appius asks, was Clodia either so familiar with Caelius that she would lend him gold or on such unfriendly terms that she would fear poison?

Wilfried Stroh observed that Appius' apparent "belief" in the personal basis for the charges of *aurum et venenum* allows Cicero to characterize her as the type of woman about whom such things could be believed, before Cicero himself goes on to dismiss these charges, like all the others, as baseless.[20] Inference and hearsay, Cicero thus implies, may be a valid source of information in Clodia's case. But "calling up" the dead Appius from the underworld in which he resides does not only demonstrate his "belief"; the technique also (somewhat humorously) lends weight to the stories about Clodia by suggesting that her dead ancestor Appius, the personification of the *gens,* has *heard* of Clodia's involvement in Caelius' persecution in the underworld and is concerned about its implications for the entire family. Appius' concern is evident in his immediate demand as to whether Clodia herself has not heard (33: *non . . . audieras*) that so many of her ancestors were consuls.[21] His subsequent insistence on the *gloria* achieved by Clodia's husband, Q. Caecilius Metellus Celer, and her illustrious ancestor Quinta Claudia likewise help frame the report circulating about Clodia as a threat to the good name of the *gens.* Appius' very blindness, which Cicero suggests will prevent him from being "pained" at the sight of Clodia, supports the passage's suggestion that Clodia's *fama* threatens that of the Claudian *gens* itself: deprived of the power of sight, we are to believe, Appius relies on what he hears—and draws ominous conclusions from the ill-report.

Through Appius, Clodia's rampant *libido* appears to threaten not only the Claudii but also elite male authority in general. Appius speaks from the heights of such authority: from the perspective, that is, of his brilliant career as a Roman statesman and civic benefactor. Appius demands ironically whether he dissolved the (proposed) peace treaty with Pyrrhus so that Clodia might daily strike "the bargains of her most shameful loves" (34). Did he build an aqueduct to bring water to Rome so that Clodia might use it for "unchaste" purposes?[22] Did he build a road so that she might frequent it accompanied by strange men?[23] Appius thus recasts a set of incriminations based on the hearsay of sexual gossip as evidence of disregard for noble *fama* and disrespect for aristocratic achievement. He presents Clodia's reputation as a detriment to these fundamental elements of institutional authority.

But Cicero's ultimate claim to speak truth about Clodia arises not simply from the concern he has the aristocratic Appius express. Cicero's portrayal of Appius adapts elite-sponsored performances with their own claim to "truth" and Cicero takes advantage of his audience's knowledge of this context. Since previous scholars' emphasis on comic drama is an essential background to my interpretation of Appius—a perspective whose limitations I hope to reveal—I review it here in offering some additional observations about this aspect of Appius' role. Linking my approach to this earlier perspective is an understanding of performance as a venue for the transmission of social meaning and an essential arena in which such meaning is produced. I diverge, however, from the previous view in that I do not see the primary rhetorical goal of the passage as humor, but as the legitimation of (nonetheless humorous) information about Clodia in the judicial arena with all the benefits, both legal and political, that might accrue for Cicero from a successful attack on his enemies, the Clodians.

Comedy and Mime

The conventions of mime and comedy, emphasized first by Katherine Gef-fcken, help Cicero both to represent Clodia's situation as ridiculous and to undercut the inflammatory techniques of his opponents. Appius' sarcastic humor is his most evident borrowing from the comic stage. But the very act of "conjuring" Appius from the underworld suggests the paratragedy upon which mime and comedy depended for so many of their humorous effects. Cicero's own contemporary Decimus Laberius wrote mimes called *Necyomantia* (*Conjuring*) and *Lacus Avernus* and ghosts are a memorable feature of Plautine comedy as well.[24] The paratragic quality of such drama becomes especially evident when one considers the long history of the conjuring-scene in Greco-Roman tragedy.[25] In Aeschylus' *Choephori*, for example, Orestes and Electra call upon their dead father, Agamemnon, to rise from the ground (138–44). In his *Persians*, the Persians actually succeed in summoning Darius from his grave (623–851). Seneca draws on this technique in the *Oedipus*, with its elaborate description of Tiresias' necromancy of the ghost of Laius; Medea's invocation of both the supernal and infernal powers, including the *di Manes*, opens Seneca's *Medea* (Sen. *Oed.* 548–658; *Med.* 10–16). In the *Tusculan Disputations*, Cicero himself quotes lines of ostensibly tragic verse that refer to the Italian Lake Avernus as a place where the spirits of the dead *excitantur* (are summoned up) (*Inc. trag.* 76 Ribbeck *ap.* Cic. *Tusc.* 1.37).[26] Like a scene from mime or comedy, Clodia's situation becomes ridiculous in part because of its contrast with serious situations in which the dead might be "called up" onstage.[27]

But just as comedy parodies tragedy, so Cicero's Appius also parodies the moralizing rhetoric of Caelius' accusers, and in this way prevents Appius' example from reflecting negatively on Caelius, a possibility about which Cicero himself expresses his concern (*Cael.* 35).[28] Scholars have not failed to discern similarities between Cicero's characterization of his opponent L. Herennius and that of Appius. Cicero claims to have noticed in particular the jury's close attention to Herennius' prosecution speech devoted to the themes of luxury, lust, and the faults characteristic of youth (25), which he suggests held the jurors' attention for its flamboyant invective rather than the applicability of the individual charges to Caelius (27). Herennius, Cicero maintains, had in contrast to his accustomed personality become *pertristis quidam patruus, censor, magister* (some gloomy uncle, censor, teacher). *Obiurgavit M. Caelium*, Cicero continues, *sicut neminem umquam parens* (he reproached M. Caelius as even a parent has never reproached anyone) (25). It is of course significant that Herennius is said to have acted like a censor, the office Appius actually held, and to have dwelt on the theme of *libido*, a term Appius also employs.[29] Likewise, the verb *obiurgare* signifies both Herennius' and Appius' reproach. The adjective *gravis* and the adverb *graviter* further link the prosecution's treatment of Caelius to Appius' treatment of Clodia: the prosecutor P. Clodius, Cicero claims, spoke *gravissime* in inveighing against Caelius; Appius' persona is *gravis* (27; 35).

Cicero's direct references to comedy in the sections of the *Pro Caelio* that follow enforce the parallels between the Appius passage and the rhetoric of Cicero's opponents. Comedy helps Cicero to reject what is *too* severe and old-fashioned in Appius' manner by allowing Cicero to present such qualities as an object of derision. Thus Cicero describes the harsh type of father from the comedies of Caecilius as *durus* (37), an adjective he also applies to Appius. Like the *pertristis* persona adopted by Herennius, the Caecilianic father is *tristis* (38) and *ferreus* (unfeeling) (37). The lines of Caecilius which Cicero actually quotes create additional parallels. One of Caecilius' fathers says his mind *ardet* (burns); similarly, Cicero describes the prosecutor P. Clodius as *inflammatus* (inflamed) (27). It is perhaps the same father who asks why his son has chosen to have dealings with a *mulier aliena* (strange woman); Appius, too, demands what business Clodia has with an *alienus*. Cicero makes his most direct jab at such parental behavior in declaring that fathers like those in Caecilius are *vix ferendi* (scarcely tolerable) (37). The same might be said, Cicero implies, about the attacks on his client's morals.

Conversely, the *lenis* type of father from the comedies of Terence meets with Cicero's approval, while eliciting an imagined reproach that further undermines the moralizing of Cicero's opponents. Cicero quotes from Terence's *Adelphoe,* in which Micio advocates an accepting attitude toward the transgressions of youth. Has a young man, Micio queries, broken down doors? They will be repaired. Has he torn someone's clothing? It will be mended (Ter. *Ad.* 120–21 *ap.* Cic. *Cael.* 38). From the perspective of this kind of father, Cicero insists, Caelius' case poses no problems: who can blame Caelius for familiarity with a woman like Clodia, when she lives in open disregard for societal norms? In anticipation of objections, Cicero notes the rarity of pure devotion to virtue, again through a contrast between the morals of the past and those of the present. Roman forefathers like Camillus, Fabricius, and Curius, he remarks, may have been capable of high moral standards, but such behavior is scarcely ever found among the present generation. Those who now preach Stoic self-denial and laborious striving after *laus* (renown) have been left *prope soli . . . in scholis* (nearly alone in their lecture halls) (38–41).[30] Through such means, Cicero stigmatizes moral rigidity like that advocated by Caelius' accusers as hopelessly outdated, the product of a dry and isolated scholasticism rather than a reflection of contemporary life. Yet, significantly, Appius Claudius Caecus is not among those invoked as *exempla* in this purely negative comparison: *his* speech is far more than an academic lecture.

Or indeed a comic diatribe: evocation of Hellenized comedy alone would hardly make a Roman audience view Appius' presentation of the gossip about Clodia in a serious light.[31] Cicero, further, cannot afford to have gossip degenerate into merely a laughing matter, since a superabundance of laughter might dissolve the distinction he has attempted to make between the stories about Caelius and those about Clodia. Thus, while previous scholars' emphasis on a Roman performance context has been well placed, we need to understand how Cicero's Appius adapts other kinds of performance designed to transmit authoritative "truth" about aristocratic houses and their members.

The Pompa Funebris, Laudationes, *and* Carmina

While gossip carried a stigma as an informal and arbitrary type of information-transmission, public performance of the Roman past was a means by which Roman elites hoped to stabilize and fix popular opinion about their families and themselves.[32] Appius enhances Cicero's own claim to be telling the truth about Clodia by his very reference to this context.

The wax *imagines* worn by actors in the aristocratic funeral procession fixed the reputation of the aristocratic dead through their very materiality: they affirmed the dead's exemplary status and were seen as tokens of aristocratic power and prestige.[33] Cicero recalls the *imagines* when he describes Appius' rough, unkempt beard as "that bristling one we see on ancient statues and masks [*imagines*]" (33); Appius, too, refers to the *imagines* of the Claudian *gens* (34). To evoke the funeral *pompa* with its *imagines* is not simply to create an aura of ethical *gravitas,* although, as recognized already by ancient critics, *gravitas* is one of Cicero's rhetorical goals at this point in the *Pro Caelio.* Through Appius, Cicero speaks (perhaps startlingly[34]) as an *imago.*[35] He thereby prepares his audience to regard what he will say as far more than mere gossip but rather as the voice of the aristocratic tradition and of publicly recognized "truth."

Appius' eulogy of the Claudian *gens* echoes the *laudatio funebris* that formed the climax of aristocratic funerals.[36] Verbalized "truth," in addition to the authoritative imagery of the *pompa,* is thus emphatically signaled as Appius' medium.[37] In the *laudatio,* a member of the family praised the *gens* and presented a list of the deceased's achievements, such as the holding of high office or conspicuous acts of bravery, that would already have been known to many. Cicero's Appius recalls such events in his own life and those of his descendants. Indeed, with its emphasis on images, reputation, and achievements, Cicero's performance collapses the two most public aspects of the aristocratic funeral, the *pompa* and the *laudatio*.

Such clear recollections of aristocratic funerals were also likely to remind a Roman audience of the broader cultural tradition of *carmina*, of which Appius himself was remembered as an author.[38] Funeral *laudationes* shared both their purpose and aspects of their presentation with the eulogistic "songs" inscribed on Roman funeral monuments. If inscription ensured the fixity, visibility, and endurance of the *fama* thus transmitted, the *carmen* itself presupposed emphatic performance like that we "see" Appius putting on.[39] Although no eulogistic verse can be associated with Appius' name, the three attributed fragments of Appius' *carmina* deal with ethical issues closely related to reputation: mental discipline as a key to right behavior, social ties as a balm for misery, and self-determination of one's own *fortuna*.[40] The sententiousness, furthermore, of Cicero's Appius recalls the very nature of his work, described as *sententiae* by Festus.[41] Appius' denunciation of Clodia's behavior can thus be taken to reflect not only aristocratic interests, but also a larger concern with aspects of personal and social comportment on which Appius was regarded as an authority. The tradition of *carmina*, another important means of transmitting aristocratic "truth," lends this broader cultural authority to Cicero's words.

Historical Drama

The elite-sponsored historical drama of the *fabula praetexta* brought the full resources of theatrical staging to the fixing and perpetuation of aristocratic *fama*.[42] In mimicking Appius, Cicero resembles not only an actor wearing an *imago* in procession or the inspired performer of *carmina*, but also a stage actor in a *praetexta*, who could have been said, in his own way, to "call up" an illustrious figure from Roman history.[43] Cicero suggests his own similarity to a stage actor when he describes his performance as Appius by saying, *gravem personam induxi* (I have brought a grave character onstage) (35).[44] Quintilian understood the Appius episode as a bravado piece of acting on Cicero's part, and modern critics, following him, have of course been justified in grouping Appius together with the actor-like portrayals of Clodius and of the harsh and lenient fathers from Roman comedy that immediately follow.[45] Yet, while Cicero's later allusions to and even quotations from comedy make it tempting to read the Appius passage as primarily an adaptation of comic norms,

Appius differs from the *Pro Caelio*'s other *prosopopoeiae* in that Cicero explicitly identifies him as a figure from Rome's illustrious past. This is essential to *his* role in the *Pro Caelio*, as opposed to the roles of the others.

As Michele Salzman reminds us, the *Ludi Megalenses* during which Caelius' trial took place are known to have involved the perpetuation of aristocratic *fama* through historical drama—an instance that Cicero himself indirectly recalls.[46] The games included a staging of the exploits of Appius' descendant Q. Claudia, famous for having conveyed the Great Mother to Rome in the form of a black stone.[47] Cicero has Appius refer to this Claudia in his eulogy of the *gens* (*Cael.* 34: *Q. illa Claudia*) and Claudia's achievement contrasts emphatically with the behavior of Clodia, who, Appius suggests, was unmoved by Claudia's good example. Recollection of the play about Claudia distances Cicero further from the perpetuation of common gossip by reminding his audience in still another way of the extent to which the activities of the Claudians are bound up with the history, well-being, and public functions of the Roman state. It is all the more legitimate to consider even casual talk about Clodia as a serious matter in light of the formal staging of Q. Claudia's *fama* that takes place during the Megalensian games. But, still more importantly, the temporally proximate performance of institutionalized "truth" about the *gens Claudia* affords Cicero perhaps his best claim to speak "truth" through Appius. When the Claudians speak from "onstage," they do not relate trivia or falsehood. The existence of the Claudia *praetexta* is especially trenchant proof of the inadequacy of comic paradigms to account for Appius as an aspect of elite strategy.

The diversity of performance traditions embodied by Cicero's Appius points to an intrinsic affinity between performance and Roman cultural memory, a relationship through which to understand Appius' function in the broadest socio-cultural terms. Tapping into the cultural anxiety surrounding the scare-figure of Clodia, Cicero self-consciously seeks to embody Appius while simultaneously attempting to replace him: he is Appius' surrogate, in Roach's terms. What is important is not that *Appius* speaks, but that Cicero speaks in his persona so as to reposition himself, his opponents, Clodia, and Caelius within the matrix of Roman power relations. Both in Cicero's text and in the performance it purports to record we observe the reproduction *and* recreation of Roman culture, even if neither of these processes is itself free from anxiety or entirely successful. On the one hand, Cicero reproduces many of the cultural values that Appius embodies simply by taking on his persona. On the other hand, Cicero recreates these values as open to a newly selective application at the same time as he recreates gossip as elite-sponsored "truth."

The Oratorical Tradition

It is from this broad perspective that we can best assess the interaction of Cicero's Appius with another, still more immediate performance context in which the passage has been read since antiquity: oratory itself and the rhetorical topos *mortuos excitare*.[48] A survey of surviving discussions and examples of the topos suggests that Cicero's exploitation of it in the *Pro Caelio* is in fact decidedly unconventional in rhetorical purpose: the emphasis of the topos was on pathetic appeals on behalf of those involved in legal or political disputes rather than on the shaming of a transgressive family member.[49] And yet Cicero's evocation of Appius benefits from an audience's knowledge of the solemnity with which *mortuos excitare* was usually imbued, its illustration of the institutional "truths" of common bloodline and familial *gloria*. In *De Oratore*, Cicero has Antonius ascribe the technique to Crassus; indeed, had Crassus been a speaker in a certain well-known case, he would have used the topos to have a dead father speak pathetically on behalf of his living son (the defendant) and commend him to the judges (*de Orat.* 1.245). Elsewhere, Cicero tells us that his contemporary P. Servilius Vatia Isauricus used the technique to evoke Q. Caecilius Metellus Celer (Clodia's former husband) as well as other Metelli so as to have them plead for the restitution of the exiled Cicero.[50] Celer's living brother, Q. Caecilius Metellus Nepos, who was Cicero's enemy, apparently put aside his private antipathies when Servilius, speaking *divina quadam gravitate* (with a kind of divine solemnity), reminded him of the deeds and outstanding qualities of their family line and common blood. In the now fragmentary conclusion of the *Pro Scauro*, Cicero claims to "see" his client's dead father and calls pathetically upon the dead man to make himself present in the jurors' minds—no doubt in order to plead for his son (*Scaur.* 49). The passage seems to have entailed a detailed physical description of the deceased, through which Cicero encouraged his audience to imagine the elder Scaurus present and recalled Scaurus' high standing. It does include the word *species* (appearance) and the proposition *etiam si forte non nosset, tamen principem civitatis esse diceret* (even if [someone] did not know him, he would nevertheless say that he was the leading citizen of the state).

Still another republican orator is known to have exploited the topos for similar purposes. Valerius Maximus records an especially memorable performance by Helvius Mancia Formianus, a freedman's son who in 55 BCE accused the annalist L. Scribonius Libo before the Roman censors.[51] Speaking in Libo's defense, Cn. Pompeius Magnus had remarked that Mancia had been let out of the underworld (*ab inferis remissum*) in order to bring the accusation—a biting commentary on Mancia's low social status. Mancia, however, turned the insult against his attacker by describing his visions *in* the underworld of the ghosts of Cn. Domitius Ahenobarbus, M. Iunius Brutus, Cn. Papirius Carbo, and M. Perperna Vento, Romans who died as a result of the civil conflicts of the late 80s and 70s BCE in which Pompeius was a commander. Mancia claims to have seen and heard the ghosts bewailing their fates at Pompeius' hands. Domitius, he says, lamented the fact that, although upstanding and patriotic, he was killed in the prime of youth by Pompeius' order. Brutus complained of having fallen victim to Pompeius' perfidy and cruelty. Carbo recalled having been imprisoned and then murdered. Perpenna hurled curses at Pompeius' viciousness. Again, such pathetic and solemn appeals, which back up Mancia's implicit claim to have been himself victimized by Pompeius, gain in force from the illustrious nature of the dead who are made to deliver them.

Cicero's Appius does far more culturally transformative work than any of the passages just cited. It goes beyond convention not only in its rhetorical goals, but also in suggesting that the values of the past are open to selection and not merely imitation. And yet the rhetorical comparanda suggest, too, that the conventions of oratory itself, its reliance on the solemn institutional "truths" of bloodline and glory, endowed Cicero's Appius with institutional gravity. Oratory's magical conjuring of the dead prepares a Roman audience to hear Appius' words as more than scurrilous gossip. [52]

While the adaptation of elite performance traditions in the Appius-*prosopopoeia* helps Cicero advance rhetorical goals tied directly to the circumstances of Caelius' trial, it also helps him attack his political enemy, Clodius, and magnify his own political standing. Every aspect of Cicero's triumph over Clodia would have diminished Clodius by implication, since Clodia's brother was closely and frequently associated with his sister in the public eye. Apparently aware, however, of the political opportunity he has afforded himself, Cicero actually turns to making a mockery of Clodius immediately after his portrayal of Appius—and thus lends still further weight to his attack on Clodia by emphasizing the decadence of the present-day Clodians in comparison with their forbearers. Cicero's stab at Clodius begins with sheer *ad hominem* attack: alluding to rumors of an incestuous bond between the siblings, he imagines the young Clodius climbing into his older sister's bed for comfort (36). Then, taking on the persona of Clodius himself, Cicero advises Clodia to drop her attachment to Caelius, since many other opportunities for amorous liaisons await her in the gardens of her property. The formal similarity of Appius' and Clodius' portraits encourages a comparison between the men themselves, even while Cicero also distinguishes them as competing influences on Clodia's behavior.[53] With this comparison in place, Cicero's evocation of the dead Appius takes on its full significance as a maneuver within the world of late-republican politics. For

Cicero thus explicitly frames his self-identification with Appius as a reason for audience and reader to prefer him over a political rival. Through Appius, Cicero claims to understand the implications of both Roman cultural tradition and ancestral achievement and to emulate their beneficial examples, while implying that Clodius, from whose own family he draws the traditions and achievements in question, comprehends neither.

Magic and Superstition

If Cicero and his contemporaries could conceive of *mortuos excitare* as similar to other types of elite-sponsored performance, so, too, they could imagine it as similar to actual magic, and Cicero also sought to exploit this cultural likeness in the competitive world of late-republican politics. An inverse aspect to the *Pro Caelio's prosopopoeia* of Appius Claudius Caecus emerges from Cicero's evocation, some years later, of none other than the dead Clodius himself in the text purporting to record Cicero's speech defending Clodius' murderer, T. Annius Milo.[54] Here Cicero uses *mortuos excitare* to stigmatize the person so evoked. On the one hand, he suggests that Roman society is better off with Clodius consigned to the underworld from which he is imagined to be summoned up. On the other hand, the very association of Clodius with the suspect world of magic and its accompanying *superstitio* (superstition) helps Cicero denigrate Clodius' memory and diminish the political standing of his followers, especially since Cicero himself professes belief in other, philosophically informed views of the dead regarded by the Roman elite as more enlightened.

A basic knowledge of events leading up to Milo's trial is essential to understanding why Cicero is so preoccupied with the idea of "calling up" Clodius from the underworld in the extant *Pro Milone.*[55] Violence between the rival gangs of Clodius and Milo culminated in January of 52 BCE when Milo's men killed Clodius after an armed conflict on the Via Appia. The event capped a period of extraordinary civil disruption instigated by Clodius, Milo, and others, as bloodshed and electoral bribery led to the postponement of both consular and praetorian elections for the year. In the aftermath of Clodius' killing, his followers immolated the Roman senate house as a pyre for their dead leader. It was not until almost three turbulent months later that Cn. Pompeius Magnus, acting as sole consul, established a special *quaestio de vi* before which Milo was to be tried.

Bound by old ties of *amicitia*, Cicero took Milo's case.[56] But Cicero now faced the challenge of justifying a violent and highly public murder for which his client had admitted responsibility. Unable to deny the act, Cicero would claim that Milo's slaying of Clodius, committed in self-defense, had rid the state of a mortal enemy. Through such tactics, Cicero must have hoped to bring Clodius' violent character and behavior to the forefront and to leave Milo's own checkered past in the shadows.[57] The Clodians, Asconius tells us, disrupted the proceedings with violence on the day before Cicero was to deliver his defense speech; they remained a disturbance on the following day, taunting Cicero with their cries as he attempted to speak.[58] Indeed, just how much of his case Cicero was able to make in public, as well as the exact argument he chose for the spoken oration as opposed to the published version, remain topics of scholarly debate.[59] In an effort to maintain order, Pompeius had his troops ring the forum. Their arms, according to Plutarch, glittered in the sunlight while Cicero spoke.[60]

The extant *Pro Milone* represents Milo as a patriotic hero rather than a murderer, while Clodius appears as a maddened transgressor devoted to the state's destruction. This appeal to the patriotism of Cicero's audience relies in part on making the topos *mortuos excitare* the occasion for rejecting a nightmarish scenario in which Clodius is "called up" from the dead to continue as the leader of his rabid followers. Elaborating his *extra causam* argument in the speech's later sections, Cicero asserts that no one would want to summon Clodius back from the underworld even if such a thing were possible.[61] He exhorts his audience to imagine that Milo could be absolved on the condition that Clodius *revixerit* (live again). Affecting surprise at his listeners' response, Cicero asks them why they cringe in fear. "What," he demands, "would be the effect of the living Clodius upon you, whom he has terrified, dead as he is, in a vain thought?" Cicero then goes on to assert that even Pompeius, who "has always been able to do what no one beside him can," would have preferred legal recourse over the chance *ipsum ab inferis excitare* (to summon [Clodius] himself up from the underworld). Even if Pompeius had wanted *evocare* (to call) Clodius up from the dead, he would never have done so out of concern for the state (79).[62] Later, after recollecting the Clodian mob's immolation of the senate, Cicero exclaims, *excitate, excitate ipsum, si potestis, a mortuis: frangetis impetum vivi cuius vix sustinetis Furias insepulti?* (Call him up from the dead, call him up if you can: will you break the onslaught of the living man when you scarcely withstood the Furies of the man unburied?) (91). Rome, Cicero suggests, should rejoice in Clodius' removal from civic life.

But Cicero himself works hard to make Clodius present as a way of driving home his point. Indeed, he goes so far as to create a tension between the mental image of the dead Clodius created by his words and the idea of a somehow animate being acting on its own behalf. The mental conjuring that Cicero encourages with the phase *fingite animis* seems to call up the dead Clodius himself in the subsequent question *quonam modo ille vos vivus adficeret quos mortuus inani cogitatione percussit?* (What would be the effect of the living Clodius upon you, whom he has terrified, dead as he is, in a vain thought?) (79). Here Clodius, the subject of *percussit* and referent of *mortuus,* possesses an independent agency: it is he himself who strikes terror into the hearts of Cicero's listeners. In what follows, Cicero relates that Clodius' henchman, Sex. Cloelius, threw Clodius' corpse into the senate house *ut eam mortuus incenderet quam vivus everterat* (so that as a dead man he might set on fire what he overturned while alive) (90). Earlier the subject of the verb *percussit,* Clodius again possesses agency as the subject of *incenderet,* a verb Cicero elsewhere uses in a very active sense.[63] Cicero enforces this image of Clodius' dead body as an active agent by asserting that the senate house could not resist Clodius' corpse: *non restiterit cadaveri curia* (91).[64] He even lends his own words an incantatory quality through the repetition of the imperative *fingite* when he encourages his audience to imagine the dead Clodius returning to life (79: *fingite animis . . . fingite igitur*).

In the *Pro Milone,* Clodius' resurrection is made to stand for a mass resurgence of civil discord. The use of such symbolism suggests the anxiety surrounding that which Cicero seeks, in Roach's terms, both to embody and replace here, i.e., *mortuos excitare* itself (a performance that may not have taken place at Milo's actual trial). For the figure of Clodius, blamed obsessively for Rome's woes, is in fact inadequate as a shorthand for Roman political dysfunction—Cicero himself must concede that Milo also led a violent gang—while the specter of Clodius will not vanish simply by denying the possibility of his resurrection: his followers live on and even threaten to grow in rabidity following their leader's death.

Even worse, however, than a resurrected Clodius would be Milo's exile as punishment for his killing (103). In the *Pro Milone*'s peroration, Cicero constructs an opposition between the rejected idea of Clodius' resurrection and the glorious destiny that Milo has in store as a hero of the Roman state. The killing of Clodius, Cicero declares, will assure Milo's lasting fame in Rome and the world. Purporting to repeat Milo's own words, Cicero asserts that through *gloria, absentes adessemus, mortui viveremus* (though absent, we are present, though dead, we live). *Gloria* makes men seem even to ascend into the heavens; it alone offers consolation for the brevity of life in the memory of posterity (97).

Disembodiment and Philosophy

Crossing the boundary between life and death is thus central to Cicero's representation of both Clodius as a menace and Milo as a patriot. The capacity of *gloria* to bring it about that, "though dead, we live" repeats the series of parallelisms through which Cicero had evoked the Clodian threat earlier in the *Pro Milone*. The words *mortui viveremus* recall Cicero's declaration that Sex. Cloelius threw his master into the senate house *ut eam mortuus incenderet quam vivus everterat* (so that as a dead man he might set on fire what he overturned while alive) (90). Cicero's questions, *ille denique vivus mali nihil fecisset cui mortuo unus ex suis satellitibus curiam incenderit?* (Would, finally, that man, if alive, have done no evil, when a single one of his henchman burned the senate house for him after his death?) and *cum tantum ausus sit ustor pro mortuo, quid signifer pro vivo non esset ausurus?* (when he [Cloelius] dared so much as a torch bearer for the dead [Clodius], what would he not have dared as a sign bearer for the living man?) (90), employ a similar opposition between the living and their posthumous influence. Likewise, Cicero's words in the peroration echo his earlier question about the mental image of Clodius he has asked his audience to conjure up: *quonam modo ille vos vivus adficeret quos mortuus inani cogitatione percussit?* (What would be the effect of the living Clodius upon you, whom he has terrified, dead as he is, in a vain thought?) (79).

What distinguishes Milo and Clodius, however, is the absence or presence of their bodies in the afterlives to which they are respectively destined. This distinction helps Cicero signal Milo's embrace of one of the highest goals recognized by the Roman elite, the pursuit of *gloria*, while it also allows him to stigmatize Clodius and the Clodians as politically and culturally backward. In contrast to the dead Clodius, whose unburied corpse becomes an agent of destruction, Milo's *gloria* is entirely independent of his body and its fate. This is particularly clear in Milo's supposed reaction to the joy that he imagines spreading through the Roman empire at the news of Clodius' death: *"quam ob rem ubi corpus hoc sit non," inquit, "laboro, quoniam omnibus in terris et iam versatur et semper hic habitabit nominis mei gloria"* ("On account of which I care not" [Milo] says, "where this body may be, since in every land the glory of my name is even now on men's tongues and here it will always dwell") (98). Here Cicero has Milo bravely face the prospect of banishment and even burial in a place other than Rome because he can count on the lasting glory of his name. Milo is a true and outstanding Roman who looks forward to the rewards most prized by someone of that station.[65]

Cicero further identifies himself and Milo with the elite by having Milo appear both inspired and consoled by philosophy. Stoicism, like that which influenced Cicero's own *Tusculan Disputations* and *De re publica*, fostered a disregard for the body through discussion of the soul's disembodiment after death.[66] Expelled from his earthly home in Rome, Milo aspires, through *gloria*, to a similarly disembodied existence in a celestial realm (97). Moreover, as Clark and Ruebel have shown, the *Pro Milone* is informed by a "theory" of tyrannicide strongly influenced by Stoic views elaborated in Cicero's philosophical works. Cicero actually calls Clodius a *tyrannus* just before drawing an overt comparison between him and the insurgent Catiline (35–37); but Cicero's general insistence on Clodius' recourse to *vis* (violence), his characterization of Clodius' actions as *dominatio* and *regnum*, and his descriptions of Clodius' manipulation of the legal system all fit into a framework within which Cicero elsewhere analyzes the rise of tyrants and their power. Conversely, Milo's link to *providentia* and divine law liken him both to the figure of the *tyrannoktonos* (tyrant-slayer) and that of the Stoic wise man. Cicero proposes that Clodius' death at Milo's hands was actually ordained by a divine force acting for the perpetual good of Rome. It was appropriate, he explains, that Clodius fell near Mount Alba in Latium, whose lakes, groves, and altars he had polluted (85). Fitting, too, was the fact that Clodius was mortally wounded near a temple of the Bona Dea, whose rites he had defiled (86). The immortal gods encouraged Clodius to attack Milo, who was the only person capable of defeating him (88): if Milo had not killed Clodius, Rome's citizens would have no *res publica* left (89).

In contrast to Cicero's association of Milo with philosophy, his identification of Clodius with popular traditions of a ghostly underworld stigmatizes both Clodius and his followers as socially inferior, blinded by ignorance, and superstition-bound. Cicero expressly equates such views with the ignorance of the masses in the *Tusculan Disputations,* and many of his peers must have held a similar opinion.[67] Cicero's methods in the *Pro Milone,* however, are subtle in comparison with the directness of his philosophy, perhaps in consideration of the plebeian element among Milo's potential supporters. It is striking, for example, that Cicero chooses not to mention Clodius' adoption into a plebeian *gens,* a decision that he derides elsewhere as mere pandering to the masses.[68] Identifying Clodius with popular traditions through the orature of *mortuos excitare* is a more effective means of diminishing his standing. Drawing on competing views of the dead and the afterlife, Cicero relegates the shade of the plebeian Clodius to a traditional underworld from which he can never be conjured up, while Milo, consoled by philosophy, stands a chance of ascending into the heavens.

Conclusion

As we learn from Quintilian and other imperial rhetoricians, the topos *mortuos* [or *defunctos*] *excitare* continued to be recommended to orators of the

Principate, and Cicero's *Pro Caelio* was often cited as an educational model.[69] Our almost total lack of imperial oratorical texts apart from declamation, however, prevents us from following the development of the technique. To what extent, we may wonder, would emphasizing the resemblance between the topos and other elite performances of the Republic continue to be a useful persuasive device once the political purpose for which these spectacles had been designed could no longer be envisioned? Conversely, to what similarities, if any, between their own techniques and those of magic would Augustan orators have called attention?

Changing social and political circumstances suggest a shift in conception and practice. Ancestral customs such as the display of the *imagines maiorum*, for example, while their use did not die out entirely under Augustus, could no longer be the vehicle for political self-promotion they once had been.[70] It is difficult, consequently, to imagine a judicial or political orator drawing, in the manner of the *Pro Caelio*, connections between his own speech and the particular set of cultural performances that interest Cicero. Augustus had, moreover, associated himself early in his career with an effort to rid Rome of magic.[71] The renewal of traditional religion was a hallmark of his regime. While magical motifs are frequent in Augustan poetry, it is hard to envision Augustan orators extrapolating, like Cicero, political conclusions from the notion of resurrecting a murder victim from the underworld. Augustan trials are likely to have been far less spectacular affairs in general than their republican antecedents.[72] The Princeps himself often delivered judgment in tribunal and sought to avoid spectacles of a macabre nature, such as a condemned man's public torture.[73] In these changed circumstances, the theatrical and inflammatory style that Cicero had employed in "calling up the dead" would have seemed anachronistically out of place. In chapter 4, however, we will see it resurfacing, transformed, in the work of the Augustan poet Propertius.

CHAPTER TWO

Domesticae Furiae:
Cicero's Tragic Universe

THE REPUBLICAN orator often had to be a dramatist. In his performance, references to the stage could help him appeal to the many audience members who attended or read plays. Techniques reminiscent of drama, moreover, were advocated by the rhetorical theorists. Rutulius Lupus, for example, in his Latin abridgment of the first-century BCE rhetor Gorgias' work, *On Figures of Speech,* describes an orator's means of building a set of *personae,* a self-performed cast of characters through which to enhance his persuasiveness. For Rutulius, oratorical *prosopopoeia* resembles the prologues of plays, where the playwright himself might speak through one of his characters (often a ghost). But the trope, Rutulius suggests, may be used not only to portray oneself the speech and action of dead persons and inanimate objects, but also to introduce descriptively a personified thing or concept (Rut. Lup. 2.6). Thus an orator might describe Nature presiding as the judge of a trial, or the State imploring its citizens to consider their freedom, their families, and their ancestors. Quintilian, offering further parallels for this technique, compares Vergil's portrait of Rumor in the *Aeneid,* Xenophon's fable of Pleasure and Virtue, and the figures of Life and Death that Ennius imagined debating in one of his satires (Quint. *Inst.* 9.2.36).[1] Methods of this sort represent an imaginative complement to the role-playing we have seen Cicero embracing through his manipulation of the topos *mortuos excitare* in chapter 1.

Indeed, Rutulius' account suggests the range of prosopopoeiac techniques that would have been familiar to Cicero from the rhetorical handbooks and from Greek orators such as Hyperides and Charisius. Nothing here or elsewhere, however, prepares the reader of Cicero's speeches for his use of one such *persona* through which to represent the dead's close involvement with the living: the Furies, personifications of the madness (*furor*) that was the dead's fearful curse, inflicted especially by murder victims upon their killers.[2] While a Greek orator might introduce similar characters for the limited purposes to which Rutulius points, Cicero's Furies pervade the Rome of his oratorical imagination, their actions closely shadowing those of living Romans who work for both the *res publica*'s demise and its preservation. Thus the Furies aid P. Clodius Pulcher and L. Calpurnius Piso Caesoninus in the destruction of Rome and drive Cicero himself into an unjust exile. But they also assist in the prosecution of the corrupt provincial governor C. Verres and hasten the expiation of Rome's crimes by seeking the punishment of the Catilinarian conspirators. As with the techniques examined in the last chapter, Cicero's boldness is remarkable when dealing with an issue of such basic importance to Roman society, the relationship between the living and the dead. What might have compelled him to push oratorical convention to such a point?

In this chapter I argue that Cicero's oratorical use of the Furies represents an appropriation of mythological tragedy for the purposes of characteristically late-republican political competition. In this way, too, it is a counterpart to his politically motivated adaptation of cultural performance through the topos *mortuos excitare*.[3] For Cicero, the Furies' political usefulness springs from the narratives of murder, madness, and vendetta-style violence, together with the powerful emotions of fear, guilt, and religious awe, with which the Greek tragedians—and their Roman translators—associated them. Adapting these features of tragedy in his oratorical works helps Cicero stigmatize opponents while suggesting that he himself can direct the drama of Roman civic life to a favorable outcome. Attuned to the interplay of literacy and oral performance signified by Joseph Roach's concept of orature, we perceive again its historical operation in the crafting of a Latin literary tradition. For the illiterate majority of audience members who attended both plays and the trials and assemblies at which orators spoke, the tragedies in which the Furies figured so prominently were performances, as were the speeches that Cicero's published orations purport to preserve. For the educated minority, however, Cicero's speeches were also highly literary documents, whose allusions to Hellenic drama would have made them at once more literary and more tied to the circumstances of oral performance. Like them, the works of the playwrights circulated as texts for refined private appreciation, itself a performance-based activity, in addition to serving as scripts for popular theatrical productions.

The tragic motif of the Furies not only informs the imagery and characterization of individual Ciceronian speeches in a deep and subtle fashion, but also lends coherence to Cicero's presentation of a range of pressing civic issues. From the Forum to the written page, Rome risks *becoming* a stage tragedy, an exemplary performance of social and political dysfunction for all time, its protagonists helpless to resist the workings of divine justice. In order to bring out this dual function of the Furies as a Ciceronian oratorical trope, I begin with a detailed analysis of Cicero's early speech *Pro Sex. Roscio Amerino*, before turning, more briefly, to a series of Cicero's later orations, including the *Pro Sulla*, the *In Pisonem*, the *Pro Milone*, and the second *actio* of the *In Verrem*. I have labeled each section according to the significant civic issue to which Cicero applies the tragic paradigm. But the full scope of political motivations underpinning the Ciceronian literary fantasy emerges from the chapter as a whole. Through the Furies, Cicero introduces the Roman dead as party to discussions of the aftermath of civil war, the recurrence of violence across generations, the exile of leaders, the return of tyranny, and the mismanagement of Rome's empire. The tragic coloring that pervades later accounts of the Republic's final decades infuses Cicero's representation of his public pronouncements on these matters—and serves his political ends.

Murderous Aftermath of Civil War

The lawlessness and disorder arising from the Roman general L. Cornelius Sulla's second occupation of Rome in 82 BCE stood out in Roman memory even in comparison with other such events marring the first century BCE. We hear of general bloodshed, an orgy of looting and killing indulged in by all who sought profit or revenge. Sulla himself was particularly merciless toward his personal enemies. The senator M. Marius Gratidianus was not only killed but also decapitated and his head carried through the streets (an act foreshadowing Cicero's own gruesome and spectacular end forty years later: his amputated head and hands displayed on the speaker's platform in the Forum). Gangs of armed men roamed the city exacting similar punishments on behalf of the victorious general. Sulla's list of the proscribed— those whose property was to be confiscated and whose lives could be taken at sight—numbered in the many hundreds. The impact of the Sullan proscriptions, a measure unlike any implemented previously by a Roman leader, was made especially grave by Sulla's insistence on depriving of their civil rights the proscribeds' sons and grandsons.

And yet the chaos of this period could be made coherent, its profound traumatic impact channeled into persuasive arguments, through adapting its events to the tragic paradigm of the Furies' dire vengeance on those implicated in murderous violence. This was Cicero's strategy in one of his earliest and most celebrated orations, the *Pro Sex. Roscio Amerino,* delivered in defense of a young man whose father had been killed and his patrimony confiscated in suspicious circumstances. A close analysis of the speech reveals Cicero's deep reliance on the tragic motif of the Furies to arouse strong emotions in both audience and reader.[4] In a case such as this, both the educated members of the elite and the popular element familiar with oratory only through attending public speeches would have expected a pathetic display on Cicero's part.[5] And Cicero makes his defense hang on the emotions considered most appropriate to tragedy, fear and pity, as well as a generalized anxiety and religious awe that he also ties to the idea of the Furies' vengeance.[6]

Serving as Sex. Roscius' advocate in 80 BCE with Rome still reeling from Sulla's proscriptions, Cicero ostensibly refers to the Furies of tragedy only to reject them as a paradigm inapplicable to his client. At a culminating moment of his extended *refutatio,* Cicero asks Roscius' judges to consider whether Roscius, who stands charged with the murder of his father, really appears as frenzied as the parricides whom his audience sees repeatedly being tormented by the Furies in plays. Roscius' docility and good character, Cicero implies, assure his innocence. A true parricide would be in a state of extreme agitation due to the guilty knowledge of his crime (66–68).[7]

In his speech as a whole, however, Cicero repeats on a far wider and less self-evident level the basic elements of the tragic paradigm whose mimesis of a present reality he seems to deny. The threat, Cicero suggests, of an unbounded and indeed furious recurrence of murderous violence pervades Rome. The bloodthirstiness of Roscius' enemies, whom Cicero equates with enemies of the state, recalls the pitiless, animal aggression characteristic of the tragic Furies' menace. The anxious memory of the many Roman dead hangs over Roscius' trial as Cicero urges the jury to put an end to the cycle of killing and vengeance that has come to typify Roman life. The Furies of the *Pro Roscio Amerino* are thus at the heart of cosmic disruption, a vision that lends urgency to Cicero's message as Roscius' defender. Therefore, the pressing need for the rule of law: Cicero insinuates that Sulla must ultimately be held responsible both for the violence with which Roscius has been plagued and for enacting reforms that will put the troubling memory of Rome's recent past to rest.[8]

The *Pro Roscio Amerino*'s *refutatio* (37–82) offers a useful point of entry into the larger pattern of pathetic language and imagery in which we will see tragedy's influence predominating. The passage owes much of its power to a pathetic discussion of the horrors of parricide, beginning with a series of reflections on the psychology of one who is capable of killing a parent and closing with praise of the ancestors' wisdom in designing a punishment to fit the magnitude of the crime.⁹ Here, the case of T. Caelius of Tarracina provides Cicero with a specific illustration of parricide's atrocity. Caelius, Cicero explains, was found strangled one morning in a room in which he had spent the night with his two sons. Although there were no other suspects, Caelius' sons were freed from all suspicion because they were found asleep in the same room with their dead father. No one, apparently, believed that a person who had broken both human and divine laws by killing his father could have then managed to sleep through the night. Criminals of this type, Cicero insists, can neither rest nor even breathe *sine metu* (without fear) (64–65).

Alluding next to the figure of Orestes, Cicero observes that the tragic poets depicted the Furies' relentless pursuit of matricides, even in cases where the violent act is undertaken by divine command (66). Yet it is not true, Cicero insists, that, as in plays, those guilty of some wrong are hunted and terrified by real Furies carrying burning torches. Rather, "each man's guilt and terror vex him the most, each man's crime hunts him and afflicts him with madness." Dark ruminations and the pangs of a guilty conscience are the *domesticae* (private) Furies who day and night seek retribution for the slaying of parents (67). With formidable adroitness, Cicero thus reaches out simultaneously to a broad popular audience of theatergoers and the best-educated among his elite peers: he recalls here not only the conventions of contemporary Roman drama but also the work of the fourth-century Greek orator Aeschines, who in his speech against Timarchus had employed a similar comparison.¹⁰

While effective in Roscius' defense, Cicero's evocation of the Furies furthers the equally important task of incriminating those upon whom Cicero lays the blame for the elder Roscius' murder and his son's persecution. These are Roscius' kinsmen, T. Roscius Magnus and T. Roscius Capito, to whom Cicero imputes direct involvement in the killing, and Sulla's freedman L. Cornelius Chrysogonus, whom Cicero portrays as wielding the political influence necessary for the prosecution of the case.¹¹ Consider Cicero's account of the effects of the parricide's *scelus* (crime) upon him. Cicero's initial portrait of Chrysogonus employs a virtually identical set of terms in emphasizing the terror and consciousness of guilt that inhabit the freedman's mind and force him "night and day" to repay the consequences of his *nefas* (impiety).¹² Chrysogonus, guilty of his own *scelus* in depriving Roscius of his patrimony, seeks to clear his mind of fear and suspicion, the *scrupulum* (source of anxiety) that torments him and keeps him from his *praedam nefariam* (impious plunder) (6). Elsewhere, Chrysogonus is overtly compared to the *furiosus*, C. Fimbria (33–34). His lack of *pietas* emerges in blatant disregard for Sex. Roscius' filial devotions and the necessity of proper funeral rites for the elder Roscius, whose ghost would thus have a reason to be restless (23–24, 146). His fitness to pay *poenas* (penalties) is a recurring theme (113, 148, etc.). Indeed, it is clear in section 67 that Cicero has a more general criminality in mind when he says that the Furies torment *eos qui aliquid impie scelerateque commiserint* (those who have committed some impious crime), words which might apply as much to Roscius' opponents as they do to the dramatic parricide. Likewise, Cicero's generalization, *sua quemque fraus et suus terror maxime vexat . . .* (each man's guilt and terror vex him the most . . .), widens the applicability of the Furies as an allegory. Even the syntax of the sentence *hae sunt impiis adsiduae domesticaeque Furiae quae dies noctesque parentium poenas a consceleratissimis filiis repetant* (These are the persistent private Furies who night and day demand from the most criminal sons the recompense owed to their parents) (67) suggests that any *impius* may be visited by Furies of bad conscience like the Furies who pursue parricidal sons in drama. The general term *impiis* stands apart from the phrase *a consceleratissimis filiis*, which is further set off by its inclusion in the relative clause that concludes the sentence.[13]

Not only is Cicero's Chrysogonus pursued by the Furies of bad conscience, but he is also, in a sense, a Fury himself and in this respect his own punishment for his criminal wrongdoings.[14] This emerges in particular from Cicero's description of Chrysogonus' brutal lawlessness and murderous nature. Immediately after mentioning Chrysogonus for the first time, Cicero asserts, *a Chrysogono peto ut pecunia fortunisque nostris contentus sit, sanguinem et vitam ne petat* (I seek from Chrysogonus that he be content with our money and fortunes and not seek our blood and life) (7). Chrysogonus' desires are inhuman: he seeks not only Roscius' life but, like the tragic Erinyes, his blood.[15] The same claim is made in the speech's peroration. If it is not enough, Cicero declares, for Chrysogonus to satisfy his greed through money *nisi etiam crudelitati sanguis praebitus sit* (unless an offering of blood is also made to his brutal cruelty), Sex. Roscius' only remaining hope is the jury's mercy (150).[16] The ritual connotations of this later passage form a particularly strong point of contact between Chysogonus and the Erinyes, to whom their victims were owed as a ritual atonement.[17] Chrysogonus' demand for Roscius' blood is an indication of the freedman's brutal, violent nature, which has led him to commit unspeakable acts. These have now become sources of anxiety, suspicion, and further wrongdoing. The seeds of Chrysogonus' criminality can be found within himself: in those aspects of his character that bear comparison to the Furies of tragedy.

In expatiating, then, upon parricide, Cicero not only seeks to dismiss the possibility of guilt in the case of his client but also magnifies an atmosphere of abhorrence for the very acts and traits he imputes to Roscius' enemies.

The latter, he suggests, are far more likely to be harried by the Furies of bad conscience than the man they accuse. Cicero could count on his contemporaries to assume that the consciousness of complicity in Roscius' murder would haunt the latter's surviving kinsmen, Magnus and Capito, while Chrysogonus would suffer from fear of prosecution and from knowing that the younger Roscius still lives—motivations that might compel him to seek Roscius' death. Cicero's characterization of Chrysogonus in particular makes the implications of violence and blood-vengeance embodied in the Furies reach beyond the specifics of Roscius' particular case to the fundamental institutions of the Roman justice system.

Turning to the *Pro Roscio Amerino*'s frame—its elaborate exordium and peroration—we find that Cicero exploits the motif of the Furies not only for individual characterizations but also to underscore his account of the generalized anxiety afflicting Rome.[18] In the exordium, Cicero insists that, rather than personal boldness or devotion to duty, it is the fear gripping other, more prominent men that has compelled him to come forward. While more established orators, he suggests, would neither be ignored nor forgiven for speaking *de re publica,* what Cicero says will either remain "hidden" or be pardoned due to his youth, even if in general the principle of pardon as well as the custom of hearing cases has been destroyed under Sulla's dictatorship (3). Is it not most shameful, Cicero goes on to ask, that the jury should be the vehicle through which Roscius' foes accomplish what formerly they brought about through violence (8)? Cicero thus warns of *periculum* (danger) in the form of a breakdown of law and public discourse (5, 7).[19] This represents both the precondition for all that he will say and a lingering threat impinging upon the court proceedings. In the peroration, Cicero suggests that the source of this *periculum* is the *crudelitas* (savagery) that has come to characterize Roman civic life (148, 150, 154). Such *crudelitas* works like an illness on both the minds of individuals and on the Roman people as a whole: it is the responsibility of those in positions of power and authority *mederi* (to cure) the afflictions from which the state *laborat* (suffers) (154). Developing the metaphor of illness and cure, Cicero continues, *vestrum nemo est quin intellegat populum Romanum qui quondam in hostis lenissimus existimatur hoc tempore domestica crudelitate laborare* (There is not a single one of you who is not aware that the Roman people, who in the past have been thought most forgiving toward enemies, suffer at this time from a savagery afflicting the state) (154).

The phrase *domestica crudelitate* here echoes Cicero's earlier characterization of the torments of a guilty conscience as *domesticae Furiae* (67). Although the sense of *domesticus* varies slightly between these, its only two occurrences in the *Pro Roscio Amerino,* a basic meaning remains unchanged:

in each case, *domesticus* denotes something peculiar to a subject defined by its inclusion within a single *domus,* whether a personal dwelling place or a civic body.[20] In addition to being like an illness in the body politic, the *periculum* of *crudelitas* is thus also like the Furies, who are themselves interpreted as an allegory of the mental affliction suffered by those involved in murderous *nefas.*[21]

Sulla, as head of the Roman state, bears the ultimate responsibility for the *periculum* of *crudelitas,* all the more heinous in that his duties as Rome's leader are religious as well as political. Like the Greek tragedian Euripides, on whom Roman playwrights such as Ennius, Accius, and Pacuvius based many of their tragic scripts, Cicero does not limit himself to psychological explanations of murder and its repercussions even while psychologizing the Furies. Rather, he infuses his defense of Roscius with a sense of religious awe. Cicero's continual invocation of the immortal gods is significant in this regard, even if the exclamation *di immortales* is entirely conventional. More telling is his description of the *religio* (religious constraint) (66) emanating from spilt parental blood. The Roman ancestors, Cicero claims, recognized its polluting power and so insisted on cutting the criminal off from air, light, water, and earth. So arose the custom of enclosing the condemned parricide in the *culleus,* or leather sack, before hurling him into a river.[22] The ancestors' practical wisdom in this as in all affairs of law and state, Cicero insists, reflects their understanding that nothing is so sacred as to be exempt from eventual violation (70–72). Earlier in the speech, Cicero has anticipated the religious tone of his rhetoric here by stating his uncertainty whether to implore the help of the jury, the Roman people, or the immortal gods (29).[23] Elsewhere still, Cicero compares Sulla's rule to that of Jupiter himself (131)—only to raise doubts about the nature and stability of the regime. If Sulla is as all-knowing as Jupiter, does this mean that Chrysogonus' apparently illegal purchase was carried out with his knowledge? Is Sulla then still to be feared as a dictator? Or—what might have been an even more fearful prospect for the senatorial members of the jury—has Chrysogonus, a former slave, gained the upper hand on his old master?[24] "May the gods prevent," Cicero exclaims, "the public courts from becoming the refuge of *sectores* [those who buy confiscated property at auction so as to resell it]!" (151).

Cicero's evocations of the Furies, through both explicit reference and a larger pattern of language and imagery, enforce the *Pro Sex. Roscio Amerino*'s argument for the rule of law by symbolizing impulses toward civil discord and anarchy that constitute a breach of divine order as well as a failure of Sulla's regime. The Furies both require and endanger the right functioning of judicial process. They perpetuate a cycle of blood-vengeance antithetical to the rule of state-sponsored law because the basis of this cycle lies instead in the severed bonds of kinship. Tragic myth located the impetus toward such retribution in the infernal realms of the dead, whose ghosts and Furies might haunt the world of the living for generations to come. Cicero, too, fears a curse on Roman posterity (153).

Recurrence of Murderous Violence across Generations

History would prove Cicero right. In spite of the fact that civil war per se would not reemerge as a problem for Rome until 49 BCE, violence between citizens resurfaced repeatedly in the intervening years, most flagrantly in the Catilinarian uprising of 63 and the continued upheavals of the 50s. Contributing to the idea of a single type of *recurring* violence that informs both ancient and modern accounts is the fact that the protagonists of the major social and political crises were either identical or closely tied to the men most prominent in earlier outbreaks. Sulla had put Catiline himself, for instance, in charge of the murder of opponents (such as M. Marius Gratidianus) in the bloody aftermath of his second march on Rome. Others who had fought with Sulla, such as C. Manlius and P. Furius, became Catiline's own lieutenants or swelled the ranks of his soldiers. Such men were often motivated by their failure to find prosperity in farming the land distributed to them through the proscriptions. Those dispossessed of land, likewise desperate, also ended up in Catiline's forces. For Cicero, the continuity of personnel across periods of social upheaval could be effectively presented in tragic terms. Two of Cicero's speeches belonging to this period, the *Pro Sulla* of 62 BCE and the *In Pisonem* of 55, show Cicero expanding his tragic vision of Roman civic life to account for the transferral of murderous violence from one generation of malefactors to another.

P. Cornelius Sulla, the nephew of Sulla the dictator, was accused in 62 BCE on a charge of *vis* for his alleged abetment of Catilinarian violence. Personal ties to the younger Sulla led Cicero (in spite of his criticism of the dictator in the *Pro Roscio Amerino*) to join a series of other prominent public figures in Sulla's defense. Recognized as the consul who had uncovered the Catilinarian conspiracy of 63, Cicero based his exculpation of Sulla on a claim to possess intimate understanding of those who were in fact responsible for the uprising.[25]

In a manner similar to his tactics in the *Pro Roscio Amerino* years before, Cicero supports his case for Sulla by arguing that the latter was nothing like the true Catilinarians in temperament or character. Here again, the motif of the Furies helps Cicero characterize the motivation of real criminals beset by the guilty knowledge of their crime. Different now, however, is the way

Cicero uses the Furies to describe the effects not only of a particular act of murder but also of murderous violence against the state and its citizens (*parricidium patriae*) as an endemic problem, lingering and festering over time. At a moment of high pathos, Cicero asks the judges to look deep into the minds of the convicted conspirators Catiline, Autronius, Cethegus, and Lentulus: what aberrant traits, he insists, what traces of *parricidia* they will find. The conspirators, Cicero goes on, were incited by the Furies *non ad perficiendum scelus, sed ad luendas rei publicae poenas* (not in order to accomplish a crime but to expiate the state's transgressions). From the state's long-term "wounds," the conspiracy "erupted" as a violent force. Only when this *vis* had been brought to issue and dispelled could the state convalesce and be healed (76).

The tragic condition of Roman civic life emerges powerfully from this memorable and complex image. Cicero here compares the Roman state itself both to a sick person and to a criminal who must perform an expiatory sacrifice as a means of atoning for his wrongdoings. The two metaphors overlap and complement each other. Rome's "illness" is its implication in the *parricidium* of the state, the actions of the Catilinarians; the Furies produced the conspiracy's final, bloody outbreak, the bursting of the state's suppurating wounds, so that the state's illness, which is also its crime, might be healed and, simultaneously, atoned for. The Furies' association here with sacrificial atonement for past crime recalls Aeschylus' *Oresteia,* in which Orestes says he has rid himself of the taint of maternal blood through the sacrifice of swine to Apollo (*Eum.* 282–83). The conspirators are Rome's sacrificial victims—Cicero actually likens them to beasts (76)—whose deaths assure the cleansing (cf. *luendas*) of Rome.

In Cicero's forceful invective against L. Calpurnius Piso Caesoninus, the *In Pisonem* of 55 BCE, we find the Furies again being used to suggest a genealogy of Roman insurrection, criminality, and madness whose roots extend back to the Catilinarian uprising of the previous decade. Piso, along with his consular colleague, A. Gabinius, and their ally, P. Clodius Pulcher, was one of those most responsible for persecuting Cicero over his decision, as consul in 63, to execute the conspiracy's captured leaders. The pressure of his adversaries drove Cicero into exile in 58 BCE, a blow to political standing and self-esteem from which he seems never fully to have recovered. In the *In Pisonem,* Cicero figures Piso's aim in opposing him as a ritual offering of Cicero's own blood to the dead Catiline and his followers at Catiline's tomb (16).[26] The Furies who avenge Catiline, Cicero suggests, are the followers of Clodius to whom Piso distributes torches for the purpose of destroying Cicero's house (26: *Furiis Clodianis*). Piso himself is portrayed as both hounded by Furies—he is madder than the tragic Orestes and Athamas (47;

cf. fr. 3, Clark's Oxford edition)—and a Fury himself, wreaking destruction on those who are presumed to be his allies (8, 91). The Furies are a sign of an evil transmitted to the present from an earlier generation, a lingering source of destruction which refuses to die with the individuals who perpetrate it. The murderous vengeance of Catiline's ghost lives on in Clodius and Piso, his equals in *nefas*.

Unjust Exile of Leaders

No act of alleged civil injustice looms larger in our record of the tumultuous 50s BCE than Cicero's exile of 58–57. Many have remarked on the deep psychological impact, as revealed especially in his letters, that exile appears to have had on Cicero, and the pessimism that it fostered in him about the state of Roman politics. But the biographical effort to form an impression of Cicero's psychology and political thought may have prevented us from understanding his representation of exile in fully cultural terms. In speeches delivered soon after his return, Cicero represents the unjust exile of Rome's leaders—both his own and those of earlier days—through tragic language and imagery so as to enhance its significance as an issue for Rome's concern.[27] The impulse may be self-aggrandizing, but the comparison is apt: in tragedy, the Furies' torments drove Orestes, who had returned from exile to kill his mother and her lover, back into exile by requiring him to seek absolution from Apollo at Athens. Euripides' Orestes rids himself of the Furies though a still more exilic journey to the distant land of the Tauri, from where he is to recover the statue of Artemis (*IT* 85–92). The tragic Orestes hopes for restitution to authority, upon his return, in his rightful position as the male heir of his family.

Linked by concern for a social order that would guarantee Cicero a position of restored personal and political authority following his exile, a series of speeches from this period exploit the image of Clodius as Rome's Fury. In the *De domo sua*, Clodius is the *fax ac Furia patriae* (firebrand and Fury of the fatherland) (102); in the *De haruspicum responso*, he shouts in furious tones (*furialis in contionibus voces mittis*) and is compared with Athamas and the tragic matricides (39). In the *Pro Sestio*, he is *Furia ac pestis* (Fury and pestilence) (33; cf. 39, 117); in the *In Vatinium*, he is called *illa taeterrima Furia* (that most savage Fury) and *Furia patriae, tempestas rei publicae* (Fury of the fatherland, destruction of the state) (33, 40). All these passages connect Clodius explicitly to the circumstances of Cicero's exile and the persecution of those who worked for his recall: Clodius the Fury makes Cicero's exile his goal. The issue of unjust exile, of which Cicero represents his own as the most recent example, thus takes its place in the tragic staging of Roman civic life that Cicero develops in his speeches *post reditum*.

Return of Tyranny

Clodius met his death in 52 BCE after an armed conflict on the Via Appia. As I have discussed in chapter 1, however, the danger represented by Clodius to Roman civic order lay not merely in his own person but also in the threat posed by his adherents, and in the still larger phenomenon of mob and gang violence that had by this time come to impinge directly on the functioning of electoral and judicial process at Rome. Such violence was exploited not only by Clodius but also by other competitors for public office and backers of controversial legislation. Already in 59 BCE, M. Calpurnius Bibulus and many of his followers had been injured by the supporters of Julius Caesar when attempting to block the passage of Caesar's agrarian bill. A. Gabinius escaped prosecution for electoral bribery (also in 59) through gang tactics. Q. Fabricius, M. Cispius, and Cicero's own brother, Quintus, met with armed violence in the Forum when attempting to support a bill in favor of Cicero's recall (57). Clodius' prosecution of Milo on a charge of *vis* in 56 degenerated into a gang war. The gangs of two of the candidates for consul in 52, Milo and P. Plautius Hypsaeus, resulted in much bloodshed on the Via Sacra, and no consuls were in office by the beginning of the year. The recourse to these and similar tactics on the part of Roman officials prompted charges of tyrannical ambition: M. Porcius Cato is said to have branded Julius Caesar a tyrant in 59 (Plu. *Cat. Mi.* 33); Gabinius called Pompeius a *privatus dictator* (Cic. *Q. fr.* 1.2.15); Cicero saw a tyrant in Clodius.

Thus when Cicero came to defend Milo for the murder of Clodius in 51, the tragic narrative of resistance to tyranny thwarted by the violent curse of the dead must have seemed a natural choice for the characterization of recent events. Even after Clodius' murder, his followers persisted in their lawlessness, igniting and destroying the Roman senate house as a pyre for their slain leader and disrupting Milo's trial. For Cicero in the *Pro Milone*, Clodius' rabid followers are his Furies. The speech, as discussed in chapter 1, is fascinating for its bold use of the topos *mortuos excitare* to summon Clodius back from the dead, but it demands our further attention for Cicero's adaptation of tragedy in insisting on the continued threat posed by the tyrannical Clodius to the Roman state.[28]

Andrew Dyck has suggested that Cicero's description in the *Pro Milone* of a divine force motivating Clodius' madness and death recalls a pattern of divine retribution implicit in the plot of tragedies such as Euripides'

Bacchae.[29] Still more central, however, to Cicero's representation of the threat posed by Clodius is the issue of returning tyranny that Cicero grounds in another tragic narrative, the story of Orestes. Cicero's justification of Clodius' death suggests a "theory" of tyrannicide strongly influenced by the political philosophy that Cicero elaborates in the *De re publica* and *De officiis*.[30] The tyrannical Clodius continues to exert his influence over Roman politics and civic life in the violent behavior of his followers. Indeed, one of these followers in particular, Sex. Cloelius, seeks to perpetuate Clodius' manipulation of the legal system, a trait typical of tyrants (33; cf. 89).[31] Milo, on the other hand, is like Orestes, whose story illustrates for Cicero the principle that killing is not always tantamount to *nefas* (8). The tragic characterization of Milo, Clodius, and the Clodians thus helps Cicero to address concerns about moral transgression and sacrilege while advancing a still larger argument for the rule of state-sponsored law over the domination of political factions. Clodius appears in the *Pro Milone* as a maddened tyrant devoted, both in life and after his death, to the dissolution of the *res publica*. And Cicero suggests that his audience knows the best outcome to the situation—the acquittal of Milo/Orestes and his deliverance from persecution by the Clodian Furies—from stage tragedy.[32]

Imperial Mismanagement

No simple formula can encompass Rome's attitude toward the government of its provinces in the late Republic; and yet whatever their motives—power, wealth, stability, Roman honor—Roman leaders were expected to adhere to the basic principle that "Rome had a duty to defend her allies and subjects and give them just government."[33] One need only consider the sequence of republican laws against extortion, each, Cicero could boast, more stringent than its predecessor (Cic. *Off.* 2.75), to gain a sense of how seriously, in principle, Rome took the issue of provincial mismanagement, even if the real grievances of wronged subjects often met with indifference from a corrupt judiciary. Inept and criminal governors were less a cause of increasing weakness in republican institutions than an effect of the cronyism that plagued them, but the problem, when skillfully presented, could nevertheless hold the attention of audiences at Rome.

In Cicero's speeches the potential for Roman civic life to become a tragedy implicates not only the city itself but also distant areas of Rome's wide-reaching *imperium*. That the issue of Rome's mismanagement of its empire should have occurred to Cicero as one appropriate for presentation in tragic terms will not surprise those familiar with imperial tragedy itself, in

which the central place of *furor* can be understood to reflect Roman awareness of the "darker consequences" of empire.[34] Seneca's Medea, as Anthony
Boyle suggests, speaks with "undisguised reference to Rome's control of the
world"[35] when she warns of a *furor* that will disrupt cosmic order:

> [M]y fury will never slacken in inflicting punishment and will grow continu-
> ously—what savageness of wild beasts, what Scylla, what Charybdis sucking
> down the Ausonian and Sicilian sea, or what Aetna weighing heavy on the
> gasping Titan will boil with such great menace? Not the swift river, not the
> blustering ocean nor the sea made fierce by the northwest wind nor the force
> of fire helped by a blast of wind will be able to check my onslaught and my
> wrath: I will overturn and lay low all things. (Sen. *Med.* 406–414)

Medea's furious desire here to "overturn and lay low all things" is the dark
reflection of Rome's drive for imperial expansion.[36]

For Cicero, already in the closing decades of the republic, the civic well-
being of the Roman provinces is afflicted with a similarly destructive *furor*
personified by the Furies of the dead who torment the provincial governors
C. Verres and L. Calpurnius Piso Caesoninus.[37] Tragedy makes an especially
apt metaphor for life under Verres' and Piso's jurisdictions, since both served
in Hellenic regions of the empire (Sicily and Macedonia, respectively). The
successful prosecution of Verres, an important milestone in Cicero's early
career, took place in 70 BCE after Verres' return from his province the previous year. Among the final pieces of evidence in the voluminous *In Verrem
II*, Cicero introduces the purported prison apologia of one of Verres' victims, a certain Furius of Heraclea.[38] Suspected by Verres of dishonesty with
regard to the distribution of ships in his control, Furius, Cicero relates, had
been blinded and imprisoned under expectation of imminent death. Looking ahead to what he views as Verres' inevitable trial for extortion, Cicero's
Furius recasts the trial as an episode from tragedy featuring the Furies and
their vengeful wrath.

Furius (whose name seems apt in this context, in spite of the difference in
vowel length between it and the noun *Furia*) predicts that Verres will not be
able to escape responsibility for his crimes through the killing of witnesses
like himself. Accompanying the "crowds" of those testifying, Furius warns,
there will come *ab dis manibus* (from the spirits of the dead) the avenging deities—here both *Poenae* and *Furiae*—of Verres' murdered victims.[39]
Furius frames his own document as a testimony from beyond the grave: for
discerning judges, he insists, he will be a more influential witness from the
dead (*ab inferis*) than if he were led, living, into court. If alive, Furius continues, he would be able to attest only to Verres' greed; now, having been killed

by Verres, he can bear witness to the latter's evil, recklessness, and cruelty (5.113). Furius' vision harks back to the final scene of Aeschylus's *Eumenides,* in which the Erinyes of Clytemnestra prosecute Orestes in a mythical prototype of the Athenian murder court. In the trial Furius imagines, the visitants from the dead likewise act on behalf of the prosecution in a procedure overshadowed by the victims' haunting memory.

If authentic, the condemned Furius' choice of a tragic motif for his final self-defense is a striking, even moving testament to the power of tragedy over the cultural imagination of a Roman provincial. But even if Furius' words are a product of Cicero's imagination, Cicero's own choice is still significant, since it once again assumes that the representation of Roman civic life in tragic terms, the threatened confusion of state and stage, is "good to think with": here, an effective way of presenting the issue of provincial mismanagement. Indeed, Cicero warns of the tragic retribution sought by murdered Roman citizens not only near the conclusion of *In Verrem II* but also, prominently, at its opening. Emphasizing the magnitude of Verres' crimes, Cicero declares, *agunt eum praecipitem poenae civium Romanorum* (The Avengers of Roman citizens are driving him headlong) . . . *Rapiunt eum ad supplicium di patrii* (The ancestral gods are dragging him to punishment) (1.7). Such imagery accords well with Cicero's emphasis throughout *In Verrem II* on the religious dimension of Verres' transgressions, as especially in the famous account of Verres' theft of images of the gods and other precious objects from sites throughout his province (4). In *In Verrem II,* Rome's tragedy is played out on an imperial scale far wider than that of the more localized bloodshed inflicted by Catiline or Clodius.

Military defeats suffered by L. Calpurnius Piso Caesoninus incurred a similar opprobrium from Cicero in 55 BCE. Cicero's *In Pisonem* represents Piso as one whose tragic madness endangers both Rome's provincial allies and Rome itself.[40] Thus, "The burning torches of the Furies have roused [Piso] up" (fr. 3, Clark's Oxford edition); Piso is "more crazed than the tragic Orestes or Athamas" (47) when, after transporting a vast army to his province, he leaves it after disbanding his troops. Piso is not only tormented by the Furies of bad conscience, but is also the *Poena et Furia sociorum* "Avenger and Fury to our allies" (91) due to his losses in Aetolia, formerly a peaceful area of Greece.

In Piso, as in no other figure from his oratory, Cicero traces Rome's civic tragedy back to its roots in the Hellenic world. The Hellenophile Piso who suffers from tragic madness in Macedonia, one-time head of the Greek states, brings the madness of the Furies with him like a contagion back to Rome. There, he has in fact already fostered a similarly destructive wrath in handing out torches to the "Clodian Furies" (26) who burn Cicero's own house, and in seeking to sacrifice Cicero himself to the restless ghost of Catiline (16).

Conclusion: The Politics of a Tragic Republic

Augustus' successful suppression of destructive political infighting rendered oratorical techniques like those examined in this chapter obsolete. Not only would the political competitiveness infusing Cicero's use of the Furies have been out of place in the changed political climate of the Principate, but the very nature of the motif, with its suggestion of a breakdown of civic order and an absence of overmastering political authority, could also have been easily interpretable as a criticism of the Augustan regime. For an Augustan orator to brand his opponents Furies might have drawn unfavorable attention from the Princeps himself, whose personal attention to the administration of justice was a noted feature of his rule.[41]

But the motif's lasting force as political critique emerges from the image of a tragic Republic, troubled by restless ghosts and Furies, that did become ingrained in the Roman literary imagination as the republican political order passed away. Augustus, in spite of the fact that he denied having waged a civil war during his ascension to power, tolerated a perception of the years *preceding* his rule as a tragic period, overshadowed by fear and anxiety like those embodied in drama. Horace's early *Epodes* and *Satires* link such ghastly imagery to the context of civil war. So, for example, the young Roman boy who, in *Epode* 5, promises to return as an avenging spirit to punish the witches sacrificing him, says he will become a *Furor* (92). His tormentors, the witches, are identifiable with Rome itself, especially in that at least one, Canidia, bears an unsettling similarity to a Roman matron.[42] Vergil, too, looking back from the first decade of Augustus' regime into the mythical past, depicts Aeneas' arrival in Latium as a time of violent conflict incited by Allecto, a Fury called from the world of the dead by a vengeful Juno. (*A.* 7.324ff.). The scene represents a tragic stylization of the civil wars of the late 40s and 30s BCE, while the eventual restoration of order by Vergil's Aeneas mirrors Augustus' deliverance of Rome from similar circumstances. Expanding in part upon the Vergilian precedent, Lucan fills the *Bellum civile* with such tragic borrowings, fearful visitations that compel the citizens of the late Republic to shed each other's blood and leave them in a state of unremitting anxiety while the memory of recent killing refuses to die.

Cicero's appropriations of tragedy in oratory suit the context of the late Republic for the particular political agenda to which he applies them. Cicero

equates the performance of oratory, both in fact and in literary representation, not only with decrying the cosmic tragedy enacted by his political foes
but also with resisting their endeavors, and so preventing Roman history
from becoming a tragedy for all time, a helpless submission to violence and
vengeance motivated by the fearful curse of the dead. Under the Principate,
while such notions lost their function as a technique of factional infighting,
they remained available and appealing as a characterization of history, an
implicit warning to those in power not to repeat the worst mistakes of the
past.

CHAPTER THREE

The *Second Philippic*
as Cultural Resistance

T he attempts by Rome's leaders to monopolize power in the 40s BCE presented Romans with a threat to both political and cultural tradition. Caesar's dictatorship was in many ways a foretaste of the Principate; a new page had in fact been turned. But for those who saw a return to traditional political forms as the only desirable option following Caesar's death, traditional cultural forms likewise retained their power and appeal, and could be enlisted as a way to make sense of the newly problematic relationship between Rome's present and its past. Consider Cicero's portrayal in the *Second Philippic* of the maddened Marcus Antonius entering the house of the dead Cn. Pompeius Magnus, whose property Antonius has claimed for himself and for whose death in the civil war of 49–46 BCE Cicero makes Antonius responsible:

> An tu illa in vestibulo rostra cum aspexisti, domum tuam te introire putas? Fieri non potest. Quamvis enim sine mente, sine sensu sis, ut es, tamen et te et tua et tuos nosti. Nec vero te umquam neque vigilantem neque in somnis credo posse mente consistere. Necesse est, quamvis sis, ut es, violentus et furens, cum tibi obiecta sit species singularis viri, perterritum te de somno excitari, furere etiam saepe vigilantem.

> Or when you look upon those famous prows [of ships captured by Pompeius] in the vestibule, do you think that you are entering your own house? It cannot be. Although you are indeed mindless and without judgment, you nevertheless recognize yourself and your possessions and people. Nor indeed

do I believe that you can be tranquil whether waking or sleeping. It must be that, although you are indeed violent and maddened, when the image of that singular man is put before you, you are roused from sleep in terror and often rave even while awake. (Cic. *Phil.* 2.68)

Here Cicero imagines Antonius haunted by a *species* (image [but also "phantom"]) of Pompeius, whose appearance rouses him from sleep and causes him *furere* (to rave). In death, Pompeius emulates Cicero's own persecution of Antonius, who in turn resembles the Fury-driven murderers of tragedy incited to madness by the curse of their victims, a motif to which we have seen Cicero returning time and time again in previous years to represent the more unsettling aspects of Roman civic life.

Now consider another, no less memorable passage from the *Second Philippic* that, together with this tragic evocation of the dead Pompeius, helps create an implicit argument for oratory itself as an essential feature of Roman culture. Near the end of the *Second Philippic* Cicero asks, rhetorically, whether Antonius is in any way to be compared with the dead Julius Caesar (116), whose incipient religious cult Antonius has fostered (110). Cicero then offers his own assessment of Caesar in response:

> Fuit in illo ingenium, ratio, memoria, litterae, cura, cogitatio, diligentia; res bello gesserat, quamvis rei publicae calamitosas, at tamen magnas; multos annos regnare meditatus, magno labore, magnis periculis quod cogitarat effecerat; muneribus, monumentis, congiariis, epulis multitudinem imperitam delenierat; suos praemiis, adversarios clementiae specie devinxerat.

> In that man there was talent, reason, a capacious memory, literary cultivation, attentiveness, the power of deliberation, and diligence. Through war, he had achieved things that, if disastrous for the *res publica,* were nonetheless great. Having intended for many years to hold regal power, he had achieved his object through great labor and great peril. He had mollified the ignorant masses though games, public buildings, distributions, and feasts. He had joined his supporters to him through rewards, his adversaries through the appearance of clemency. (Cic. *Phil.* 2.116)

While ambivalent and highly qualified, Cicero's praise of Caesar in this passage recalls the traditional republican *laudatio funebris* delivered at aristocratic funerals. The bare list of Caesar's achievements and attributes mirrors the similar lists that structured republican *laudationes* and formed a point of continuity between the *laudatio funebris* and the *elogia* inscribed on the tombs of the Roman elite.[1] A list, for example, of public offices, military achievements, and personal virtues appears in the earliest surviving fragment of a Roman *laudatio funebris,* the eulogy of L. Caecilius Metellus (consul in 251 and 247 BCE).[2] The traits praised in Metellus are markedly similar to those with which Cicero credits Caesar: prowess in war, skill as an orator, superior mental powers, and the favor of his peers. Traditional *laudationes* and inscriptions compare the recently deceased to the ancestors of his family; Cicero, too, uses his assessment of Caesar to draw a comparison—in this case with Antonius, who fails to match Caesar's example in everything except desire for despotic power (116: *dominandi cupiditate*). In addition to the list form, the specific personal qualities singled out, and the act of comparison, Cicero's syntax and diction likewise suggest the *laudatio* and its companion genre, the epitaphic inscription.[3]

Cicero's adaptation of traditional funereal rhetoric is startling in an assessment of a man whom he despised, and, indeed, whom he cannot help criticize even in the midst of praise. As so often in his later work, Cicero here makes Caesar responsible for the destruction of the *res publica* through ambition for regal power.[4] Caesar, Cicero insists, resorted to self-serving populism and the bribery and deception of his supporters (116). What, then, motivates Cicero's "*laudatio funebris*" of Caesar in the *Second Philippic,* and the opposition that Cicero thereby creates between reacting to Caesar's memory in this fashion and, like Antonius, worshiping Caesar, an act Cicero implicitly equates with being haunted by Pompeius' ghost?[5]

In answer, this chapter approaches my main thesis from a somewhat different angle, and by articulating a different perspective on Ciceronian oratory than either of the previous two. I argue that in the *Second Philippic,* written and circulated—but never delivered—amid a disintegration of Roman public discourse and traditional political practice, Cicero makes the literary representation of oratory into a means of resistance, not only to his great political enemy Antonius but also to changes in Roman culture portending the monopolization of power by a sole emperor. He does this by characterizing oratory's traditional evocations of the dead as a preferable alternative to Caesar's emergent cult. The prospect of Caesar's divinity had by this time given rise to ostentatious religious observances on the part of the chief competitors over Caesar's legacy, Pseudo-Marius, Octavian, and Antonius. Cicero opposes oratory to such activities by associating the former with the preservation, and the latter with the dissolution, of the *res publica* and its traditions. The "*laudatio*" of Caesar near the end of the *Second Philippic* constructs this opposition directly: it occurs soon after Cicero's declaration that Caesar's cult perverts traditional religion (110–11). But the full rhetorical force of the differentiation emerges only by tracing, within the *Second Philippic* as a literary artifact, the ongoing opposition of oratory to Antonius' behavior toward the dead in general, including his attempts to profit from Caesar's death, his selfish consumption of the dead Pompeius' possessions, and his failure to mourn those who had died in the recent civil war. Antonius' worship of Caesar is the culminating example of such behavior, the illustration whose themes encompass those of all the others.

Although much of the *Second Philippic* is devoted to low attacks on Antonius' character, the main body of the speech is in fact framed by evocations of the illustrious dead: on the one hand, dead senators and Pompeius (12) and, on the other hand, Julius Caesar (116). In a speech devoted largely to scurrilous and even humorous abuse, such a frame serves the important rhetorical function of grounding Cicero's attack in matters of the utmost solemnity. This feature of the text, however, acquires an even more pointed significance from the very fact that the *Second Philippic* was never spoken in public by Cicero himself. For while there was nothing unusual about the publication of an undelivered speech in the Rome of Cicero's day (witness the second *actio* of Cicero's *Verrines*), the orature of the *Second Philippic* presents us with a situation unlike Cicero's other published orations simulating oral performance, in that Cicero himself names the breakdown of civic order as the cause of his silence in this instance. He situates this, his most scathing attack on Antonius, in the senate meeting of September 19, 44 BCE; and yet in the *Fifth Philippic* Cicero reports that he was absent from the meeting on that day, and alleges that Antonius' willingness to use armed force made him fear for his life (*Phil.* 5.20).[6] Given the text's acknowledged fiction about itself, the distinctions that the *Second Philippic* makes between oratory and other types of behavior become prescriptive statements about free oratory's value to the Roman state and the implications of its present exclusion. Cicero, in other words, not only makes his readers wish for the live speech by treating them to a virtual *contentio dicendi* (contest of speaking) (2) in which he matches Antonius point for point and often illustrates the inadequacy of Antonius' abilities as a speaker.[7] The *Second Philippic* also looks ruefully toward the performance that might have been: Cicero "objectifies" hitherto "unformulated" aspects of traditional oratory, in the sense of these terms as employed by the sociologist Pierre Bourdieu, and makes an implicit argument for the social benefits of oratory in the circumstances of its imagined delivery.[8]

In striking testimony to the cultural importance Cicero attributed to oratory—and the sympathy with his views he expected among fellow adherents of the "republican" cause—Cicero's later *Philippics,* which were delivered, put the cultural distinctions of the *Second Philippic* into practice. In the latter part of this chapter, I will show that Cicero persists in positing the distinction between oratory and aberrant attitudes toward the dead as a basis of traditional Roman culture, whether he is treating the issue of vengeance for the dead Caesar and the brutal murder of C. Trebonius in the *Thirteenth Philippic*; the correct commemoration of Ser. Sulpicius Rufus in the *Ninth Philippic*; or the celebration of the war dead in his final preserved speech, the *Fourteenth Philippic*. In the *Philippics*, oratory, when properly practiced, is a beneficial mediation between the dead and the living, between time-honored tradition, the recent past, and a public audience. Oratory works to help the living learn from the *exempla* of the dead, to preserve these *exempla*, and to preserve the conditions that Cicero considers most suitable for oratory itself.

Close study of Cicero's *Philippics* not only illuminates Cicero's conception of the dead's function in oratory, but also encourages reflection on the nature of cultural change between the Roman Republic and Principate, a larger theme of this book. It reminds us in particular that some aspects of culture in this period, even if they did not become part of the main stream of Augustan culture, were nevertheless innovations of traditional republican cultural forms in resistance to the emerging circumstances of imperial rule. The domain of such tactics included not only the written or spoken word taken by itself but also referential play between text and performance, unsettling gestures of surrogation through orature. The *Philippics* are often read in political terms as Cicero's doomed "last stand for Republicanism." When critics do address culture, it is mainly in pursuit of Cicero's influence on the young Octavian, i.e., on the cultural program that Augustus would eventually—and successfully—pursue. A fully cultural reading, however, adds an important layer of complexity to the familiar picture of Cicero as an Augustus *manqué*. The cultural transition between Republic and Principate is neither entirely "revolution" nor simply progressive "evolution." Cultural change, we recognize afresh, occurs together at Rome with cultural resistance.

Julius Caesar and the Cult of the Dead

In the latter part of 44 BCE, traditional channels of senatorial debate and assemblies of the people—and with them, oratory—seem to have to mattered far less to Rome's rival claimants for power than ostentatious religious observances for the dead Julius Caesar.[9] Indeed, the elevation of Caesar to a status comparable to that of the high gods represented a pointed threat to one of the republican orator's basic assumptions. For while the orator routinely asserted a spiritual bond between himself, his audience, and the illustrious Roman dead, he did not go so far as to worship the dead among the high gods. Roman religion would not have sanctioned such a view of the *di Manes.* Behind religious belief lay the common interest of the republican political class. To allow any orator to express his worship of a dead Roman as a high god would have been to risk a monopolization of power in the hands of the single orator who could claim the strongest bond to this figure (see below on Pseudo-Marius). The republican speaker looked rather to a wide range of godlike "great men," any of whom, in theory, could be evoked to support the claims and enhance the authority of a particular individual.[10]

We can only guess at exactly when the popular worship of Caesar as a god actually began to take hold among his admirers; a state-recognized cult of Caesar was not decreed by law until 42 BCE and a temple to the new god would not be officially dedicated until August of 29.[11] Soon after the Ides of March, 44, however, a shadowy figure known to scholars as Pseudo-Marius saw an opportunity and, having already put together a following, built an altar on the site of Caesar's pyre.[12] His claim to be the grandson of C. Marius enforced his professed position as Caesar's avenger. His plan to establish sacrifices to Caesar as to a god met with great popular enthusiasm. The effectiveness of his efforts comes glaringly to light in the fact that Antonius, acting as consul, had him put to death without trial. Two weeks later, Antonius' colleague, P. Cornelius Dolabella, demolished Caesar's altar. Such popular influence as Pseudo-Marius possessed was not to be tolerated.

Octavian, too, hoped for public and spectacular affirmation of his tie to his adoptive father, the *divus Julius.* Twice in 44 he attempted to enforce a decree calling for the display of Caesar's gilded chair at all theatrical games. This was not the throne that had been decreed for Caesar's personal use while he lived, but another intended expressly to carry his golden crown and identifiable as a divine rather than simply a regal attribute.[13] Antonius successfully blocked Octavian's attempts to display the throne on these two occasions. In July, however, a comet appeared in the Roman sky during the *ludi Victoriae Caesaris.*[14] Octavian, apparently following popular belief, would come to identify it as Caesar's *anima;* as proof, that is, of Caesar's literal immortality.[15] Octavian—and then Augustus—capitalized on the phenomenon in diverse ways, including a famous series of representations of the comet on coinage, in art, and in literature.[16] In November of 44, he swore an oath at an altar to Caesar, an act that may signal his own restoration of the altar demolished by Dolabella.[17]

Antonius at first pursued a tentative course with regard to the issue of Caesar's supposed divinity, although he later embraced the comet motif. Perhaps compelled by the wishes of Caesar's veterans and of the Roman plebs, he quickly enacted some of the honorific decrees proposed before Caesar's death. The name of the sixth month was accordingly changed to *Iulius.* The anniversaries of Caesar's victories were made the occasion for new sacrifices. At this time Antonius also proposed *supplicationes* (thanksgivings) to or for Caesar in what may also have been an effort to put into effect honors already decreed while Caesar still lived.[18] In September, moreover, in response to Octavian's claims to be Caesar's true heir, Antonius set up his own statue of Caesar on the *rostra,* and had the statue engraved with the words *parenti optime merito* (to a most deserving parent). But, perhaps wary of the benefit for Octavian if Caesar were formally declared a god, Antonius put off having all of Caesar's proposed honors formally ratified at this time. A couch, cult-statue, and temple remained unrealized. So, too, Antonius delayed having himself inaugurated as Caesar's *flamen* (priest), an office for which he had been selected while Caesar was alive.[19]

For Cicero, however, Antonius' status as Caesar's worshiper and priest is as good as established already in September of 44 and Antonius' hesitancy is merely self-serving inconsistency. In both the *First* and *Second Philippic,* Cicero stigmatizes Caesar's honors as a perversion of traditional religion. In response to Antonius' proposal of *supplicationes,* Cicero claims that he could never be induced to support any measure that would "confuse" the traditional festival in honor of the dead, the *Parentalia,* with public thanksgivings. It would introduce *inexpiabiles religiones* (inexpiable religious taints) into the state to decree *supplicationes mortuo*—"for" (perhaps in the sense of "to") a dead man. Even in the case of the tyrannicide L. Iunius Brutus, ancestor of Caesar's assassin, Cicero's position is firm: *adduci tamen non possem ut quemquam mortuum coniungerem cum deorum immortalium religione; ut, cuius sepulcrum usquam exstet ubi parentetur, ei publice supplicetur* (I could nevertheless not be persuaded to associate any dead man with the worship of the immortal gods, so that public thanksgivings should be offered for [or "to"] one whose tomb was anywhere extant, at which one might perform rites in honor of the dead) (Cic. *Phil.* 1.13).[20] The final sections of the *Second Philippic* contain Cicero's most intense denunciation of Antonius' supposed role in Caesar's divinization. "And you," he demands of Antonius, "are you devoted to Caesar's memory? Do you love [*amas*] him even in death?" What greater honor, Cicero cynically continues, could Caesar obtain than a couch, a cult image, a pediment, and a priest? Antonius should seize the opportunity to ratify what has already come about in effect: "O detestable man," Cicero exclaims, "whether because you are the priest of a tyrant or of a dead man" (Cic. *Phil.* 2.110).

Both the *First* and *Second Philippic* reject divine honors for Caesar in so many words; however, as I suggested in the introduction to this chapter, the *Second Philippic* opposes traditional oratorical *laudatio* to the worship of Caesar and in this way advances an implicit cultural argument. Looking, now, more closely at the speech's concluding sections, we see that Cicero does not merely indicate his personal preference for the former practice over the latter, but actually emphasizes the contrasting social and cultural effects of each. Antonius' measures erode cultural tradition, in Cicero's opinion, because they destroy religion (110: *religionem tolle*). By contrast, the proper assessment of Caesar's example teaches Romans "whom to trust and whom to beware of" and so can bestow at least one "good" on the Roman people, who have otherwise suffered so cruelly from Caesar's "evils" (117).[21] A performance such as Cicero's own mixed "*laudatio*," unlike mere worship, can thus be thought to contribute to this beneficial outcome. Backing up this contrast, moreover, is Cicero's condemnation of Antonius for having delivered his famous—but untraditional—eulogy at Caesar's cremation, an event to which Cicero refers with the utmost irony and contempt as *illa pulchra laudatio* (that beautiful eulogy) (90) and whose principal effect, he insists, was to inflame the Roman mob to violence.[22] Cicero's own "*laudatio*" of Caesar is thus a correction of Antonius at once as Caesar's public *laudator* (eulogist) and, still more importantly, as his *sacerdos* (priest).

The latter part of the *Second Philippic* sets traditional oratory against worship; earlier parts of the text, however, anticipate the later characterization of Caesar's cult and thus encourage the reader to equate it with a whole series of culturally inappropriate attitudes toward the dead, of which it is the culminating example. In each case, Cicero makes traditional oratory the preferable alternative to such behavior, so that the concluding opposition becomes, in this way, too, all the more powerful. Let us now consider how the speech sets up the basic cultural distinctions that ultimately lend their force to its conclusion.

The pattern begins to take shape early in the text, when Cicero inserts an account of the way that Antonius has turned Caesar's death to his own profit (35–36). Cicero maintains that if Antonius were taken to court over Caesar's killing he would be vulnerable to the famous question of the stern judge L. Cassius Longinus Ravilla, *cui bono?* (Who stood to gain?). Since Caesar's death, Cicero goes on, Antonius has not only been delivered from servitude like other Romans but has also begun to "rule" (*regnas*). Antonius has misappropriated state funds on the basis of Caesar's supposed records. He has removed many possessions from Caesar's house and raised money through his trade in false memoranda and other documents purporting to be in Caesar's handwriting (the notorious *commentaria* and *chirographa*).[23] The money so raised has in part been squandered and in part used to pay down Antonius' debts. Later, Cicero will express his belief that Antonius' worship of Caesar is also motivated by personal gain (111: *quaestu*) rather than a sincere defense of Caesar's acts.

Significantly, Cicero describes Antonius' appropriation of Caesar's docu-ments directly after a display of oratorical *laudatio* for Caesar's assassins, who, living but in exile at the time Cicero wrote the *Second Philippic*, are treated as figures who perpetuate ancestral glory and, in turn, will be glori-fied long after their deaths (25–33). In answer to Antonius' charge that he instigated Caesar's assassination, Cicero identifies by name eight of the men actually implicated in the killing. Saying that he wants to show that these men were self-motivated and needed no prompting from him, Cicero does in fact marshal convincing evidence for this point by recalling aspects of the men's personal experience (26–27). But Cicero also uses the naming of Caesar's assassins to glorify their memory and that of their families. He evokes ancestors of M. Iunius Brutus, C. Cassius Longinus, and Gn. Domi-tius Ahenobarbus, and suggests that each man lived up to the *exempla* of his *gens*. Sometimes Cicero refers only obliquely to self-motivation *per se*. He praises C. Trebonius, for example, for placing the freedom of the Roman people above the demands of friendship and choosing to overthrow despo-tism rather than participate in it. He singles out L. Tillius Cimber for forget-ting personal obligations and remembering the *patria* (27). Similarly, after criticizing the phrasing of Antonius' charges (28–32), Cicero concludes the passage with an even more elaborate *laudatio*, marked by anaphora:

> Quid enim beatius illis quos tu expulsos a te praedicas et relegatos? qui locus est aut tam desertus aut tam inhumanus qui illos, cum accesserint, non adfari atque appetere videatur? qui homines tam agrestes qui se, cum eos aspexerint, non maximum cepisse vitae fructum putent? quae vero tam immemor posteritas, quae tam ingratae litterae reperientur quae eorum glo-riam non immortalitatis memoria prosequantur? Tu vero ascribe me talem in numerum.

> Whose situation could be happier than that of the men you boast of having driven out and banished? What region is either so remote or so uncivilized that it will not seem to address them in greeting when they approach? What human beings are so boorish that, when they lay eyes on those men, they will not think themselves to have attained life's greatest reward? What future age will be found so unmindful, what literature so ungrateful as not to bestow everlasting remembrance upon their glory? Yes, indeed, enroll me in the number of such men. (Cic. *Phil.* 2.33)

All of his praise of Caesar's assassins, Cicero will go on to specify, per-petuates the memory of a deed that is *expositum ad imitandum* (set forth for imitation), since, like the killing of earlier aspirants to monarchic power, the killing of Caesar delivered the Roman state from servitude (114). The transmission of such *exempla*, Cicero implies, is the duty of speakers and writers alike, and among the greatest benefits they can bestow upon posterity. Cicero clearly hoped that the *Second Philippic*, as a text for reading, would play a part in transmitting the assassins' memory to later generations: he in fact mentions *litterae* as a way that future ages will glorify the conspirators (33). The performance of oratory, however, signifies the freedom to do so at the present moment and in public. In view of the fact that Cicero felt he was prevented from delivering the *Second Philippic* by the breakdown of free society, his placement in the undelivered speech of an extended passage glorifying Caesar's killers becomes a part of his call for freedom (cf. 27: *libertatem;* 113: *libertas;* etc.): only freedom, Cicero reminds his readers, will assure that speakers can declare such views aloud. Thus the passage both perpetuates the assassins' memory and comments implicitly on the preferable way to do so. Cicero here draws a specific contrast between such oratory in commemoration of Caesar's assassins and Antonius' appropriation of the dead Caesar's legacy for personal gain alone.

If personal gain motivates both Antonius' use of Caesar's legacy and his worship of Caesar, so, too, in Cicero's view, Antonius' appropriation of the dead Pompeius' possessions should be equated with the worship of Caesar because each displays Antonius' failure to consider what the dead in fact deserve. Antonius, Cicero insists, has ignored Caesar's actual worthiness (111: *dignitate*); nor does he acknowledge that Pompeius is deserving of admiration and praise (69: *admirandus . . . laudandus*). The account of Antonius' purchase and dissipation of Pompeius' possessions dominates the middle sections of the *Second Philippic* and contains some of the most vivid invective in the speech. Here we witness Antonius' cronies, people of low social status such as actors and actresses, indulging in an orgy of drinking, gambling, and robbery. The sheer speed, Cicero exclaims, with which they consumed Pompeius' goods is a prodigy, comparable to the voracity of Charybdis or of Ocean itself (67). Presiding over all we find Antonius, who now appears in his tragic guise as a delusional, fury-driven madman, haunted by Pompeius' phantom (68).

In the midst of this account, Cicero interjects a plea that his audience recognize Pompeius' legacy as an outstanding Roman, and asserts implicitly that the best way to perpetuate this legacy is through oratorical *laudatio:*

> Me quidem miseret parietum ipsorum atque tectorum. Quid enim umquam domus illa viderat nisi pudicum, quid nisi ex optimo more et sanctissima disciplina? Fuit enim ille vir, patres conscripti, sicuti scitis, cum foris clarus

tum domi admirandus, neque rebus externis magis laudandus quam insti-
tutis domesticis.

For myself, I pity the very walls and roof. For what had that house witnessed
except what was chaste and derived from the best established custom and
most sacred discipline. For as you know, conscript fathers, that man was
both famous for his life in public and admirable for his life at home, nor was
he more deserving of praise for his conduct abroad than for his domestic
habits. (Cic. *Phil.* 2.69)

Cicero makes Pompeius' house, the physical devastation of which he is in the
midst of recounting, part of Pompeius' spiritual legacy to all of Rome. He
suggests that the house embodies and perpetuates Pompeius' virtues (which
it has "witnessed")—even as Cicero's own text perpetuates these same virtues to the reader now that Pompeius is gone. The inclusion, however, of the
pathetic vocative *patres conscripti* recalls specifically the circumstances of live
performance at this key moment, while the gerundive *laudandus* (deserving
of praise) is a self-referential signpost, suggesting acts of public praise like
the one that is being represented here. Antonius may have squandered Pompeius' physical wealth, Cicero implies, but the freedom to praise Pompeius
in public oratory brings still more lasting spiritual rewards.

Indeed, the details of Cicero's language would make a Roman reader
especially aware of the social importance of public praise for the dead by
recalling (albeit in a less obvious way than Cicero's later "*laudatio*" of Caesar)
the traditional rhetoric associated with aristocratic funerals. Cicero's recollection of Pompeius' devotion to moral behavior and ancestral tradition
repeats topics familiar from funereal inscriptions and the surviving fragments of funeral *laudationes*. Likewise, the distinction between conduct at
home and in public helps structure individual *laudationes,* as especially in
the eulogy of L. Caecilius Metellus.[24] Cicero's generalization of his own grief
(his 'pity' finds larger expression in the lamentation of the people over the
auction of Pompeius' possessions) also suggests the *laudatio funebris,* which,
as Polybius (6.53) indicates, sought to make the loss suffered by the grieving
aristocratic family into a loss suffered by the state as a whole. Cicero's appeal
to his audience's shared opinion about Pompeius ("For as you know, conscript fathers . . .") recalls the funereal inscriptions' similar appeals to consensus.[25] Even the phrase with which Cicero begins his praise of Pompeius,
fuit ille vir, suggests texts like the Scipionic inscriptions in the designation of
Pompeius as a *vir* at phrase-end.[26]

Praise of the dead implies mourning. Antonius' failure to mourn the dead

Pompeius and other victims of civil war is still another aspect of his behavior assimilated, in the *Second Philippic*, to the worship of Caesar, in that both are based on apparent obliviousness to reality. Antonius appears oblivious, that is, both to the copious mourning for Pompeius going on around him (64) and, later in the text, to the fact that Caesar is a dead man (110: *mortui*) and not a god. Where the civil-war dead are concerned, Cicero nowhere associates even pity or sorrow, let alone actual mourning, with Antonius and his followers, while he repeatedly singles out greed and abuse of the deceased's rights as typical of them (cf. 40–41, 62, 109).

Effusive mourning expressed in (written) oratory is Cicero's response. Before recounting the destruction of Pompeius' property, he interjects an expression of his own personal grief: *miserum me,* he laments, "even when tears have run dry, pain stays deeply embedded in the heart." He goes on to recall the Roman people's public lamentations over the auction of Pompeius' possessions (64). He expresses "pity" for Pompeius' house, a sentiment in which he suggests all Romans should share (69). The expression of grief here, again, signifies freedom: in spite of the servitude to which the Roman people were subjected, their "groaning," Cicero specifies, was "free" (64: *liber*). And the sympathetic reader, aware that Cicero felt unfree to deliver the *Second Philippic,* wishes, again, for the circumstances in which Cicero's own expressions of grief could in fact have been freely expressed and heard. The display, moreover, of both mourning and praise for the victims of the civil war is a recurring feature of the *Second Philippic* and in this way the speech as a whole contrasts with Antonius' callous behavior. Cicero must have believed that such rhetoric would have been one of the most effective aspects of the *Second Philippic* in a performance before the Roman senate, since he repeatedly singles out dead senators by name. A passage like the following, for example, from early in the speech, reads like an act of collective mourning for the senate itself:

> Non placet M. Antonio consulatus meus. At placuit P. Servilio, ut eum primum nominem ex illius temporis consularibus qui proxime est mortuus; placuit Q. Catulo, cuius semper in hac re publica vivet auctoritas; placuit duobus Lucullis, M. Crasso, Q. Hortensio, C. Curioni, C. Pisoni, M.' Glabrioni, M.' Lepido, L. Volcatio, C. Figulo, D. Silano, L. Murenae, qui tum erant consules designati; placuit idem quod consularibus M. Catoni, qui cum multa vita excedens providit, tum quod te consulem non vidit. Maxime vero consulatum meum Cn. Pompeius probavit . . . Sed quoniam illis quos nominavi tot et talibus viris res publica orbata est, veniamus ad vivos. . . .

Marcus Antonius disapproves of my consulship. But Publius Servilius approved of it—I name him first among the consulars of that time because he was the last to die. So did Quintus Catulus, respect for whom will live forever in this state. So likewise the two Luculli, Marcus Crassus, Quintus Hortensius, Gaius Curio, Gaius Piso, Manius Glabrio, Manius Lepidus, Lucius Vulcatius, Gaius Figulus. So also the consuls-elect, Decimus Silanus and Lucius Murena. The consulars' approval was shared by Marcus Cato, who in taking leave of life showed great foresight, not least because he did not see you as consul. Above all, Gnaeus Pompeius approved my consulship. . . . Since, however, the state has been bereaved of all those distinguished men whom I have named, let me come to the living. . . . (Cic. *Phil.* 2.12–13)

The roll of the dead, even when read to oneself, possesses a powerful, cumulative emotional force, but a reader senses, too, how much more effective it would have been if actually delivered in the context Cicero imagines. Here again, Cicero reminds a reading audience of oratory's power to focus public mourning so as to help living Romans come to terms with loss and preserve what is best about their dead compatriots' lives. This is suggested, too, by Cicero's reply to the reproach that he spent time in Pompeius' camp before the bloody and decisive battle of Pharsalus in 48 BCE. *Dolebam, dolebam* (I was grieving, grieving), Cicero declares, that the Republic was so soon to perish. Desire for life, Cicero claims, was not at the root of his grief. He wished, rather, that the outstanding men who had died in the war were still living: "so many ex-consuls, so many former praetors, so many of the most upright senators, the whole flower of nobility and youth besides, and armies of the best citizens." If all these men were alive, Cicero concludes, the *res publica* would still stand (37).

The Cicero who expresses his grief over the dead in the *Second Philippic* seems a far cry from the philosopher of the *Tusculan Disputations*, in which, through a discussion of the passions strongly influenced by Stoicism, Cicero seeks a cure for grief and expresses his disapproval of extended mourning. Cicero had written a *consolatio* (now lost) to himself after the death of his daughter, Tullia, in which he combined the approaches of various philosophical schools, and the hope for an end to personal grief also colors the *Tusculans*, as Erskine has shown. But the Cicero of the *Second Philippic* is likely to rely on the human tendency, recalled in the *Tusculans* as the focus of Chrysippus' views on consolation, to regard mourning as a duty, as something right, proper, and obligatory (*Tusc.* 3.64; cf. 72, 76). Victims of grief, Cicero observes, may even think that the dead will be gratified by the intensity of their grief and fall victim to a certain *superstitio muliebris* (womanish superstition) that, by admitting how devastated they are by their loss, they will more easily satisfy the gods (72). Cicero himself, it is worth remarking, was unable to contain his own mourning over the loss of his daughter, and even expressed his doubt as to whether he should or should not seek to hide his grief. In *Att.* 12.14.3 he writes, "I do everything to compose not my soul but my face itself, if I am able. When I do this, I feel sometimes that I am doing wrong, but at other times I feel that I should be doing wrong if I did not do so." Others, Cicero must have hoped, would in a similar way feel it was somehow wrong to cease lamentation for the civil war dead, and find themselves eager for situations of public remembrance in which such emotions could be expressed.

To sum up: the reader of the *Second Philippic,* having encountered example after example of Antonius' profit-seeking, neglectful, and oblivious behavior toward the dead, is in a better position, at the end of the text, to believe Cicero's assertion that Antonius' worship of Caesar is also profit-seeking, neglectful, and oblivious. Likewise, the reader who has been reminded repeatedly that the traditional orator evokes the dead so as to perpetuate an attitude of community-mindedness, sensitivity to tradition, and engagement with social reality, and who has seen Cicero demonstrate the preferability of his attitude to Antonius' on occasion after occasion, has all the more reason to accept Cicero's words when, in the manner of speaker at a funeral, he passes judgment on Caesar just after condemning his emergent cult. This reader hopes, ideally, both for Cicero's return and for the return of the social, political, and cultural order that would allow Ciceronian oratory to thrive.

Solidarity with the Dead

Ancient rhetorical theory was all but inadequate to help Cicero advance the strategy I have described here. While topoi for evoking the dead were known and widely used, no rhetorician could have envisioned the particular way in which Cicero mobilizes tradition, since ancient theory, far from imagining that the worship of a dead aristocrat might threaten oratory's political function, assumes a stable social role for oratory itself. But the undelivered *Second Philippic* functions like a work of theory in calling attention to certain aspects of oratory on which the handbooks were silent so as to inculcate them as part of the "right" way of life Cicero wishes to defend. Lacking ancient terms, we are helped by those of the twentieth-century sociologist Pierre Bourdieu. Through the circulation of his undelivered speech, Cicero "objectifies," in Bourdieu's sense, what was in essence a part of oratory as a "practical scheme."[27] Because, that is, it was obvious that praising or mourning the dead was practically useful in a variety of rhetorical situations, rhetoricians felt no need to call attention to this fact per se. They might describe and clarify the exact techniques to be employed, but the value of these techniques was clear to any orator. The fundamental act of showing solidarity with the dead was so ingrained in Roman culture as to be an "embodied" practice governed by Bourdieu's "*habitus*," the "principles of the generation and structuring of practices and representations which can be objectively 'regulated' and 'regular' without in any way being the product of obedience to rules."[28] As Bourdieu suggests, however, the need to objectify "unformulated experiences"—to endow them with the status of rule-governed behavior—is never more strongly felt than in situations of social crisis "in which the everyday order . . . is challenged, and with it the language of order."[29] In the autumn of 44 BCE, Cicero felt a challenge to free oratory as the language of order, and the *Second Philippic* has the quasi-theoretical function of "objectifying" oratory's preferability to the outright worship of the dead where previously no discourse on this subject was needed.

But if the *Second Philippic* is in some sense "theoretical" in its Bourdieu-esque "objectification" of what at an earlier time had gone without saying, the later *Philippics*, which were delivered in something close to their published form, in fact put its cultural distinctions between right and wrong ways of relating to the dead into practice. This is striking confirmation both of the importance of these distinctions to Cicero himself, and of the sympathy with his views that Cicero must have expected he would find among the other adherents of the "republican" cause.

With respect to Caesar, the later *Philippics* extend Cicero's condemnation of Antonius' worship to include the notion of vengeance that Antonius himself had made a central component of his ideological justification for war, and that came to the fore after the murder of C. Trebonius at the opening of 43 BCE. Formerly one of Caesar's supporters, Trebonius had turned against the dictator and participated in his assassination. While serving as proconsul of Asia, he was tortured and violently put to death by Antonius' colleague Dolabella, then on his way to take up the governorship of Syria. In the *Thirteenth Philippic*, Cicero belittles Antonius' claim to avenge Caesar as a pathological devotion to Caesar's ghost. Conversely, Cicero's *laudatio* of those fallen in the civil war both signals and enacts what he considers an appropriate form of devotion to the cause of the *res publica*.

In the second half of the *Thirteenth Philippic*, Cicero professes to cite a letter from Antonius to the effect that Trebonius' killing was a justified act of vengeance and an expression of piety toward the dead Caesar, a claim that Cicero vehemently denies. It is a matter for rejoicing, Antonius is made to assert, [d]*edisse poenas sceleratum cineri atque ossibus clarissimi viri et apparuisse numen deorum* (that a criminal has paid the penalty to the ashes and bones of a most outstanding man and the will of the gods has been revealed) (22). In a scornful retort, Cicero insists that had Antonius' own troops not recently deserted him to D. Iunius Brutus Albinus, *non Dolabella prius imperatori suo quam Antonius etiam conlegae parentasset* (Dolabella would not have offered a sacrifice [literally: "performed the rites of the *Parentalia*"] to his dead commander [i.e., Caesar] before Antonius, too, had done so to his colleague) (35)—before Antonius, that is, had murdered D. Brutus as a sacrifice to Caesar. Thus, as we have seen him do before, Cicero reduces Antonius' attitude toward Julius Caesar to a perversion of traditional religion.

In the same speech, Cicero takes pains to amplify the idea that his own cause is no mere vendetta on behalf of a ghost by demonstrating his devotion to the *memory* of the dead senators and linking their glory to that of the *res publica*. He praises the consulars L. Afranius, P. Lentulus, M. Bibulus, L. Domitius, Appius Claudius, and P. Scipio, then recalls Pompeius as well as Cato and the other ex-praetors, the ex-aediles, ex-tribunes, and ex-quaestors. "Why," he asks his audience, "should I commemorate the remaining illustrious men? You know them all. I am more afraid that you will think me tedious in enumerating them than ungrateful in leaving someone out" (29–30). The passage demonstrates what Cicero will later assert in response to Antonius' insinuation that the republicans are fighting *quo facilius reviviscat Pompeianorum causa totiens iugulata* (so that the cause of the Pompeians, a cause whose throat was so often cut, should more easily return to life). If the Pompeian cause *had* been *iugulata*, Cicero retorts, it would never have risen to action; "may this," Cicero snaps, "be the fate of you and yours" (38). Cicero goes on to say that Octavian, whose cause he supports, is *nulla specie paterni nominis . . . abductus* (led astray by no show of his father's name), but understands rather that "the greatest loyalty is in the preservation of the fatherland" (46). Through *laudatio* of the dead senators, Cicero both shows that the memory of his fallen countrymen is still fresh in the minds of himself and his audience and subordinates any idea of personal vengeance to this larger cause.

Elsewhere in the later *Philippics*, we find a still more exuberant embrace of oratory as a fitting memorialization of the dead. In February of 43, Cicero entered enthusiastically into the senatorial debate over honors for Ser. Sulpicius Rufus, who had died while taking part in the senate's embassy to Antonius during the siege of Mutina in January.[30] Cicero uses the *Ninth Philippic* not only to recommend honors for the dead Sulpicius, but to reaffirm the importance of public commendation in keeping the memory of the dead "alive." Cicero urges the senate to "restore" to Sulpicius, through the decree of a statue, the life it has "taken away" from him by sending him on the embassy: *vita enim mortuorum in memoria est positum vivorum* (For the life of the dead is placed in the memory of the living). In a moment of self-reference, Cicero declares that the *fama* (report) of all mortals will celebrate Sulpicius' dignity, constancy, faithfulness, patriotism, and wisdom (i.e., just as Cicero himself is doing). *Nec vero silebitur* (Nor indeed will there be silence), Cicero goes on, regarding Sulpicius' incredible and "almost divine" knowledge of law and equity (10).

Cicero professes to speak as though he were transmitting Sulpicius' own wishes from beyond the grave. He asserts that *si qui est sensus in morte* (if there is any consciousness in death), Sulpicius will be more pleased by a bronze statue of himself represented on foot rather than a gilded statue on horseback (13). This will be in keeping with Sulpicius' own preferences, for Sulpicius, Cicero asserts, felt great esteem for the restraint of the ancestors and censured the indulgence of the present age.[31] Cicero claims to be making his proposal as if he were consulting the man himself (13: *ut igitur si ipsum consulam quid velit . . .*) and acting on Sulpicius' own authority and wishes (*ex eius auctoritate et voluntate*). Such is the privilege and the duty, Cicero reminds his listeners, of the republican orator: to create a bond with the illustrious dead through which to preserve and perpetuate the *res publica* and its traditions. Evoked in oratorical performance as a model of republicanism, the dead Sulpicius becomes Cicero's source for the terms of commendation applied to him.

Cicero's praise of Ser. Sulpicius Rufus in the *Ninth Philippic* anticipates in both its occasion and its form what is arguably the most culturally innovative *laudatio* of the dead in all of Cicero's oratory, that of the fallen soldiers of the Martian legion in the *Fourteenth Philippic,* delivered in April of 43. A record of Cicero's last known speech, the text represents as well one of his final expressions of resistance—both political and cultural—to those he viewed as the *res publica*'s antagonists. Ultimately, Cicero himself became one of the "honorable dead." On December 7, he was murdered by henchmen of Antonius and Octavian, who, now reconciled and acting together, had embarked on a campaign of bloody proscriptions. Given the canonical status that Cicero's speeches would enjoy so soon after his death, it is sadly ironic that his mutilated body—his severed hands and head placed on the *rostra*—became a grim "monument" to his prowess as both writer and orator as well as to his misestimation of Octavian.[32]

Commemorative protocols were once more the subject of intense debate when the senate convened on the 21st of April, 43. Antonius had retreated before the victorious forces of the consul A. Hirtius, but D. Iunius Brutus Albinus remained under siege at Mutina. C. Vibius Pansa Caetronianus, the other of the year's two consuls, had been mortally wounded. P. Servilius Vatia Isauricus spoke first and proposed that the senators assume for one day the toga, the garment of peace, as opposed to the *saga,* the military cloak indicating a state of war. Servilius also proposed a public *supplicatio* in gratitude for the victory. In the *Fourteenth Philippic,* Cicero opposes adopting the toga on the grounds that a full victory has not yet been achieved. He supports, however, a *supplicatio* in honor of the two consuls and Octavian, to all of whom he seeks to extend the honorific title *imperator.* Bestowing the title, Cicero points out, would brand Antonius as an enemy of the state, since no Roman had ever received it for fighting against fellow citizens. The bravery of the dead soldiers of the Martian legion, by contrast, deserves to be recorded for all time.

Cicero's solidarity with the fallen soldiers culminates in the apostrophe that dominates the concluding portions of the speech (32–33). The passage is memorable for its superlatives: the Martian legion was "born for its country"; the god Mars himself engendered it for Rome (32); in exchange for their mortal lives, the soldiers have achieved *immortalitas* (33). The valor of the dead soldiers, Cicero insists, must not be buried by forgetfulness or the silence of posterity (33). Addressing the soldiers themselves, Cicero assures them of the status their spirits will enjoy: theirs will be a beatific afterlife in the *sedes piorum* (abode of the pious). Those fighting against Rome, on the other hand, "will pay the penalties of the parricide in the underworld" (32).

Cicero calls for an unprecedented adaptation of the traditional *laudatio* to mark the achievements of the Martian legion's fallen soldiers. He encourages the senate to join with him in consoling the soldiers' relatives, then expresses the wish that an oration similar to his own could be addressed to the soldiers' families to make them put off their mourning and rejoice in the fate of their kinsmen (34). The speech Cicero here proposes is reminiscent of the Greek *epitaphios logos,* a collective, public eulogy of the dead, like that famously described in Thucydides' account of Pericles' speech following the first year of the Peloponnesian War (2.34–46). It represents a departure from Roman practice: such collective eulogy was a Greek rather than a Roman custom.[33] But it is (or would have been) an especially effective means of reasserting "republican" cultural values. Had Cicero delivered the speech, his voice would have become that of the whole Roman state, his *laudatio* the acknowledged praise of the state itself for its dead liberators.[34] Cicero's idea of the Roman state's self-representation in a collective eulogy comes at the end of a speech in which he has condemned Antonius' ruthlessness toward the living and the dead alike (cf. 7–8 on the forging of wills and the treatment of C. Trebonius). The spirits of the republican war dead, noble but lamentable, semi-divine and yet in need of public commendation, achieve a meaningful *immortalitas* not in actual worship but in the perpetuation of their *fama*. The authority to perpetuate this *fama* in its most immediate and affecting form rests, for Cicero, with the orator.

Conclusion

The interpretation of the *Philippics* as a feature of Roman culture has, from Cicero's own day forward, had to contend with the fact that their very status as "classics" depends in part on a comparison, implicit or explicit, with the *Philippics* of Demosthenes (a parallel first drawn by Cicero himself).[35] Even more so, perhaps, than in the case of many other Roman cultural artifacts, a Greek standard overshadows our critical perceptions. The assessment, moreover, of Cicero's achievement in the *Philippics* has traditionally been tied to the assessment of his political views. The *Philippics* are part of Cicero's "last stand for Republicanism," and this is a stand that is fundamentally doomed.[36] The most that can be salvaged for Cicero as a political agent is misplaced devotion, however dedicated and courageous, to a lost cause. When Roman culture is discussed through a reading of Cicero's *Philippics*, it is usually in search of the ways that Cicero's prescriptions for the Roman state may have inspired the young Octavian and future Augustus.[37] The *Philippics*, then, are traditionally an index of their author's claim to rival a Greek model, a testament to misguided devotion to a doomed political system, or an expression of cultural values whose virtue lies in their usefulness to the first Princeps. It is no wonder that they have been relatively ignored for their careful and effective adaptation of traditional republican culture.

Certain general attitudes, moreover, toward late-republican "culture" itself may have lent their weight to this tendency, since it has long been tempting to see a cultural failure, a disjunction between traditional form and moral or ethical substance, attendant on the political failure of the Roman republic. This is a primary concern, for example, of Lucan, whose late Republic becomes a breeding ground for civil war precisely because of such failure. In addition to the personal motivations of Caesar and Pompeius, the causes of the war, in Lucan's view, include an excess of wealth, luxury, greed, effeminacy in personal habits such as dress, scorn for poverty and traditional agriculture, rejection of the pleasures of peace, a propensity for crime and violence, bribery, and usury (1.158–82). It is no coincidence that in Lucan we find Cicero lending his supreme eloquence to an "invalid cause" (7.67: *invalidae . . . causae*), the encouragement of Pompeius to engage in battle with Caesar at Pharsalus. One can trace a related strand of thinking in the modern period by tracking, as Peter Baehr has done, the development and interdependence of Republicanism and Caesarism through nineteenth- and twentieth-century political and sociological thought. At the extremes of a complex dialectic lie two polarized notions of the "Caesar phenomenon": either Caesar is the product of decadence and corruption or he is the ruler who calls to order a society lapsed into chaos because of an overdependence on the untutored and irrational impulses of the people.

The criticisms of Oswald Spengler represent the most virulent twentieth-century indictment of Roman cultural poverty in the later years of the Republic. For Spengler, Rome itself was devoid of "culture," and embodied instead an epoch of increasingly sterile "civilization" following the Greeks' cultural achievement and decline. Spengler's Cicero is a "weakling," responsible for formulating the "obsolete party-ideal" adopted by Augustus (for whom Spengler likewise expresses his contempt).[38] Spengler's *Decline of the West* is now seen as little more than a period piece, but his views were taken up and extended by a series of writers who developed the parallel he had suggested between the late Roman Republic and modern America, a parallel that continues to influence popular perceptions of the ancient world. Aumaury de Riencout, to take one notable instance, viewed American culture as "identical to that of Rome in the latter years of the Republic" in being "democratic, equalitarian, impersonal, standardized, urban, philistine, unitary, conservative and behavioristically minded, pragmatic, hero-worshipping, effeminate."[39]

My goal in this chapter has hardly been to resuscitate Cicero as the icon of a Roman Republic opposite in nature to the society imagined by a Spengler or a Riencourt ("individualistic, vital, original, masculine," etc.). Rather, I have described one area in which traditional views of Cicero and of republican Rome, in addition to a classicizing impulse initiated by Cicero himself, have made it difficult to perceive the richness of a classic text's engagement with its cultural context. But the view of the *Philippics* I have advanced here does have implications for this study's larger regard on the nature of cultural change between Republic and Principate. A cultural reading of the *Second Philippic*, that is, complements recent work foregrounding culture in the study of the "Roman Revolution." For Syme, who coined the term, culture was of secondary importance to the shift in political personnel resulting from the victory of Octavian. This emphasis, too, has had the detrimental effect of obscuring the ways that culture is in fact central to contemporary responses to the phenomenon in question—an "analytical category" in its own right.[40] Rome's cultural transition, of course, must be understood in its complexity over time rather than with recourse only to an idea of sudden, radical transformation or "revolution."[41] The close study of the *Second*

Philippic can further our understanding of the gradual and complex cultural change surrounding the emergence of Roman ruler-cult.

Octavian, and then Augustus, and then Augustan culture more broadly, drew inspiration from republican culture, rescuing and reshaping its forms in the nourishing environment of social and political order. But republican culture did not simply or entirely fail in the face of unprecedented cultural developments tied to the monopolization of power. Some Romans of 44 BCE had seen Cinna and Sulla: the tactics of tyranny were familiar to them, as Cicero himself points out.[42] Even a religious cult for an individual was not an entirely new development at Rome, although, as Weinstock argued, it had never endured in the manner of Caesar's cult. The *Second Philippic* reminds us of another aspect of the picture: the adaptation, through both voice and text, word and bodily act, of traditional republican forms in coherent resistance.

CHAPTER FOUR

Propertian Elegy
as "Restored Behavior"

N o two poems of Propertius have together exerted more fascination on modern readers than Elegy 4.7 (the visitation of his dead mistress, Cynthia, to a dreaming Propertius: *sunt aliquid manes*) and Elegy 4.11 (the so-called Queen of Elegies: the monologue of the aristocratic Cornelia's ghost to her living husband, L. Aemilius Paullus Lepidus).[1] The poems stand out within their ancient context as well, for while both allude copiously to the Greco-Roman poetic tradition extending back to Homer, nothing in ancient poetry before or since approximates the way Propertius here summons the ghosts of dead women to have them deliver extended mock legal orations to their surviving partners. These Augustan poems thus represent a tantalizing illustration of a problem addressed so far through discussion of republican oratory: the dead's striking "imitation" of the living in Latin literature of the first century BCE.

The genre and political circumstances of Elegies 4.7 and 4.11 seem to carry us far from the world of Cicero's speeches; but in fact the nature of Propertius' cultural mimicry encourages us to draw connections with the very rhetorical techniques we have seen Cicero exploiting. Here an Augustan poet summons the dead in the circumstances of imagined trials, while in the Republic, orators had evoked the dead in actual trials so as to have them speak for themselves. Pursuing the similarities between Propertius' poetry and the oratorical techniques observed in Cicero, this chapter argues that Elegies 4.7 and 4.11 adapt the rhetorical topos *mortuos ab inferis excitare* from republican oratory into Augustan elegy. A far different political purpose, however, distinguishes the *prosopopoeia* of the dead in Propertius from its Ciceronian antecedent. For while the ambitions of republican politics motivated Cicero's efforts to place the dead before the eyes of audience and reader, Propertius' elegiac use of the technique reflects the Augustan restoration of the *res publica* and suppression of the ruinous political competition that formed the backdrop for Cicero's career.

By revealing, then, a change in the political motivations behind Roman literary fantasy, I continue to develop a perspective on Latin literature's interrelationship with the wider field of Roman cultural performance—a view of literature as orature in Joseph Roach's sense. All ancient poetry, even texts as self-consciously literary as those of the Augustan poets, was normally voiced, whether to oneself or an audience. The fact that poetry was thus performed would have helped both author and audience make connections between it and other types of performance, such as oratory, that might to our eyes seem unrelated. Republican oratorical texts—Cicero's above all—became models for rhetorical training in the imperial period and circulated as works for private appreciation, which would also have involved performance on the part of readers. Propertius' poems refer both readers and listeners to the familiar ground of such established texts and practices even as they set out to craft something new. For a full understanding, however, of Elegies 4.7 and 4.11 in terms of performance, we benefit not only from Roach's views but also from Richard Schechner's concept of "restored behavior." Schechner argues for the social seriousness of performance that brings the past back to life: the ritual function of such representational play in restoring past actions for a contemporary audience (see the introduction to this study). Propertius' playful version of elegy serves the very important purpose of ritually assimilating republican oratorical traditions to the changed political circumstances of the Principate.

Oratory was the dominant form of verbal performance in the Republic and, although a tool of republican political infighting and clan-centered competition that had become intolerable under Augustus, it remained worthy of emulation by the Augustan poets. Indeed, Propertius' elite audience clearly gravitated toward other republican traditions similar to the genealogical techniques of oratory, transformed to suit Rome's new society. The celebration, for example, of genealogy through the display of *imagines maiorum* did not, as Harriet Flower reminds us, disappear with the coming of the Princeps, in spite of the fact that its political function for families other than the *gens Iulia* had now to be greatly muted.[2] There is evidence, rather, that Augustus' own appropriation of ancestral imagery became a model for senatorial families' private use of *imagines* and related images: not only did surviving members of the old elite cling to traditions, but their example also inspired new senators, like the "new men" of an earlier day, to adopt habits common under the Republic.[3] Augustan declamation favored the imitation of Cicero, with speakers both quoting and adapting the words of the master and focusing on the very episode of his life that could most easily be assimilated to the circumstances of Augustan rule: Cicero's conflict with Marcus Antonius (Sen. *Controv.* 7.2; *Suas.* 6, 7).[4] Finally, actual orators must have employed the topos *mortuos excitare* itself in imperial trials, since it reappears (more than once) in Quintilian.[5] The political incompatibility of republican oratory was a determining factor in the rise of organized poetic *recitatio* (recitation) among the Roman elite. As Maria Wyke points out, the emergence of *recitatio* as a cultural institution coincides with the disappearance of *oratio* in its institutionalized republican form, "for with the establishment of the principate exercise of power moved [out of the hands of individual members of the elite] to the imperial palace."[6] *Recitationes*, therefore, served a compensatory purpose for an elite deprived of traditional forms of self-expression and in search of new ones.[7]

Recent readings of Roman erotic elegy have shed welcome light on its response to the failure of republican institutions. With its (anti)heroic lover, its focus on a female love-object, and glorification of erotic rather than political life, Augustan elegy, such work has shown, seeks to dramatize the rents in the social fabric and the individual subject created by the trauma of the civil wars that brought Augustus to power.[8] Although in this chapter I follow this general scholarly trend, my greater aim is to elucidate how even the performance of elegy can be thought of as a response to—and a partial remedy for—the changed circumstances of elite life under Augustus: a gesture of mastery and control, albeit shadowed by the social, cultural, and political anxieties accompanying social upheaval of this magnitude.[9] On the one hand, Augustan audiences would have been drawn to performances that recalled republican oratory's emphasis on genealogy, with the suggestion of traditional authority that this aspect of oratory could lend a poet and his genre. On the other hand, Propertius' celebration of erotic bonds connecting the living and the dead represents a sly, witty *imitation* of Augustus, a counter-genealogy expressed in mock oratorical performance. Propertius revises the oratorical evocation of dead by favoring the erotic *over* the genealogical—and thereby asserts his own sort of mastery in a central area of Augustan cultural innovation.

Adapting *mortuos excitare* helped Propertius use the dead Cynthia and Cornelia as "exemplary" figures in a manner more suited to Augustan elegy than the way the exemplary dead had traditionally been evoked in oratory and call attention to the fact that he was doing so. We perceive this change best by reading the poems closely with what became the textbook example of the *mortuos excitare* topos, Cicero's *prosopopoeia* of Appius Claudius Caecus in the *Pro Caelio* (Cic. *Cael.* 33–34).[10] In spite of the unconventional rhetorical purpose, noted in chapter 1, behind Cicero's evocation of Appius, the passage nevertheless provides a rich basis for comparison by illustrating the similarities—and the profound differences—between Propertius' version of the topos and its original use in oratory. The comparison suggests, too, Cicero's speech as a subtext of Cornelia's monologue in Propertius 4.11, insofar as speech and poem share striking similarities in form and content. When we read Propertius 4.7 and 4.11 with Cicero's *Pro Caelio*, however, we do far more than enhance our understanding of the poems' (un)conventionality or allusiveness. Through his use of the topos, Propertius seeks to persuade his audience of the appropriateness, in the Augustan context, of his version of elegy, with its complex, ambivalent, even humorous relationship to traditional *exempla*. Propertius' poems, with their respective emphases on vituperation and praise, are "speeches" *about* elegy and *as* elegy; by treating them as both at once, we come closer to grasping their full cultural import and the nature of cultural change during Rome's political transition.

But why, of all the Roman elegists, did Propertius choose to restore the oratorical conventions for evoking the dead? In this regard, Elegies 4.7 and 4.11 are unique. While in Cicero's case, the virtual absence of surviving texts makes detailed comparison with contemporaneous oratory impossible, in the case of Propertius, we can see just how his technique relates to that of other elegiac poets, and so situate it more firmly in its cultural context. In the last part of the chapter, I argue that Elegies 4.7 and 4.11 in fact develop and extend Propertius' particular conception of the dead's role in elegy, a conception distinctive of him in comparison with his republican predecessor Catullus and Augustan contemporaries Tibullus and Ovid. They suggest a heightened sensitivity, fostered by the traumatic experience of civil war, to the problems and importance of commemorative performance itself. The ostentatious imitation of the exemplary dead and the elaborate representation of circumstances in which Propertius himself hoped to be commemorated after his death are both typically Propertian behaviors remodeled—indeed, like the oratorical tropes, restored—in these two poems.

Propertius 4.7: The Dead's Censure

Let us return to Cicero's *Pro Caelio*, a speech that, in spite of some scholars' emphasis on its comedic and trivializing effects, is rife with politically charged invective and self-promotion. To recapitulate the argument advanced in chapter 1: Cicero's *prosopopoeia* of Appius Claudius Caecus represents a culminating moment in the *Pro Caelio*'s political, as well as its strictly forensic, agenda. Cicero introduces Appius to bear witness to an essential point in his argument, namely, that the charges of *aurum et vene-num* leveled against Caelius attest not to any wrongdoing on Caelius' part but to a love affair between Caelius and Clodia, whom Cicero makes entirely responsible for Caelius' prosecution. Through Appius, Cicero stigmatizes Clodia's brother and his own political archrival, Clodius: he juxtaposes a *prosopopoeia* of the latter with his performance as the grave Censor, Appius, whose stature helps to set in relief the moral laxity he imputes to Clodius. Appius acts, at the same time, as an *exemplum* of *gravitas*. He recalls a series of his own achievements and those of other exemplary men and women from the Claudian *gens* of which he is patriarch. Cicero exploits Appius' gravity to lend authority to his attack upon Clodia and her brother, Clodius, and to his own public persona. He seeks to magnify his own image and belittle that of his opponents through aligning himself with the most august civic traditions, as embodied by Appius. The *Pro Caelio* is very much a part of the infighting of the late-republican elite, so unwelcome in the Rome of the new Princeps, Augustus.

For its emphasis on bearing witness to guilt and its reliance on exemplary figures from the past, the dead Cynthia's reproach of Propertius in the context of a legalistic self-defense might well have recalled the *Pro Caelio* to the minds of Propertius' educated audience. In spite of the fact that Elegy 4.7's frame and certain of its details echo closely the visitation of Patroclus' ghost to the sleeping Achilles in *Iliad* 23.59–92, what Propertius actually *does* though his performance as Cynthia is oratorical at the same time as it is epic.[11] Elegy 4.7 mimics a legal indictment and self-defense; Cynthia's language and subject-matter are that of a suit:

> Lygdamus uratur—candescat lamina vernae—
>   sensi ego, cum insidiis pallida vina bibi—
> aut Nomas—arcanas tollat versuta salivas;
>   dicet damnatas ignea testa manus.
> quae modo per vilis inspecta est publica noctes,
>   haec nunc aurata cyclade signat humum;
> at graviora rependit iniquis pensa quasillis,
>   garrula de facie si qua locuta mea est;
> nostraque quod Petale tulit ad monumenta coronas,
>   codicis immundi vincula sentit anus;
> caeditur et Lalage tortis suspensa capillis,
>   per nomen quoniam est ausa rogare meum.
> te patiente meae conflavit imaginis aurum,
>   ardente e nostro dotem habitura rogo.

non tamen insector, quamvis mereare, Properti:
  longa mea in libris regna fuere tuis.
iuro ego Fatorum nulli revolubile carmen,
  tergeminusque canis sic mihi molle sonet,
me servasse fidem. si fallo, vipera nostris
  sibilet in tumulis et super ossa cubet.

Let Lygdamus burn—let the iron grow hot for that slave—I sensed it was
she when I drank the wine that poison had discolored. Or Nomas—let
her cunningly destroy the deadly ingredients she keeps hidden, the fiery
potsherds will reveal that hers are the guilty hands. She who was recently
visible in public selling herself cheaply by night now sweeps the ground
with her gold-hemmed dress; but if a servant chatters about my beauty,
she unfairly assigns her baskets with a heavier weight of wool. And because
dear Petale brought garlands to my monument, the old woman is shackled
to the shameful wooden block. And Lalage is hung up by her twisted hair
and beaten, because she dared to ask for something in my name. With your
consent she melted down my golden image, so as to obtain a dowry from
my burning pyre. Yet I do not pursue you, though you may deserve it, Propertius: my reign in your books was a long one. I swear by the song of the
Fates that no one can retract—and may the three-headed tog sound softly
for me—I kept faith. If I lie, let a viper hiss in my tomb and lie on my bones.
(Prop. 4.7.35–54)

Cynthia's use of the verb *insector* (pursue) (49), as well as her accusations of
poisoning (36–38), demands for the torture of slaves (35–38), and oath of
innocence (51–54) all connote judicial process, and this is one of Propertius'
most significant additions to his Homeric model. Propertius ends the poem
on a similar note, the verb *perago* (prosecute) (95) and the noun *lis* (quarrel)
(95) likewise suggesting a trial: *haec postquam querula mecum sub lite pere-
git, / inter complexus excidit umbra meos* (when she had prosecuted her case
with quarrelsome plaintiveness, the ghost slipped out from my attempted
embrace).[12] Just as the dead Appius bore witness to Clodia's sexual indis-
cretion and the devotion of female members of his *gens,* so Cynthia's ghost
bears witness to Propertius' faithlessness and to her own devotion. In the *Pro
Caelio,* a charge of poisoning and a suspicious exchange of *aurum* formed
the basis for Appius' revelation, while in Propertius Cynthia charges the
slaves Lygdamus and Nomas of poisoning her and accuses Propertius' new
mistress, Chloris, of melting down her golden statue so as to have a "dowry"
(35–38, 47–48).[13] Appius cited a series of exemplary figures from the legendary history of the *gens;* Cynthia goes on to liken herself to the mythical

exempla Andromeda and Hypermestra, with whom she shares a place in the Elysian Fields (63–69). The Appius passage recalled the *laudatio funebris* in structure and content, while in its later sections Cynthia's monologue achieves, as Warden has suggested, a solemn tone of commemoration reminiscent of the *laudatio*.[14]

But more significant than the similarities between Propertius' adaptation of *mortuos excitare* and Cicero's *prosopopoeia* of Appius is the way that Elegy 4.7, as it exploits the topos, also calls attention to the differences between the simultaneously private and public world of Propertian erotic elegy and the republican civic context of politically charged invective. This signaling of different contexts while employing a well-known performance convention makes Propertius 4.7 a self-conscious restoration of behavior rather than simply another instance of a common rhetorical trope. Propertius, in other words, here adapts an important component of republican oratorical culture *and* lets his audience know that this is what he is doing.

As the invective of a woman and a *meretrix,* Cynthia's words naturally carry far less political weight than those of a male civic *exemplum* such as Appius Claudius Caecus. Propertius, however, does not simply leave this fact to be assumed by his audience. Rather, he signals it emphatically by having Cynthia reverse the priorities of the public moral discourse in which a figure like Appius participated:

> iamne tibi exciderant vigilacis furta Suburae
>   et mea nocturnis trita fenestra dolis?
> per quam demisso quotiens tibi fune pependi,
>   alterna veniens in tua colla manu!
> saepe Venus trivio commissa est, pectore mixto
>   fecerunt tepidas pallia nostra vias.
> foederis heu taciti, cuius fallacia verba
>   non audituri diripuere Noti.

> Had you already forgotten our stolen loves in the watchful Subura and my windowsill rubbed smooth with nightly trickery? How many times I let down a rope through it and descended to you, lowering myself, hand over hand, into your embrace! We often made love at the crossroads; with our breasts crushed together, our cloaks made the roadway warm. Alas for the silent pact, whose deceitful words the South Wind snatched away, unwilling to listen. (Prop. 4.7.15–22)

Even as Cynthia takes Propertius to task for faithlessness, she reproaches him for forgetting their "stolen love" (15: *furta*), their lovemaking at the crossroads (19: *trivio*), and their "silent pact" (21: *foederis . . . taciti*), admissions that would, from the perspective of an Appius Claudius Caecus, themselves be a basis for reproach. Indeed, Appius asks if he built a road (the Via Appia) so that Clodia might frequent it accompanied by strange men and rebukes Clodia for striking daily "pacts" (*foedera*) with her lovers (Cic. *Cael.* 34).

Appius' invective was backed up by his standing as a political figure and civic benefactor; other republican orators likewise depended on the political standing of the personages they evoked through the figure *mortuos excitare*.[15] Again, however, Propertius does not merely assume that Cynthia could have no political persona, but rather takes pains to distance her from the power centers of Roman politics through his description of her funeral. Cynthia was "recently buried near the end of the road" (Prop. 4.7.4: *murmur ad extremae nuper humata viae*).[16] The noun *murmur* here conveys, as Richardson has noted, a sense of the road's edge: it suggests the stream of passers-by who do not stop to watch Cynthia's funeral as they might have watched the spectacular burial of a Roman from a wealthy or aristocratic family.[17] *Extremae* likewise displaces Cynthia from center to perimeter: to the "end," that is, of the Via Tiburtina.[18] Indeed, a lack of recognition and a demand for a more prominent grave monument (one that will attract the attention of the messenger "running" by her grave in verse 84) is precisely Cynthia's concern in verses 77–86, where we also learn that Cynthia's tomb is to redound to the credit of Tibur, her place of birth (85):

> et quoscumque meo fecisti nomine versus,
> > ure mihi: laudes desine habere meas.
> pelle hederam tumulo, mihi quae praegnante corymbo
> > mollia contortis alligat ossa comis.
> ramosis Anio qua pomifer incubat arvis,
> > et numquam Herculeo numine pallet ebur,
> hic carmen media dignum me scribe columna,
> > sed breve, quod currens vector ab urbe legat:
> HIC TIBURTINA IACET AUREA CYNTHIA TERRA:
> > ACCESSIT RIPAE LAUS, ANIENE, TUAE.

And whatever verses you composed for my sake, I ask you to burn them: stop winning praise through me. Cut back from my tomb the ivy that with heavy clusters surrounds my delicate bones in its dense foliage. Where the fertile Anio descends to water orchards and, by Hercules' god-head, ivory never yellows, inscribe verses worthy of me in the middle of a column; but make them short, so that a messenger running from the city might read them: HERE ON

TIBURTINE LAND LIES GOLDEN CYNTHIA; GLORY, RIVER ANIO, IS ADDED
TO YOUR BANKS. (Prop. 4.7.77–86)

Cynthia's description of her funeral and resting place calls attention to the
fact that she has not been buried near Rome.[19] This distances her, quite literally, from the most prominent families of the Roman elite, whose tombs
lined the roadways immediately surrounding the city. Propertius distinguishes Cynthia, in death, from a figure of wide public recognition, one
whom an orator might "call up from the dead."[20]

An audience familiar with "Cynthia," the multi-faceted persona of Propertius' oeuvre, would recognize, of course, the potential humor and irony
in all this, and would be unable to segregate entirely the "obscure" Cynthia
evoked in Elegy 4.7 from the many other depictions of her that undermine
this aspect of her (self-)portrait here. It must be granted that, on the one
hand, Cynthia's ghostly form in Elegy 4.7 embodies and speaks to the guilty
knowledge of a personal betrayal rather than the fall from public standards
of morality represented by a figure such as the stern Appius of Cicero's *Pro
Caelio*. The threats posed by Cynthia and Cicero's Appius to those they
rebuke stand to this extent in opposition to each other. Cicero's Appius is
threatening, for example, because his rebuke implies a diminishment of
good *fama* among the community at large. His bearded form is reminiscent,
Cicero suggests, of the *imagines maiorum* carried in the public ceremony of
an aristocratic funeral (Cic. *Cael.* 33). Conversely, Cynthia's ghost, looking
uncannily the same as Propertius remembers her when, as a corpse, she was
carried to burial (with the "same hair," the "same eyes" and the "accustomed"
beryl ring on her finger [Prop. 4.7.7–9]) is troubling to Propertius primarily
on a personal level. She reveals his infidelities in order to move him personally rather than to destroy his public standing (70: *celo ego perfidiae crimina
multa tuae* [I hide the many transgressions of your faithlessness]). Her
request that Propertius burn his poetry about her is hardly as devastating
as Appius' assault on Clodia's public reputation. Indicating that she will not
"pursue" Propertius while he lives, she predicts that soon he will be hers, as
they "grind bone on bone" in the grave (49; 93–94). Propertius creates an
opposition between Cynthia, insofar as she *claims*, in 4.7, to be an *exemplum*
of erotic devotion, and the kind of public exemplary figure evoked by orators.

Elsewhere in Propertius' work, on the other hand, Cynthia's public
reputation—often highly questionable—is very much at stake as Propertius
asserts his ability to make or break them both with his poetry. In Elegy 2.3,
Rome's youth burns for Cynthia (33), the subject of a new book of Propertius' poems (4): she will be the "glory" of Roman girls (29), while his own

lack of self-restraint, Propertius laments, will redound to his discredit (1–4). In 2.1, Propertius imagines the illustrious Maecenas reading aloud the poet's epitaph at his tomb: *huic misero fatum dura puella fuit* (a hard girl was this man's demise) (78). In 3.2, Propertius asserts that his poetry will impart everlasting fame to the woman he celebrates (17–26); but in 2.5, Propertius has said he will ruin Cynthia's reputation for all time, and find another girl who wants to be celebrated in his poetry, this in retaliation for the bad *fama* Cynthia has already earned (1–2, 5–6, 27–30). Propertius and Cynthia's affair is, in Elegy 2.20, that which "no street-corner" is silent about (22); in 3.24 Propertius is ashamed that Cynthia has become famous through his verse (4).

A glance at "Cynthia" in Propertius' larger oeuvre, therefore, reminds us that no simple opposition between public and private concerns is applicable to Propertian elegy's adaptations of oratory, and that the oratorical presentation of Cynthia in Elegy 4.7 is only one among a series of competing views of her that Propertius' audiences are encouraged to adopt.[21] As Barbara Gold suggests, it is helpful to understand these competing views as projections of the desires and anxieties of "Propertius" (that is, the poet insofar as he can be identified with his persona in the text), as versions of "what Propertius wants or fears for himself."[22] Indeed, part of what Propertius "wants" (and wants us to know he wants) in Elegy 4.7 is to show that Cynthia *can* fit the model—the revised, ambivalent, Propertian model—of an oratorical *exemplum*.

Propertius remodels oratory in a complex, ambivalent manner by embedding the public in the private. To identify with the "model" Cynthia in Elegy 4.7, he implies, is to be like the mythical heroines Andromeda and Hypermestra: to assimilate oneself, that is, to figures worthy of praise. And yet these "models" can in fact be interpreted as the basis for a paradoxical apologia of erotic elegy in a collection (Book 4) supposedly devoted to etiological poetry.[23] We discover in them, with Micaela Janan, a bravura "indictment" of elegy itself as a genre embracing a reductive view of Woman and exploiting a subjugated female object.[24] Cynthia rails at Propertius in a manner we are free to find serious or funny, appropriate or incongruous.[25] And yet our view of her ultimately has a strong bearing on our view of Propertius. Cynthia wants to be heard *because* of her subjugation, just as Propertius, the subjugated hero/lover, wants himself to be heard. Even as an oratorical *exemplum,* she is a projection of Propertius' own desires.[26]

But whether we read Propertius 4.7 as an "oratorical" defense or indictment *of* erotic elegy, it is important to hear in it oratory *as* erotic elegy: essential to the cultural import of the poem are the means by which Propertius brings Cynthia on the scene. Elegy 4.7 refashions the evocation of dead ancestors known to a republican speaker such as Cicero by asserting that the private-public world of elegy has a claim to rival the public sphere for the significance of its interpersonal attachments, each with its own power and validity—as well as risks—for those involved.

Propertius 4.11: The Dead's Praise

Propertius' Cornelia, as he portrays her in Elegy 4.11, might seem at first glance inextricably associated both with a politically charged context of republican self-promotion, and specifically with Cicero's *Pro Caelio*. As has long been recognized, Propertius has Cornelia allude to conventions of judicial oratory as well as of the aristocratic funeral, such as the *laudatio funebris* and the wearing of *imagines*, both central aspects of the ceremony as political self-advertisement.[27] Because Cornelia engages in ancestral *laudatio*, the fact that she is a woman does not necessarily distance her from a political context (in the way that Cynthia's sex, for instance, distances her from political invective):

> si cui fama fuit per avita tropaea decori,
>   Afra Numantinos regna loquuntur avos:
> altera maternos exaequat turba Libones,
>   et domus est titulis utraque fulta suis.
>
> . . . .
>
> testor maiorum cineres tibi, Roma, colendos,
>   sub quorum titulis, Africa, tunsa iaces,
> †et Persen proavo stimulantem pectus Achille,
>   quique tuas proavo fregit Achille domos,†
> me neque censurae legem mollisse neque ulla
>   labe mea vestros erubuisse focos.
>
> . . . .
>
> quaelibet austeras de me ferat urna tabellas:
>   turpior assessu non erit ulla meo,
> vel tu, quae tardam movisti fune Cybeben,
>   Claudia, turritae rara ministra deae,
> vel †cuius rasos† cum Vesta reposceret ignis,
>   exhibuit vivos carbasus alba focos.

If reputation from ancestral trophies has ever been a source of glory for anyone, the African kingdoms speak of my sires who captured Numantia:

on the other side a host of forbears makes my mother's family, the Libones, equal, and each house is strengthened by the report of its memorial inscriptions. . . . I call to witness the ashes of ancestors cherished by you, Rome, and under the fame of whose memorials you, Africa, lie beaten, and the one who, although you, Perses, were incited by the spirit of your ancestor, Achilles, destroyed your house although its ancestor was Achilles, that I never weakened the censor's law and that your hearth never blushed red through any transgression of mine. . . . Let any urn bear the stern voting tablets: no woman will be shamed by appearing beside me in court, whether you, Claudia, matchless handmaid of the turreted goddess, who moved the stranded Cybebe with a rope, or you, whose fine white linen garment, when Vesta called you to account for the [extinguished] flame, revealed a living hearth. (Prop. 4.11.29–32, 37–42, 49–54)

Although women did not perform actual *laudationes*, it was a traditional Roman custom to deliver funeral orations for older women and the first *laudatio* for a young noble woman was delivered by Julius Caesar for his wife Cornelia, with whom the subject of Propertius 4.11 shares membership in the Cornelian *gens*.[28] It is possible that Propertius' decision to have Paullus' wife deliver her own "funeral oration" reflected the fact that her relative was the first woman so honored. Augustus himself had helped set a precedent for continued *laudationes* of women by having spoken, as a boy of twelve years, at the funeral of Julius Caesar's sister Julia in 51 BCE.[29]

The similarities, moreover, between the use of *mortuos excitare* in Cicero's *Pro Caelio* and Propertius 4.11 are so striking as to suggest Cicero's speech as a subtext for Propertius' poem. Both Cicero and Propertius "call up" an exemplary dead aristocrat who recalls other exemplary figures from his or her family, and the families in question are in fact related, so that one *exemplum*, Q. Claudia, is invoked by both Propertius and Cicero and in a remarkably similar way (cf. the references, in quick succession, to Q. Claudia and a Vestal Virgin at Prop. 4.11.51–54 above and Cic. *Cael.* 34).[30] Cicero's Appius is among Cornelia's ancestors, both in fact and in the performance tradition linking Propertius to his republican forbear, Cicero.

As Judith Hallett has observed, Propertius' Cornelia possesses not only female but male traits that associate her with the public realm of Roman elite life, the very realm in which Cicero's *Pro Caelio* is situated.[31] As in the case of Elegy 4.7, we cannot resort to a simple dichotomy between public and private to characterize Propertius' representation of Cornelia. We can say, however, that Propertius signals his distance from the political self-promotion of the Republic through a series of important details in this poem, thereby making the *Pro Caelio* far more significant as a subtext.

Cornelia does hope to perpetuate her good name among a wider audience. But instead of the very broad public audience that would have thronged to the forum to hear the *laudatio* of a republican aristocrat, she addresses her husband, her children, and certain residents (as well as physical features) of the underworld. She is careful to emphasize the self-enclosure of the underworld and its removal from the world of the living (3–4: *cum semel infernas intrarunt funera leges, / non exorato stant adamante viae* [once the corpse has entered the jurisdiction of the underworld, the road back stands closed in inexorable adamant]). While she refers to aspects of the aristocratic funeral with its *imagines maiorum*, she does not mention the *pompa* that formed a focal point of the ceremony as a form of political advertisement.[32] Cornelia removes herself in still another way from this context in recalling that her achievements as a living woman merited no public display comparable to that of the military triumph a man might enjoy (71–72: *haec est feminei merces extrema triumphi, / laudat ubi emeritum libera fama rogum* [this is the highest reward of a woman's triumph: when uninhibited speech lauds her deserving pyre]). Cornelia is concerned specifically with the domestic sphere, above all the care and raising of her children (61–98). While her reference to Augustus' distress at her death (58) may point to a public display of grief, it also suggests that Propertius' commemoration of her is not an act of aggressive self-promotion on the part of her clan but is carried out with the emperor's approval.[33] Propertius thus indicates his distance from public oratorical performance such as judicial oratory and the funeral *laudationes* of individual clans even as he draws on these traditions.

Further distancing Propertius 4.11 from Cicero's *Pro Caelio* is the fact that attestations to the transgressions of others, so prominent a part of Cicero's speech, are greatly muted in Propertius' poem, and true invective is entirely absent. Although her speech seems to contain veiled criticism of her husband, Paullus, real transgressors are limited to the sinners in the underworld (23–24), whose guilt cannot be debated.[34] Conversely, Cornelia herself is so emphatic about her own blamelessness that scholars have wondered whether the scene evoked is primarily that of a trial or a legal induction (as a "naturalized" citizen into the company of the underworld).[35] In light of the poem's echo of the *Pro Caelio*, the suggestion of a trial becomes readily apparent, but this trial lacks any politically charged disparagement of opponents. It is most unlike the republican procedure in which Cicero defended Caelius.

Like Elegy 4.7, 4.11 invites ironic and even humorous interpretations of Cornelia's self-eulogy, readings that might appear to call into doubt Propertius' interest in adapting republican oratorical conventions for the purpose of aligning his version of elegy with the concerns of the Augustan elite. If an audience must hesitate before identifying with Cornelia as an "oratorical" *exemplum*, why should it (or we) be convinced by those aspects of Propertius' poem that contribute to her representation in this light? Scholars such as La Penna, Hallett, Hubbard, and Sullivan have found Cornelia's virtue cold and uninspiring.[36] Richardson discerns a condemnation of Augustan gender codes, a view that Janan further develops in describing Cornelia's self-denying attitude in 4.11 in terms of the Hegelian "sacrifice of the sacrifice." In Janan's view, Cornelia renounces the very possibility of a meaningful, coherent outcome to the tensions and contradictions imposed upon her as a woman of the Augustan elite.[37] In a more whimsical vein, W. R. Johnson points out the potential embarrassment to Augustus in Propertius' mention of Cornelia's mother and Augustus' first wife, Scribonia, whom he divorced after a short time to marry Livia, his wife at the time of Elegy 4.11's composition.[38] Johnson's reading, on the surface foreign to a traditional understanding of the poem's solemnity, is very much in keeping with the humor that so marks Propertius' poetry, and the spirit of *recusatio* that pervades the poet's work from Book 2 onward. Having refused so often to write an "Augustan epic," why should Propertius not subtly resist when praising a prominent member of Augustus' own family?

The complexities of Cornelia's persona in Propertius 4.11, or of the social situation occasioned by her funeral, do not detract, however, from seeing the poem's performance as a culturally transformative gesture, a restoration of behavior. Indeed, they even enhance its effect as such. As recent critics of Roman erotic elegy have emphasized, one of the ways the genre most appealed to the concerns of an Augustan audience was its response to "the moments of ideological contradiction and aporia"[39] that accompanied Rome's transition from Republic to Principate. That is, Propertius and his audience were very much aware of a failure in Roman aristocratic institutions and the difficulties imposed upon them by the need to redefine and reinvent social roles, and yet they sought out occasions for collective expression of such difficulties. Restoring those aspects of republican oratory that were most suggestive of the traditional authority of the orator and his genre could be a stabilizing act implying mastery over the very tensions it might generate.

In a manner even more pointed than Propertius 4.7, 4.11 signals its own contrast with oratorical techniques that would have been highly inappropriate in an Augustan judicial context. Cicero had co-opted the exemplary figure of Appius in the service not only of a judicial argument but also of political self-promotion and display. Propertius' Cornelia is concerned not about the image she projects to a broad public, which goes all but unmentioned,[40] but about the opinion of her ancestors and close family. "Called up" from the underworld, in which she nevertheless remains firmly located, Cornelia offers herself as an *exemplum* of devotion and other feminine virtues—without entirely disguising the contradictions and tensions inherent in this gesture. The poem does not aim to exploit Cornelia's genealogical ties for political advancement but uses them to establish the basis of praise for her virtuous behavior in the realm of erotic life. And this praise is potentially as ambivalent, problematic, and funny as Cynthia's vituperation of Propertius in Elegy 4.7.

The restoration of republican values and institutions central to Augustus' ideological program allowed for a great deal of interpretation, and even dissent, on the part of poets and other literary performers whose activities he encouraged. But some of the uses to which performance had been put under the Republic were simply incompatible with the rule of a *Princeps*. To be sure, oratory flourished under the Principate and imperial rhetorical handbooks took over republican techniques in virtually all their forms. But judicial speeches in service of political competition would now cede to a form of speech that, if no less varied in its effects, would nevertheless have to keep its distance from politics in comparison with its republican predecessor.[41] For Augustus, restoring the *res publica* meant co-opting political power so as to oversee all its forms of expression, including the invective and self-promotion of public performances such as oratory. Romans, including Augustus himself, sought new ways to understand, fashion, and display the relationship between the present and the past as a means of addressing and repairing the damage to the social fabric caused by the traumas of the civil wars.

Where Roman identity is concerned, the restorative quality of Propertian elegy, in the Schechnerian sense, is nowhere more evident than in Propertius 4.7 and 4.11.[42] The performance of these poems has the ritual function of integrating past and present, the living and the dead, in a politically acceptable—if ambivalent, ironic, and even humorous—manner. But, likewise in a ritual fashion, Propertius wittily imitates Augustus. Performing and listening appreciatively to such poems, the Augustan elite emulates its Princeps, but in a way that leaves open the possibility of laughter and love alongside gravity and civic-mindedness. We might put ourselves in the place of Augustus' subjects, surrounded by the ever-increasing evidence of the Princeps' dominance and the power of the ideology he fostered. The Forum Augustum, for example, a central component in Augustus' building program, was an imposing sight, its colonnades filled with statues of exemplary Romans, including members and ancestors of the Julian *gens*. The Forum was a powerful symbol, in spite of internal tensions and contradictions, of "Augustus' efforts to impose unity on Rome's eclectic heritage" to "coax a totality from the division and incoherence of Roman cultural identity."[43] In the face of such overwhelming assertions of ideological will, what kinds of responses might be open to the Roman elite besides simple acceptance or resistance? Propertius and his audiences could respond by favoring the erotic *over* the genealogical, but in the process they produced and ritually displayed their own counter-genealogy, one that was as particular and appealing to them as Augustus' was impressive and imposing.[44] Elegies 4.7 and 4.11 venture into an area of cultural innovation especially important to Augustus himself. They not only describe bonds between erotic partners but also foster a bond between successive generations of those who take an interest in elegy and in Propertius' poetry. The ghostly Cynthia and Cornelia are ancestors, in spirit, of Propertian elegy's future audiences and interpreters everywhere.

Propertius' Poetic Use of the Imitatio maiorum

I have argued thus far that the evocation of the dead in Propertian elegy was one means of negotiating the social, cultural, and political changes accompanying Rome's transition from Republic to Principate. Given the distinctiveness, however, of the two poems on which I have focused, it remains to be explained why Propertius in particular took advantage of this opportunity and why his techniques are neither anticipated in the elegiac poems of the republican poet Catullus nor paralleled in Tibullus and Ovid, the other principal Augustan elegists. In the second part of this chapter, I will argue that Propertius was particularly well-placed to incorporate the oratorical topos *mortuos excitare* into elegy, because it harmonized with the conception of the dead's role in elegy that he had been developing throughout his career and with the "behaviors" this conception led him to stage in elegy previously. At least two features of his earlier work anticipate his adaptation of oratorical behavior in the later poems, 4.7 and 4.11: his ostentatious imitation of the exemplary dead and the elaborate representation of his own posthumous commemoration. Propertius' interest in representing such acts seems to have still deeper roots in his personal sensitivity to the ambivalent nature of such performance, a trait fostered in him by the brutal experience of civil war in the late 40s BCE.

Returning, then, with a fresh eye to our main texts, we find that Elegy 4.11, at least outwardly, accords the noble Cornelia an exemplary status that Propertius uses his evocation of her ghost to imitate (by speaking in her voice) and thus recommend. Cornelia comes from an illustrious family and can at least claim to have lived up to the expectations incumbent upon her in widely acknowledged areas of female virtue: marital fidelity and the bearing of children. To this extent, she deserves to be regarded as a successor to the famous ancestors she mentions and imitating this aspect of her conduct, Propertius implies, can be understood as a worthy goal. As we have seen, this is one of the features of the poem that ties it to Cicero's *Pro Caelio.* When Cicero has Appius Claudius Caecus rebuke Clodia, his performance itself is an illustration, although clearly tinged with humor and irony, of the *imitatio maiorum* that he believes Clodia herself ought to practice. Speaking as Appius, Cicero asks Clodia whether, if the images of the male members of the Claudian *gens* did not move her to abandon her interest in the young M. Caelius, the examples of Quinta Claudia and Claudia the Vestal did not compel her to be *aemulam* (emulous) of the achievements of the *gens* (34). And Cicero himself emulates Appius as an authoritative public figure.[45]

Even before Book 4, however, Propertius had claimed an analogous role for the elegist.[46] In Elegy 3.1, Propertius evokes his poetic models Callimachus and Philetas as ghosts who, as denizens of the Muses' sacred grove, will welcome and inspire him as he performs "Italian rites in Greek dances" (3.1.1–6). The prominence of this technique at the opening of the book suggests not only Propertius' devotion to Hellenistic aesthetics (which has already been amply confirmed in the poems of Book 2), but also an intense interest in representing elegy as both an imitative and a competitive genre, inspired by the spirits of important poetic ancestors. Propertius says he hopes to outdo a "crowd" of emulous writers, whom he imagines following his "triumphal" procession (9–14, cf. 21). This, he claims, will help assure his lasting reputation among Romans (35–38).

Somewhat later in Book 3, Propertius develops this idea still further by expressly equating his inspiration by poetic ancestors with traditional Roman *imitatio maiorum* (3.9). In an arch example of *recusatio,* Propertius here bases his refusal to write an epic poem for Augustus on the premise that he is actually following the lead of his patron, Maecenas, to whom the poem is addressed. Propertius insists that just as Maecenas has rejected a higher, more public status for himself, so he himself will adhere to his modest, sheltered role as an elegiac rather than an epic poet. While Maecenas' wisdom, Propertius claims, will lead men to consider him equal of Camillus, the famous Roman general and statesman of the fourth century BCE (31–32), Propertius aspires, once again, to be the peer of Philetas, whom he addresses in verse 45 (. . . *et cecinisse modis, Coe poeta, tuis* [. . . and to have sung, Coan poet, in your meters]).

Propertius' expressed admiration for Maecenas' behavior in Elegy 3.9 invites our skepticism: the force of the *recusatio* seems to cut two ways, suggesting both self-deprecation on Propertius' part and sly criticism of Maecenas for his subservience.[47] But Propertius here shows nevertheless that he *can*, through the performance of elegy, display his own imitation of the ghostly Philetas evoked in 3.1—and justify this practice as analogous to Maecenas' own ancestrally sanctioned behavior. "I am compelled," Propertius declares, "to outdo you by your own example": *cogor et exemplis te superare tuis* (22). It will be enough "to have been judged pleasing in comparison to Callimachus' books. . . . Let these writings enflame boys and girls and let them declare me a god and bring me sacred offerings!" (43, 45–46). *Mutatis mutandis*, Elegy 3.9 would have had, in performance, an effect not unlike a passage such as Cicero' *prosopopoeia* of Appius Claudius Caecus, in that Cicero, too, displays his imitation of the dead Appius (in which he has outdone Clodia) and promotes the practice of such imitation in general. He strives to be an *exemplum* for Rome's youth (cf. *Cael.* 6–14 and 37–47) in part through his self-association with the revered, semi-divine figure of Appius.[48] Propertius represents inspired imitation of the exemplary dead as a practice central to elegy.

Adding to the foreshadowing of oratorical behavior in Propertius' evocation of Callimachus and Camillus in Elegy 3.9 is the fact the poem gives the overall impression of a rhetorical tour de force, in which a speaker praises his audience, gradually builds a case in his own defense through the accumulation of *exempla* that support his position and bear on his character, and concludes with a recapitulation of the matter at hand and an appeal to the emotions of his audience. Propertius begins with a formal address of Maecenas (1–4), whom he praises, in a manner reminiscent of the oratorical *captatio benevolentiae*, as *eques Etrusco de sanguine regum* (equestrian from the Etruscan blood of kings) (1).[49] He then proceeds to introduce, in a delayed priamel, a series of Greek artists whose greatness consisted in a particular aspect of their style or talent: Lysippus achieved glory though his life-like statues, Calamis sculpted perfect horses, Apelles excelled in painting Venus, and so on. Parrhasius, Mentor, Mys, Phidias, and Praxiteles are all adduced in support of the principle that "each man follows the seeds of his own nature" (20).[50] Ethical accounts of Maecenas' and Propertius' natures and habits follow (21–46),[51] before Propertius concludes with a recapitulation and an appeal to the emotions of his patron: if Maecenas will lead the way, Propertius will go beyond the role of elegist and sing of *arma;* would that Maecenas favor the work that Propertius' has begun (47–60).[52] Structurally, Propertius' poem invites comparison with a speech.

The dead Cynthia and Cornelia, then, find poetic precursors in Propertius' earlier work simply in being "exemplary" spirits who inspire Propertius' poetic activity and whom he ostentatiously imitates. But they are even more suggestive of Propertius' earlier poetic practice in what they do: in their elaborately imagined perpetuation, that is, of their own posthumous fame. Propertius' repeated staging of the circumstances through which *his own* fame as a poet/lover will be perpetuated after his death is a second type of elegiac behavior restored in his oratorical evocations of the dead. Cynthia's speech in Elegy 4.7, for instance, calls attention to the honor due to her now that she has become famous. Cynthia glorifies herself—this is, in fact, a form of poetic self-promotion on Propertius' part, since Cynthia's "fame" refers to Propertius' success as a poet. Similarly in 4.11, when Cornelia insists that her own reputation for virtue will outlive her, she implies that Propertius' own reputation will outlive him.[53] Comparing, again, Cicero's Appius-*prosopopoeia*, we see that Cicero hopes that his audience will transfer its reverence for the Claudians' fame to himself and that this will boost both his persuasiveness in Caelius' trial and his own political standing. Cicero thus has one of the Claudians recall his own glory and that of his *gens*, while Clodia's failure to be moved by the illustrious members of her own family invites his scorn. The passage is typical in this regard of Cicero's speeches generally, which frequently cite the honor due to the dead as a means of enhancing Cicero's own position.[54]

But the honor and glory due to himself as the hero of his erotic world—and the means by which his renown will be perpetuated posthumously—has been a recurring focus of Propertius' poetry long before. This is perhaps nowhere more true than when, in Elegy 2.1, Propertius imagines his new patron, Maecenas, commemorating him after his own death. This poem, one of only two from Propertius to Maecenas, concludes with a pentameter meant to be understood as the poet's epitaph, *huic misero fatum dura puella fuit* (An unyielding girl was this man's demise) (78). Elegies in the form of epitaphs were common in the Hellenistic Greek tradition on which Propertius drew so heavily for models. Elegy 2.1, however, transplants this convention to a Roman context by concluding with an image of Maecenas arriving at Propertius' tomb and there tearfully speaking aloud Propertius' epitaph:

> quandocumque igitur vitam mea fata reposcent,
>   et breve in exiguo marmore nomen ero,
> Maecenas, nostrae spes invidiosa iuventae,
>   et vitae ut morti gloria iusta meae,
> si te forte meo ducet via proxima busto,
>   esseda caelatis siste Britanna iugis,

taliaque illacrimans mutae iace verba favillae:
'Huic misero fatum dura puella fuit.'

> When, therefore, my fates will demand my life, and I will become a brief
> name on a slight piece of marble, Maecenas, the envied hope of our youth,
> and the rightful glory of my life as of my death, if by chance your way will
> lead you near to my tomb, halt your Britannic chariot with its engraved yoke
> and, weeping, utter such words to my silent ashes: "An unyielding girl was
> this poor man's demise." (Prop. 2.1.71–78)

Here, Maecenas is an agent of Propertius' fame among a wider audience. He
is *et vitae ut morti gloria iusta meae* (the rightful glory of my life as of my
death) (74). His favor, we are to understand, will assure that Propertius does
not remain merely a "slight name on a piece of marble," but enjoys posthumous *fama* as a figure worthy of envy (73): an *exemplum* to which other
Romans will aspire. And Propertius seems to locate some of the power to
perpetuate his own *gloria* in his patron's verbal performance at his tomb (as
overheard, perhaps, by Maecenas' attendants and transmitted from there to
a wider public[55]). Through the favor Maecenas shows to Propertius' "silent
ashes" in weeping over them and commemorating the life and the death of
the departed poet, Maecenas glorifies Propertius (rather than—what was in
fact the case—the other way around).[56]

Idealizing the circumstances of literary patronage in this fashion, Propertius points to—as he distances himself from—a well-established function
of public speech at Rome: broadcasting the dead's claim to be honored.
Maecenas' tearful utterance of Propertius' epitaph at his tomb recalls both
the purpose and the circumstances of the Roman *laudatio funebris* as it was
in the process of developing under the Principate, and so looks forward
especially to Cornelia's speech in Elegy 4.11, which recalls this genre all but
explicitly. Roman epitaphs and *laudationes* were intertwined from early days
as companion genres. With the rise of Augustus, *laudationes* were largely displaced from the Forum and more personal eulogies may actually have been
performed at the gravesite.[57] But, again, as in Elegies 4.7 and 4.11, Propertius
signals his distance in 2.1 from a traditional oratorical context by inverting
techniques and conditions assumed by the orator. The republican orator's
performance had belonged to the power centers of the Roman capital, above
all to the Forum. Maecenas' glorification of Propertius takes place at a road-
side tomb whose location is not specified, and Maecenas does not actually
perform *at* Propertius' funeral but at some later time. While the republican
orator found one of the surest bases of his own authority in the historical

exempla he invoked, Propertius concludes Elegy 2.1 by emphasizing the conditions in which *he himself* may become exemplary. A *puella*, rather than military or political prowess, is his ambition and cause of death. Propertius' relationship to his *puella* is not the basis of social or political authority but its very opposite: marginality and subordination. Having embraced, however, this typically elegiac position of subservience already in 2.1 and throughout Book 1, Propertius is now redeemed by Maecenas' favor. His marginality and subordination—and even his death—are thus, he hopes, undone.

As Elegy 2.1 suggests, staging the circumstances of his own posthumous glorification is a Propertian preoccupation. While Maecenas fills the central role in 2.1, Cynthia calls attention to the honor due to the dead Propertius elsewhere. In Elegy 2.24, Propertius imagines Cynthia declaring over his bones that he was faithful, although his ancestry was not noble and he himself was not rich (35–38). Elegy 2.13, the haunting depiction of the funeral and tomb that Propertius wishes Cynthia to prepare for him, again includes the poet's epitaph (35–36) and imagines his burial place becoming as well-known as Achilles' (37–38). In addition to Maecenas and Cynthia, Propertius' other admirers, such as the "youths" who read his verse, are more than once imagined perpetuating his fame after death (e.g., 1.7.23–24; 3.1.35–38; 3.9.45–46; etc.). Sometimes, too, it is Propertius himself who announces the form he wishes his posthumous glory to take. Elegy 2.20 concludes with an oath (similar, in fact, to those sworn by the ghosts of Cynthia and Cornelia: cf. 4.7.51–54 and 4.11.27–28), in which Propertius hopes that if he is unfaithful, he should be punished in the underworld by the Furies and Aeacus, and subject to tortures like those of Tityrus and Sisyphus (28–32). *Hoc mihi perpetuo ius est,* he concludes, *quod solus amator / nec cito desisto nec temere incipio* (This is my rule for ever, that I be the only lover who neither ends abruptly nor begins rashly) (35–36).

As befits a poetry book (*Elegies,* Book 4) in which Propertius has claimed to renounce erotic elegy for patriotic etiological poetry (and yet in which the themes and concerns of Propertius' earlier work are still very much in evidence), Elegies 4.7 and 4.11 no longer imagine others' glorification of the dead Propertius as an (anti)heroic poet/lover. Rather, two figures reminiscent of Propertius' erotic poetry, the ghosts of Cynthia and Cornelia, glorify themselves—and in fact continue the earlier glorification of Propertius in a different form. The transposition of this elegiac behavior, its restoration in a new form ostensibly more suited to Augustan ideology, is a sign both of Book 4's departure from the earlier books and of its self-conscious refiguring of their conventions.[58]

Poems from across his literary career show that Propertius' attraction to the evocation of the dead in oratory reflects his conception of the dead's role in elegy. The final two poems, however, in *Elegies,* Book 1 suggest, movingly, that the origins of this conception may lie in a deep-seated view of commemorative performance itself. Propertius recounts that, having lost his father at an early age, he saw his family property reduced in the proscriptions of 41–40 BCE (4.1.127–30). The siege of Perusia in 41 seems, additionally, to have cost him a relative, a figure mentioned in Elegy 1.22 and often identified with the Gallus who speaks in 1.21. Is Elegy 1.21, like Elegies 4.7 and Elegy 4.11, spoken by a ghost, the spirit of this relation? Some have thought so, but given any of the poetic personae that scholars have proposed for this obscure and difficult poem, Elegy 1.21 draws our attention to Propertius' profound interest in the personal bond between the living and the dead, as it relates to and even conflicts with public perspectives.[59] As Bruce Heiden has eloquently suggested, Elegy 1.21's very obscurity reflects the experience of a populace stricken by civil war and torn by conflicting loyalties to both Octavian and his opponents. To identify explicitly with either side the dying (or dead) soldier who speaks in Elegy 1.21 would have been a partisan act Propertius would have wished to avoid. Elegy 1.21 stands rather as a trace of war's brutality, recalling the deep feelings and precise memories of individuals, but yielding little more of its secrets than the epitaphic poetry on the tombs of the dead of Perusia, now all but anonymous to the masses who passed their resting places every day.[60]

Like Elegy 1.21, 1.22, its themes and form again suggestive of an epitaphic inscription, intimates that the personal commemoration of the dead will be one of Propertius' major concerns.[61] The poem's first lines report Tullus' question to Propertius as to his status and the origin of his family: *qualis et unde genus . . .* (Of what sort I am and from where my lineage comes . . .) (1.22.1), etc. While expressing grief over the loss of a relative at the battle of Perusia, 1.22 also calls attention to the fact that Propertius' *gens,* although it may have been locally prominent (4.1.121: *notis . . . Penatibus*), has not been publicly celebrated at Rome. To remember Propertius' family, the poem's opening lines suggest, is rather an activity for family members and friends.

And yet in his revelation to Tullus about his Umbrian origins, Propertius points to the advantages of belonging to a relatively obscure family, one whose members are not well-known figures through whom Propertius might be identified with either side in the conflict at Perusia. Disturbingly, the very anonymity of the family members who now lie as mere *proiecta membra* (cast-out limbs) on the Etruscan soil (6–8) becomes, from Propertius' perspective, a kind of advantage. This emerges from Tullus' assurance to Propertius that he is inquiring about the latter's family *pro nostra semper amicitia* (in the name of our eternal friendship) (2), words that recall the divisive context of civil war and suggest a potential danger in revealing the identity of one's *gens*. Elegy 1.22 conjures up an atmosphere of suspicion and uncertainty in the wake of the civil wars, a setting with important implications for how the dead are to be remembered. Augustus would make it his task to quell partisan enmities, partly through reining in familial self-assertion like that on which so much of republican civic life depended. Already at the end of *Elegies*, Book 1, Propertius has embraced an attitude that would predispose him to this position.

Many have remarked Propertius' curious obsession with death and the dead: the far greater frequency and imagination with which he treats these topics in comparison with the other Roman erotic elegists. The forgoing survey, however, suggests a specific set of qualitative differences between Propertius' approach to the dead and that of the others.[62] Catullus' famous epitaph for his brother (poem 101), for example, focuses throughout on Catullus' own emotional state. The overwhelming impression is of loss, sorrow, and feelings of futility, sentiments echoed in Catullus' other impassioned expressions of grief over his brother's death in poems 65 and 68. Of these latter, two are part of apologias for poetic failure (65.5–14; 68.19–26) while one is interjected in such a way as to recall personal grief and loss in the midst of recounting the myth of Laodamia, to whom Catullus compares the mistress supplied him by his friend, Allius (68.91–100). Thus ideas of exemplarity and posthumous honor cede to a concern with the here and now. Catullus 96, a poem of consolation to Calvus over the death of his wife, tempers the suggestion of futility in its opening lines (1–2: *si quicquam mutis gratum acceptumve sepulcris / accidere a nostro, Calve, dolore potest* . . . [If anything welcome or pleasing to the silent dead can result, Calve, from our grief . . .]) with the hope that Quintilia's ghost will take pleasure in the testament to love that is Calvus' grief. But, again, the emphasis is intensely personal: there is no stress on exemplary qualities of the deceased or the importance of wider commemoration. Catullus is not entirely uninterested in poetry's power to transmit the glory of the dead to a public audience, and indeed hopes for poetic "immortality" himself (1.9–10; 68.47–50). But this theme, too, is overpowered in the *libellus* as a whole by a focus on the joys and sorrows of present life and love. It is telling that the closest Catullus comes to a poem in true commemoration of the dead is the parodic poem 3 on the death of his girlfriend's sparrow.

Propertius' contemporary, Tibullus, a poet engrossed by the depiction of life and love in a pastoral world, is, like Catullus, all but uninterested in portraying his poetic activity as in some way an imitation of ancestral figures. He does sometimes claim, in his persona as a poet/lover, that honor will be due to him after his death. The tone of such assertions, however, is much more muted and tentative than what we find in a poem such as Propertius 2.1, nor is Tibullus as concerned with imagining the circumstances through which dead lovers' claims to honor will become widely known. At the end of Elegy 1.1, Tibullus briefly predicts that youths and maidens will return weeping from his own funeral (65–66). The focus of the passage as a whole, however, is on Delia's actual grief (61–64, 67–68), and Tibullus shifts quickly back to the here and now, to the importance of enjoying love while you can (69–78). Tibullus 1.3 seems at first quite similar in circumstance and form to Propertius 2.1: here the poet is ill, and expresses his hopes that Messalla will remember him. He imagines his own epitaph: *hic iacet immiti consumptus morte Tibullus, / Messallam terra dum sequiturque mari* (here lies Tibullus, consumed by a cruel death while he followed Messalla on land and sea) (55–56). And yet Tibullus worries over the fact that he has no mother with him to gather his bones, no sister to pour Assyrian perfumes on his ashes, and is also without his lover, Delia (5–9). He hopes that Messalla and his cohort will remember him but does not imagine them in the act of commemorating him, in the way that Propertius does emphatically imagine Maecenas. Following the poet's epitaph, the scene shifts to the underworld, which is described as the final destination of both Tibullus himself and his detractors.[63] Then, once again, we are back in the here and now of an imagined encounter between Tibullus and Delia, and on this note the poem concludes. Similarly, in Elegy 2.4 Tibullus imagines a *puella* commemorated after her death not by the public at large but by a single lover, now grown old (47–50). In 2.6, when Tibullus begs Nemesis for mercy by the bones of her sister, who has died before her time (29–40), he seems more interested in concealing the identity of the deceased than in celebrating her memory: Nemesis' sister is not even named.[64]

Ovid's driving interest in his own poetic immortality takes many forms, but the *Amores* contain no elaborate scene of commemoration in which the dead poet is glorified for his persistence as a lover.[65] When Ovid celebrates the dead Tibullus (*Amores* 3.9), he assumes that the latter's immortality is beyond doubt. He feels no need, that is, to imagine or insist upon *how* Tibullus' fame will actually be perpetuated (although the poem itself has this function). Rather, clear symbols of fame populate the poem's world. Ovid inserts the allegorical figures *Elegia* and *Amor,* whom he depicts, along with Tibullus' mother, sister, and literary loves Delia and Nemesis, as mourners at Tibullus' funeral. As in Tibullus' own poetry, Ovid's overriding concern is with the here and now (coupled with his general irreverence toward tradition) which leaves little place for erotic elegy as a behavior modeled on that of the exemplary dead. It is especially illuminating that Ovid's parodic

Amores 2.6 on the death of a parrot, an extended allusion to Catullus' poem 3 on the death of Lesbia's sparrow, is the nearest Ovid comes to a poem such as Propertius 2.1. The parody ends with an epitaph announcing, in the parrot's voice, the honor due for his mistress's favor and for his own *ora docta* (learned mouth). Ovid's parrot squawks his claim abroad in verses that commemorate his status as an exemplary "lover" and a "poet" capable of composing his own epitaph.[66]

Conclusion

It will always be tempting to read Roman erotic elegy as a window onto the personal passions of the elegiac poets themselves. As I have argued elsewhere, the tendency of early Propertius scholarship to trace the history of his love affair with Cynthia through poems such as Elegy 4.7 gave way to a trend emphasizing self-conscious intertextuality, but substituting, nevertheless, a belief in access to Propertius' passionate devotion to poetry for the confident biographical narrative of earlier days.[67] The ghost of Cynthia became the ghost of elegy. The central force behind *Elegies,* Book 4 emerged as Propertius' programmatic struggle to situate the old style of erotic poetry he claims to have renounced beside patriotic, etiological works in a Callimachean vein, such as Elegies 4.2, 4.4, 4.6, 4.9–10, and, indeed, 4.11. Personal affect remained front and center. Elegy's own subject matter has thus been responsible for sidelining the collective desires of Propertius' audience as an influence on the poetry's formal and thematic traits. An emphasis on performance, however, and especially on the ritual workings of restored behavior, brings the interrelationship between personal and collective desire to the fore. If Propertius' ghosts speak to us of love and betrayal, individual honor and sacrifice, his performances, hovering between the written page and now-lost voices and bodies, point all the same to social upheaval and an urgent need for transition, a collective experience in which he found distinctive parts to play.

CHAPTER FIVE

Vergil's Alternatives
to Republican Performance

I N PURSUIT of a distinctively Roman literary fantasy, the "imitation" of the living by the dead, this book's trajectory has led from republican oratory to Augustan elegy and now, in its last part, turns toward Augustan epic. Rather than simply a terminus, however, this final chapter also represents a culmination. For of all the texts central to our study, Vergil's *Aeneid* 1–6 infuses the language and actions of the dead with the most complex reminiscences of Roman cultural life. Here the dead Hector transfers Troy's religious objects to Aeneas, the ghost of Anchises discusses philosophical matters with his son, spirits await reincarnation as Roman heroes in an underworld *pompa funebris,* and still other characters and scenes somehow suggest the proximity of the dead's behavior to that of the living. Like his Augustan contemporary, Propertius, then, Vergil restages familiar cultural performances of the Republic to make them appropriate, at least in outward form, to Augustan society, but on a far grander scale suited to the universalizing aspirations and more public orientation of his epic poem.[1] Indeed, notwithstanding the ambivalence toward Augustus that critics have often discerned in the *Aeneid,* Vergil's cultural ambition, his crafting of alternatives to a wide variety of republican traditions, outstrips anything in other poetry of the period.[2] Understood as performances themselves, Vergil's evocations of the dead are the quintessentially Roman restoration of behavior through self-conscious orature, a powerful confirmation of Richard Schechner's and Joseph Roach's views at once.[3] In Vergil's hands, Augustan epic rivals Ciceronian oratory for its creative refashioning of the broader culture. The juxtaposition of these two authors' work, however, highlights the very different political purposes espoused by each. Cicero struggled for dominance in the political maelstrom of the Republic's final decades; Vergil seeks to make his epic the central Augustan literary text. By grounding the *Aeneid* in the visible, bodily expression of what it means to be a Roman citizen under the new Princeps, he creates a mythic precedent for Augustan culture, not only as it was perceived and understood by its participants, but also as it was lived by them.[4]

The successive and cumulative structure of my argument in this chapter is intended as evidence for this main point. I have labeled each of its six sections according to the restored behavior in question. But Vergil neither engages with nor transforms all of the traditions that concern him in the same fashion, and here again scrutiny of the *Aeneid* complements our earlier perspective on Propertian elegy by illustrating the sheer variety of ways that Augustan poetry models cultural renewal through its own use of *prosopopoeia* and related techniques. In at least one case, the evocation of Rome's fratricidal curse, the difficulty of an already existing practice from the perspective of Augustan Rome is inherent in the practice itself. The conflict between Romulus and Remus was the prototype for Roman civil war, a problematic issue for the new regime. Vergil thus concentrates on the evocation of a very different sort of ghost, that of Hector, whose hopeful transfer of Troy's legacy becomes a cultural alternative to the curse inflicted by Remus on Roman posterity. In another instance, the Polydorus episode of Book 3, Vergil characterizes the republican version of a familiar practice as problematic and then offers an alternative to it. Here Vergil recalls the corrupt trials of the Republic by pointing to the trial of Polymestor in Euripides' *Hecuba*, before refashioning the conclusion of Polydorus' story in the pious funeral accorded him by the Trojans. The "Review of Heroes" presents still another paradigm, as Vergil restages republican funeral ritual by imagining its prototype as an underworld procession. Because of such variations in Vergil's technique, my own methods and conclusions in the different sections of the chapter vary as well. The *Aeneid*'s heterogeneity, however, points in at least one sense to a unified vision. Through his epic, Vergil looks comprehensively at the late Republic as a time of distorted interactions between the living and the dead, a situation now, he hopes, to be set right.

Hector and the Evocation of Rome's Curse

What explains Aeneas' behavior following his dream of the dead Hector at *Aeneid* 2.270–97? Why, that is, does Vergil have Aeneas, upon waking and viewing Troy's destruction first hand, take up arms in a maddened, self-destructive frenzy (314–17) in spite of the fact that Hector has warned him to flee Troy and entrusted him with the Trojan household gods (289–97)? The passage has long been interpreted as an illustration of the Homeric temperament—"rash, impulsive, brave, seeking when all is lost the glorious death"—from which Vergil gradually distances Aeneas as a new kind of hero appropriate for Augustan Rome, and Aeneas' own words (314–17) lend credence to this view.[5] But another explanation, not exclusive of the first, emerges through hints in Vergil's text of the civil-war discourse informing a poem such as Horace's *Epode 7* and deeply resonant within the *Aeneid* as a whole. By recalling here the Roman concern with civil war, Vergil encourages his Roman audience to recognize its own history of self-destructiveness in Aeneas' behavior. This association is of crucial importance for our understanding of the Hector *prosopopoeia* itself.

Consider the similarity of Vergil's language, imagery, and thematics in his account of Aeneas' impulsiveness to those employed by Horace. Decrying the curse of continued civil war, Horace asks where Romans are "rushing" (*Ep.* 7.1: *quo . . . ruitis?*), why they unsheath swords against each other rather than against their historical enemies, Carthage and the Britains (1–10). Is it blind *furor,* Horace demands, or some keener force or guilt that compels them to treat each other more savagely than the beasts (11–14)? *Responsum date* (respond), Horace insists (14), but the Romans he claims to address remain pale and silent, their minds overcome (16: *mentesque perculsae stupent*). So it is, the poet concludes, that the curse of Remus continues to determine Rome's fate:

> . . . acerba fata Romanos agunt
> scelusque fraternae necis,
> ut immerentis fluxit in terram Remi
> sacer nepotibus cruor.

> . . . harsh fate drives the Romans and the crime of a brother's murder, since the blood of innocent Remus, a curse to his descendants, flowed upon the earth. (Hor. *Ep.* 7.17–20)

Vergil's Aeneas, of course, when confronted with Hector's ghost, finds himself in circumstances quite different from those of Horace's Romans. Aeneas bears no responsibility for Hector's death. The anger he feels upon waking from his dream is over Troy's destruction by the Greeks rather than the fratricidal violence of civil war. And yet *furor* (316) drives both Aeneas and the Romans, who are likewise abandoned to fate just as Aeneas and his followers

(294). Vergil's Troy *ruit* (falls headlong) (290) while Horace's Romans "rush headlong" (*ruitis*) to their destruction. Aeneas is *amens* (mad) (314), fury and wrath *praecipitant* (drive) his *mentem* (mind) (316–17); the Romans' *mentes* are *perculsae* (struck senseless). The shepherd to whom Aeneas is compared as he looks upon the burning Troy *stupet* (is stunned) (307); the Romans' minds *stupent*. Troy commends its *sacra* (holy things) to Aeneas (320), while Remus' blood is *sacer* (a curse [the word's usage in this sense reflecting the two-sided nature of the Roman idea of "sacredness"]). Vergil stresses the senselessness of fighting in Aeneas' case (314: *nec sat rationis in arma* [nor is there any sense in taking up arms]), while Horace's repeated questions (*quo, quo . . . ? cur . . . ? parumne . . . ? furorne . . . ?*) make the same point in a different way. Somewhat later in Book 2, Aeneas and his companions, who have adopted Greek armor as a disguise, are actually attacked by their own countrymen (410–12), while Vergil has already made the Trojan War itself symbolic of Rome's recent civil wars, insofar as it represents the major collective trauma to the body politic in response to which the Trojans are struggling to proceed as a people at the *Aeneid*'s opening.[6]

Aeneas' behavior and the events that follow from it frame Vergil's summoning of Hector as an alternative to a cultural performance not confined to epic poetry alone: the evocation of Rome's ancient curse, most characteristically embodied in the ghost of the murdered Remus and still felt, it was said, in the civil wars that brought Augustus to power.[7] In Hector, a ghostly figure of a kind all but visible at the close of Horace's Epode 7 voices hope for the future, although self-destructiveness threatens to overwhelm the awakened Aeneas, a detail that helps underscore, in retrospect, the Hector-Remus connection. Vergil here makes one of the violently slain dead whom his poem of sacrifice and foundation places center-stage symbolize social renewal in an Augustan vein: Aeneas receives Troy's legacy just as Augustus could claim to have received Rome's, while Aeneas' eventual diversion from self-destructiveness by a priest of Apollo (318ff.), a deity with whom Augustus claimed to have a special relationship, focuses Rome's hopes for a future free of civil war on the Princeps and his rule.[8] Thus Vergil opposes Aeneas' brother-in-law to Romulus' brother.[9] Concord between the living Aeneas and kin slaughtered in community-ravaging conflict marks the opening of Aeneas' journey even if the curse of fraternal strife disfigures Rome's actual founding. Hector preempts Remus.

Playing this new Hector against his cultural counterpart, Remus, Vergil reembodies centuries of tradition. As Peter Wiseman has recently confirmed, the association of Remus with Roman civil unrest is most plausibly traced, if not to the origins of Rome, then at least to an era predating the emergence of Latin literature itself.[10] The evocation of Remus is a cultural practice with deep extra-literary roots, even if our most abundant evidence for the idea of Remus' curse comes from the work of Vergil and his literary contemporaries. And even in the Augustan poets' work, we must confront the interplay of orality and literacy in the perpetuation of the Roman myth. Within some four or five years, for example, before he began work on the *Aeneid* (the conventional date is 26 BCE), Vergil could have heard Horace himself performing Epode 7 with its clarion call to reject the senseless destruction of civil war. This poem shares its concerns with other Horatian Epodes as well as Horace's first Book of Satires, collections that allude repeatedly to the bloody conflicts of the 30s during which they were composed.[11] The *Furor* into which the Roman boy of Epode 5 says he will be transformed suggests the perpetuation of Remus' legacy in Roman civil strife: the boy predicts a violent confrontation between the Roman mob and his tormentors, the witches (97–98), one of whom resembles a Roman matron and so symbolizes Rome itself.[12] Wolves and birds, the boy prophecies, will scatter the witches' bones on the Esquiline hill (99–100), site of a notorious graveyard in the years preceding Octavian's consolidation of power and, additionally, the setting, in *Satires* 1.8, for the necromancy though which Horace's witches call up ghosts to assist them with their spells. In this latter poem, the witches' malevolent activities tie them to a republican context of invective and dissension among the Roman elite, phenomena deeply implicated in the civil conflicts of Horace's day.[13]

For Horace, epode and satire are a means of recalling Remus' curse in order to ward it off. Similar expressions of anxiety were heard repeatedly in the circles of both Maecenas and Messalla. Propertius, for example, refers memorably to Remus' murder in describing the nationalistic epic he refuses to write. Only if Maecenas, he says, will lead the way in departing from inherent nature will he devote himself to epic themes, including *caeso moenia firma Remo* ([Rome's] walls made firm with Remus slain) (Prop. 3.9.50). Drawing on Vergil's account of Hector, Ovid depicts Remus as a ghost in a dream, ostensibly to exculpate Romulus from guilt in his brother's death (*Fast.* 5.457–76).[14] Vergil, too, concludes the second Book of the *Georgics* with an account of the peaceful life enjoyed by *Remus et frater* (2.533), a time comparable to the Golden Age, before warfare came to the earth.[15]

The *Aeneid* itself represents one of the more complex elaborations of the curse of Remus, including its prehistory before Rome's actual founding, in Latin literature. Vergil mentions Remus by name only once in the poem, when he has Jupiter refer to a future in which both Romulus and Remus will "deal out justice" together: *Remo cum fratre Quirinus / iura dabunt* (1.292–

93). This passage, too, looks forward to peace from civil war, but Vergil's mention of both the twins seems to tell a darker tale. While we may agree with Helen Bacon that the image reflects a truth existing in the world of the spirit, we are nevertheless justifiably struck, with Dennis Feeney, by the way that Vergil here reminds us of Remus' murder even while singing the praises of Rome's founder, Romulus.[16]

In fact, the whole trajectory of Aeneas' journey in the *Aeneid* keeps the history of Rome's internal conflicts before the minds of Vergil's audience. In addition to Jupiter's pregnant reference to Remus in Book 1, the underworld sequence of Book 6 includes prominent mention of the civil war between Julius Caesar and Cn. Pompeius Magnus, who appear in the "Review of Heroes," narrated for Aeneas by the ghost of Anchises (826–31). Anchises even pauses in his account to exhort Romans to avoid the horror of civil war (832–35). And yet Vergil figures the war between the Trojans and the Italians as war between kin, a proleptic civil conflict anticipating later civil war.[17] The war in Italy can be understood as an effect of Dido's curse on Aeneas and the Trojans at the end of Book 4, where she also foretells Rome's foreign conflict with Carthage (625–27). Dido's curse is in this sense the antecedent to Remus': Dido's own history is in fact marked *fraterna caede* (by fraternal blood) (4.21) through her brother Pygmalion's killing of her first husband, Sychaeus; in her curse on Aeneas, Dido seeks to perpetuate her own misfortune.[18] Indeed, although it may be true that the Carthaginian component of Dido's curse is "exorcised" at *Aeneid* 6.845–46 by Anchises' reference to the conqueror of Carthage, Q. Fabius Maximus Verrucosus (Cunctator), the threat of civil war also contained in her words remains active at the *Aeneid*'s very conclusion, with its closing image of Aeneas killing Turnus.[19]

But while Remus' spilled blood was the vehicle for his curse upon Roman posterity, Vergil introduces Hector through a description dominated by the sight of his mutilation and blood only to have him emerge as a purveyor of hopeful prophecy (*A*. 2.293–95). Aeneas first reacts to Hector as a savior: he is *lux Dardaniae* (light of Dardania) and *spes fidissima Teucrum* (most trustworthy hope of the Teucrians) (281). Aeneas asks Hector why he has been delayed in his arrival and where he comes from (282–83). He stresses the Trojans' suffering in Hector's absence and long expectation of his return (283–85). Only then seeming to notice Hector's wounds does he ask how and why they were inflicted (285–86). Although Aeneas' deluded and amnesiac response to the vision of Hector is deeply infused with pathos—we pity Aeneas' implicit wish to undo Hector's death as much as we pity the sufferings of Hector and Troy—Aeneas' hope is in part justified by Hector's transfer of the Trojan legacy and by his prophecy of a new city to come.

The hopeful legacy of Hector *as an alternative* to the destructiveness embodied in Remus is brought out still further through Hector's proximity to the other ghosts in *Aeneid*, Books 1 and 2, those of Sychaeus and Creusa. The *fraterna caedes* of Sychaeus' death and his appearance as a ghost in Dido's dream at *Aeneid* 1.353–59 are implicated, like the murder of Remus, in the founding of a city, Carthage. And Carthage is doomed, as the *Aeneid* both dramatizes and forecasts. So too, a Rome in the grip of Remus' curse is doomed to self-destruction. A Rome guided, however, by the promise of Hector's prophecy can hope for salvation. Hector's function as a guiding, prophetic spirit is doubled in *Aeneid*, Book 2 by Creusa, who adds to Hector's words in specifying the name of the land (Hesperia) to which Aeneas must travel, the river (Tiber) on which he will settle, and his future marriage to a regal wife (Lavinia), while indicating that she herself will remain, as a ghost, in Troy, rather than be carried, as a slave, to Greece (781–88). Vergil links Creusa closely to the forces of procreation: she identifies herself as the daughter-in-law of Venus (787), whom she specifies as the deity who "detains" her in Troy rather than allowing her to follow Aeneas to Italy (788). The mention of Venus *genetrix* recalls Creusa's position, as the mother of Iulus, at the head of the Julian line, and so looks forward to the Augustan regime.

The pattern continues in Book 3. At the moment when Aeneas finds Andromache at Buthrotum, she is pouring libations and calling upon Hector's spirit (303: *Manisque vocabat*) to visit his cenotaph at the miniature Troy where she and her new husband, Helenus, now reside.[20] In the midst of this imitation Troy, Andromache still weeps at Hector's empty tomb, where we do *not* see Hector's ghost appear, as he does for Aeneas in Book 2. Indeed, to the startled Andromache, it is Aeneas who seems to be the ghost that she has summoned[21]: her reaction (312: "Where is Hector?") points to the fact that the "New Troy" at Buthrotum will fail to become the political and cultural heir of the ruined Troy, as Rome will. Hector's spirit, absent here, has already conferred this heritage on Aeneas, who can now take Hector's place, while Andromache continues to call upon a past that induces only continued suffering. Andromache's attempted evocation of Hector is in this sense still more like calling upon Remus, Rome's curse, than is Vergil's own "successful" summoning of Hector in Book 2. She is an alter-ego of Vergil himself within the *Aeneid*, her fruitless performance of rites for Hector the opposite of Vergil's poetic craft.

Through Horace's Epode 7 and other performances of Vergil's day, Romans accounted for the violence of the present through grim reference to the curse of the past. Vergil evokes Hector to suggest a more promising inheritance.

Polydorus and the Murder Trial

Aeneid 3, a book replete with *monstra* that form some of the most memorable episodes in the poem, opens with a scene whose very presence is still puzzling to scholars: Aeneas' encounter with the ghost of the murdered Polydorus in Thrace, where he has attempted to found the first of a series of unsuccessful colonies. As Aeneas builds an altar to Venus, the myrtle saplings he uproots come away from the earth covered with blood. Although horrified by this finding, he continues to pull the shoots away, and on the third attempt is addressed and warned off by the agonized ghost of Polydorus, whose corpse lies here covered by spears that have now taken root. Why did Vergil include this gruesome scene, for which no antecedent can be found in the myths of either Polydorus or Aeneas?[22] In an influential reading, David Quint has suggested that Vergil uses Polydorus to develop a parallel in Book 3 between the Trojans, confronted with painful memories of their traumatic past, and Augustan Romans in need of putting to rest memories of civil war.[23] For Quint, Book 3 thus locates the Trojans in a cycle of unsuccessful repetitions of past trauma. The failed colonies in Thrace and Crete and the strange Troy-in-miniature built by Helenus at Buthrotum all anticipate, and act as foils for, Aeneas' successful foundation of a city in Italy.

A reconsideration, however, of Vergil's Euripidean source for the myth of Polydorus shows that his restaging of its conclusion could have also reminded Vergil's contemporaries of Augustus' efforts at judicial reform.[24] By having the Trojans opt for the reburial of Polydorus' corpse, and by passing over in silence the corrupt trial of Polydorus' killer, Polymestor, as recounted in Euripides, Vergil dramatizes the benefits of relegating to the past the corrupt judicial procedures that Augustus himself took pains to prevent. Epic's emphasis on linear narrative here stands opposed to tragedy's interest in exploring the ambiguous implications of legal conflicts. But the linearity of epic in this case suggests specifically Rome's passage away from one, imperfect approach to the communal problem of murder toward another, more promising one. In Vergil's present-tense narration of a plea from the dead and a pious funeral, the *prosopopoeia* of a murder victim like that which a republican orator might have used to direct ire toward his killer instead occasions a performance of ritual piety and social cohesion.

Both those favorable and unfavorable to Augustus could agree that his influence over the judicial system had the beneficial effect of reforming corruption and other abuses left over from the late Republic and perpetuated during the civil wars of the 30s. Suetonius points in particular to brigandage, organized crime under the façade of the guilds, blackmail, and various impediments to the execution of the law (Suet. *Aug.* 32.1–2). He recounts

Augustus' personal administration of justice in tribunal. One anecdote illustrating Augustus' conscientiousness and leniency in fact pertains to a trial for parricide, in which the emperor, apparently to avoid the archaic and macabre spectacle of the condemned's punishment in the *culleus,* sought to inhibit an outright confession through a leading question to the accused.[25] Even Tacitus admits the popularity of Augustus' reform of the judicial system in the provinces, where "feuds among those in power" and "the greed of the magistrates" had left the public vulnerable to a system disrupted by force, canvassing, and wealth (Tac. *Ann.* 1.2.2: *vi ambitu . . . pecunia*). The people's favorable opinions of Augustus after his death, Tacitus reports, included the observation that he assured *ius apud cives* (law among the citizenry) (1.9.5).

Virtually the same kinds of corruption in a legal system as Augustus was credited with reforming overshadow the conclusion of Euridipes' *Hecuba.*[26] Here, Polymestor and Hecuba present their cases to Agamemnon, who, acting as judge, finds Polymestor guilty of the murder of Polydorus. The procedure, however, is mere pretense: earlier in the play, Agamemnon had granted Hecuba the right to avenge herself personally on Polymestor, after she concedes his wish to avoid supporting her openly for fear of dissent among the Greek host (850–904). At the end of the public trial, Agamemnon orders Polymestor, who has been brutally blinded by Hecuba, to be taken to exile on an island, and allows Hecuba to bury her two dead children (1284–88).[27] While the outcome of the trial is thus immediately favorable to Hecuba, Euripides portrays judicial procedure undermined by personal and political influences.[28]

The similarity of these influences to those deplored by Tacitus is especially close.[29] Polymestor's greed and betrayal of Priam lead to the murder of Polydorus and the attempt to disguise it (cf. Tac. *Ann.* 1.2.2: *certamina potentium . . . avaritiam . . . pecunia*). Agamemnon fears the power of the Greek host (cf. *vi*) and is convinced by Hecuba's canvassing to grant her the personal vengeance she craves (cf. *ambitu*). Euripides provides Vergil with a staging of the problems seen as endemic to the Roman judicial system.

But, while alluding to Polymestor's corrupt trial through a series of verbal and thematic echoes of Euripides, Vergil does not refer to it directly, and so consigns it to the past while recreating it as the funeral that now marks a new and unprecedented conclusion to Polydorus' story. After the Trojan leaders, assembled for the purpose of deciding how to respond to the *monstrum,* opt for departure from the "accursed land" and its "polluted hospitality," the Trojans "start afresh" Polydorus' funeral (62: *instauramus Polydoro funus*). Vergil stages the rite's pious unfolding: *stant Manibus arae* (an altar stands for the ghost) (63); *animamque sepulcro / condimus* (we lay to rest the spirit in the tomb) (67–68). The Trojans—and Vergil—perform *de more* (according to custom) (65). The funeral allows them to move on: Aeneas' next words (69–72) portray the Trojans sailing to Delos.

Vergil even characterizes forensic inquiry itself as secondary to the goal of piety and absolution from guilt achieved through the proper rites for a murder victim. He involves Aeneas, seeking to discover the cause of the *monstrum*, symbolically in the murder of Polydorus.[30] The episode's first movement creates a sense of Aeneas' implication in the crime through the repeated gesture of plucking the bloodstained saplings from Polydorus' corpse. The repetition of the noun *sanguis* in the text of verses 28, 30, and 33 presents this idea in iconic fashion: having been horrified by his first sight of blood (28: *atro liquuntur sanguine guttae*), Aeneas feels his own blood run cold (30: *gelidusque coit formidine sanguis*), only to discover blood once again in seeking out the "hidden causes" of the *monstrum* (33: *ater et alterius sequitur de cortice sanguis*). The first drops of blood "stain the earth with their damp corruption" (29). And yet on his third attempt, after prayers to the Nymphs and to Mars to change the bad omen to good, Aeneas drops to the earth and struggles, knees against the sand (34–38). He then hears Polydorus' ghost asking him to "spare the buried," and to refrain from "defiling" his untainted hands (40–42). But Aeneas has already gone too far. He, like the land he touches, is *sceleratus;* he is driven by a motivation that we best understand, in Michael Putnam's words, as "intellectual greed," a "desperate need for understanding, even at the cost of further hurt."[31] Aeneas' motives do indeed, as Putnam suggests, run parallel to the murderous greed for wealth of Polymestor. In this, they help make Polydorus' funeral all the more appealing as an alternative to Polymestor's corrupt trial, since the Trojans themselves, Vergil indicates, have implicated themselves in ritual corruption.

In the Polydorus episode of *Aeneid* 3, inquiry into a sign of past violence leads only to further violence that awakens the ghosts of the past. The myth becomes a parable of not looking further—both in what Vergil says and what he does not say. Understood in such general terms, the performance of Vergil's text points hopefully toward reform of judicial corruption, and, beyond this, to the resolution of Augustan Rome's larger problems in the relationship to its republican past. Corruption in the courts had been an aspect of the political infighting that fanned the flames of civil war. Also, the question of how—and how much—to remember the violence of the civil wars was a central one for Augustus.[32] Vergil's Trojans exclude the possibility of further conflict between the leading families of Troy and Thrace by looking to the future. They focus not on vengeance for a dead kinsman but on his funeral, a ritual through which his agonized ghost may be laid to rest and their journey continue. The threat of a fratricidal curse is felt but averted: Aeneas defiles himself through, and then seeks absolution from, bloodshed that is almost fraternal. Like Hector, Polydorus had been one of his *sororii* or brothers-in-law.

Dido and the Stigmatization of Magic

While the Trojans' departure from Thrace in *Aeneid* 3 symbolizes Augustan Rome's desire to leave behind the judicial corruption of the Republic and its ghosts haunting the present, Vergil uses Aeneas' departure from Carthage in *Aeneid* 4 to distance Rome from another troubling practice, magic, that had been of enough concern to inspire legislation during the period of Augustus' rise to power. While Maecenas was in charge of Rome and Italy in 33 BCE, Agrippa passed a bill expelling astrologers and witches from the city.[33] The necromancy of Horace's witches in *Satires* 1.8 is a topical reference to threatening behavior associated, as DuQuesnay has shown, with Octavian's opponents.[34] Horace's *Satires* and *Epodes* in fact illuminate Dido's recourse to magic in *Aeneid* 4 more than has been recognized.[35] Comparison between these texts reveals that Vergil has revised personal invective of the kind favored by Horace so as to present a far more wide-reaching opposition between the supernal and the infernal powers appropriate to the *Aeneid's* broader poetic and cultural ambitions. While Greek epic and Roman elegy anticipate Dido's recourse to magic in the context of a love affair, Vergil here works also in another Roman performance tradition exemplified before him by Horace: that of the politically motivated stigmatization of magic.[36] In the *Aeneid,* the guiding force of the supernal gods identified with the Augustan regime trumps the destructive power of the infernal deities associated with magic, a practice that Vergil attributes to an exotic, alien queen—Dido—and relegates to a foreign land—Carthage—destined to fall to Roman might in the future to which the *Aeneid* looks forward.

Like Vergil's Dido, Horace's witches belong to the outside not only of Roman culture but also of the geographical space of Rome, and in this way they help Horace define, quite literally, a new social and political order. We see this best in Satire 1.8, which expels the powers of magic from the Esquiline cemetery by way of articulating the role of Horatian poetry within the circle of Maecenas and Octavian.[37] The fig-wood statue of Priapus who narrates the poem expresses his concern over the witches' nightly visits to the cemetery (17–22). He goes on to describe their rites (23–44), and concludes by recalling his fortuitous fart, which put them to flight (44–50). The scene is a satiric allegory of Maecenas' own establishment of an elegant garden on the site. Further, the transformation of the garden stands symbolically for a hoped-for deliverance of Rome from the horrors of civil war, whose indiscriminate destruction is recalled in the bones of the dead littering the ground (16). Other Horatian poems likewise associate witches and their magic with a geographical outside, as for example Epode 5, in which Horace notes that the witch Folia is from the Umbrian town of Ariminum; her doings are of interest in "idle Naples and every nearby town" (42–44).[38]

Rather than, like Horace in Satire 1.8, expelling magic from part of the physical space of Rome, Vergil in *Aeneid* 4 delivers the founder of the Roman race from a marginal land, where magic exercises a pernicious force, toward the part of Italy where Rome will eventually rise. Dido's recourse to magic in the climactic scenes of Book 4 (a reminiscence of the Euripidean Medea) identifies her with that which Aeneas, journeying on to the fulfillment of his mission, must reject and leave behind. Indeed, all that makes Dido a threat to the fulfillment of Aeneas' mission—sexuality, vulnerability to the passions, a capacity for deception, and a tie to divine powers alien to the will of Jupiter—is on display here. We first become aware of Dido's intention to employ magic during her deceptive speech to her sister, Anna, at *Aeneid* 4.478–98. Here she says that she has enlisted the services of a Massylian priestess either to restore Aeneas to her or to free herself from love for him (the latter may be true, but the former certainly is not, since Dido has already determined to die). The priestess, Dido reports, is the guardian of the far-distant precinct of the Hesperides and keeper of the dragon protecting the apples of Juno. Dido says she is skilled in the magic conventionally ascribed to alien figures of her kind: the halting of rivers, the reversal of the stars, and the conjuring of ghosts. Informing Anna of the priestess's arrival, Dido instructs her to build a pyre on which to burn Aeneas' belongings. Dido will, of course, use the pyre to immolate herself, after cursing Aeneas and falling on his sword.

Vergil associates Dido ever more strongly with the infernal powers as Book 4 moves toward her suicide and consecration to Dis. Indeed, no other figure in surviving Latin poetry before Vergil dies a death so elaborately represented as a union with the powers of the underworld. Far from mere ornament, this feature of Book 4 represents a stigmatization of infernal magic, a familiar performance in Augustan circles. Vergil's reference to the *di Manes* in verse 490 (*nocturnos movet manes* [she summons the nocturnal spirits]) is developed in his account of the magical rite in 504ff., where the priestess calls upon Erebus, Chaos, and Hecate, and sprinkles water said to be from Lake Avernus, while Dido prays nearby. Later, Dido imitates the priestess in summoning the powers of the underworld to hear her curse: Hecate and the Furies are among those upon whom she calls to torment Aeneas and his race (609–10). In a prophetic reference to Hannibal, she prays that an avenger arise from her bones to punish the Trojan colonists (625–27). Resolved to pass *sub umbras* (660), she asks that Aeneas bear with him the omen of her death (662). Her actual death is represented as Proserpina's consignment of her person to Stygian Orcus, after Iris has made a sacred offering to Dis of a lock from her head (693–705).

The cultural and political implications of Aeneas' departure from Carthage bear a superficial resemblance to those of Horace's witches' flight from the Esquiline cemetery in *Satires* 1.8. Both poems, that is, put distance, physical and temporal, between Rome and the powers of magic in looking hopefully toward a new social and political order with Octavian/Augustus at its head. But Vergil, with the conventions of epic at his disposal, has located the basis for rejecting magic in obedience to the will of Jupiter, doubled by the good favor of Venus, Aeneas' mother and origin of the Julian line. Magic, with its ties to a morbid erotic force presided over by Hecate, stands opposed to and outside Jupiter's divine plan. Vergil transforms the conflict between magicians and their opponents from a clash of individual personalities into a clash of these major divinities. He thus rephrases the political aspirations of an earlier poetic style in far grander terms, while pursuing a sympathetic portrayal of Dido, even as one who seeks to exploit magic for her own designs. Horace, by contrast, sees only objects of horror and ridicule in figures such as Canidia and Sagana.

Anchises and Parentatio

Vergil develops the contrast between the suspect realm of magic and the legitimate political and religious order represented by Jupiter's plan for Aeneas in the *aetion* of state-sponsored ancestor cult *(parentatio)* that opens *Aeneid* 5 (42–103).[39] Immediately after depicting Dido's attempt to summon the infernal powers for destructive, personal goals, Vergil is quick to portray Aeneas engaged in the worship of his father's spirit for the good of the larger Trojan community. The close juxtaposition of the two rituals, one "magical" and the other "religious" in nature, helps Vergil present an "official" version of *parentatio* appropriate to Augustan Rome. For Vergil here endorses the ritual's use in celebrating the preeminence of a single family (the Julian line) while both making his ceremony conform to traditional religious precepts and distancing it from the atmosphere of political competition that characterized the ancestral devotion of the republican elite. Vergil emphasizes the place of *parentatio* in a larger religious structure existing for the advancement of the Trojan people and the Roman state rather than for an exclusive personal bond with the deceased. From this perspective, we see that the famous serpent appearing at the end of Aeneas' *parentatio* in fact helps Vergil save the ritual from taking on an atmosphere of magic or political self-promotion by allowing him to tie it to a larger religious structure and delay direct contact between Aeneas and Anchises to the end of the Book. The encounter that does occur there is not as easily associated with such practices as it might have been had it occurred directly after Aeneas' performance.

The politically inclusive atmosphere of Aeneas' *parentatio* is evident from the start. Aeneas begins at dawn by summoning all the Trojans, who are described in words that emphasize the inclusiveness of this gesture: *socios in coetum litore ab omne / advocat Aeneas* (Aeneas summons his companions from all parts of the shore into an assembly) (43–44). Here the general terms *socii* and *coetus,* like the prominent use of *omnis* at line-end, mark the occasion as open to all. The fact that other religious ceremonies performed collectively by the Trojans, such as Polydorus' funeral, call for a limited council of nobles (cf. 3.58–59) makes the presence of the whole community here stand out all the more. Vergil positions Aeneas where he will be visible to all, on a raised mound (44). He has Aeneas address the Trojans with a title calling the utmost attention to their identity as one people: *Dardanidae* (45). Aeneas emphasizes, too, the Trojans' shared descent as a *genus* from the "high blood of the gods" (45). Later in his speech, he explicitly invites all the Trojans to share in his tribute to Anchises: *laetum cuncti celebremus honorem* (58); similarly, he invites "all" (70: *cuncti*) either to take part in or be spectators of Anchises' funeral games. He calls for both the Trojan Penates and those of their host, Acestes, to share in the feast (62–63).

Vergil is careful to tie Aeneas' *parentatio* for Anchises, as a religious occasion, to the divine will motivating the action of the poem. He thus grounds the claims and practices of the Julian line, prefigured here, in a traditional religious structure. Aeneas expresses his belief that the *numen divum* (will of the gods) provided the opportunity to perform the ritual at Anchises' tomb in Sicily (55–57). He refers to "the bones of my divine parent" (47: *divinique ossa parentis*), words which, although they activate, as Servius recognized, the memory of the divine honors bestowed upon Julius Caesar by Augustus, do not depart entirely from the traditional ambiguity surrounding the spirits of the dead, who shared certain privileges with the immortal gods while still inhabiting a subterranean underworld.[40] Indeed, for John Scheid, who reminds us of this fact, Vergil's exploitation of such ambiguity is the key to understanding the connection between this episode in *Aeneid* 5 and the "official" version of *parentatio* performed in Pisa for L. Julius Caesar following his death in 2 CE and recorded in *ILS* 139.[41] Vergil's text anticipates the Pisa inscription, Scheid demonstrates, not simply in the details of the ritual it describes, but in that the honor shown to Anchises (as to L. Caesar) rests on a traditional view of the divine nature of the dead rather than on the assumption of a full apotheosis, which was reserved for the dead Princeps alone. The Pisa inscription thus makes us keenly aware of Vergil's sensitivity here to the Augustan context.

The appearance of the serpent at the end of Aeneas' *parentatio* (90–93) has been the source of much scholarly debate, stemming ultimately from Aeneas' own doubt as to whether the animal is some *genius loci* (local spirit) or the *famulus* (attendant spirit) of his father (95).[42] Rather than reopen the question of the serpent's identity (of which Aeneas himself is uncertain), I prefer to focus on what the serpent does to shape our perception of the ritual Aeneas has just performed and the bond between Aeneas and Anchises that it exists in part to affirm. We need to interpret the serpent's appearance from the perspective of what it would not have been unreasonable to expect as the ritual's outcome: a manifestation of Anchises' ghost like that which, separated from Aeneas' *parentatio* by the entire account of Anchises' funeral games and the burning of the Trojan ships, Vergil does in fact insert near the end of Book 5. Why does Vergil postpone contact with Anchises until Aeneas has withdrawn from his public role as leader of the Trojan host and, in a moment of solitude, anxiously ponders the future? Why not include an unambiguous sign of Anchises' pleasure in Aeneas' ritual offering, such as the imaginative universe of the *Aeneid* would seem to allow?

Part of the explanation lies in the contrast drawn between Aeneas' *parentatio* and the magic practiced by the maddened Dido at the end of Book 4. Vergil runs the risk of implying an equation between the two kinds of ritual. They are similar in that each centers on a request for further contact and exchange between the living and the dead. Calling, like the Massylian priestess, on the infernal powers (609–10), Dido prays to Hecate and the *Dirae* to be able to torment Aeneas and his line. She calls for an avenger to rise from her bones (625: *ossibus*) so as to facilitate the hatred between the Carthaginians and the Romans that will be a source of gifts to her ashes (623: *cineri*). Aeneas, standing before his father's *ossa* and *cineres* (5.55), asks to be able to perform the same ritual once the Trojan's new city has been founded and a temple dedicated to Anchises. The crucial difference, however, lies in the essentially personal aims of Dido and the community-centered goals of Aeneas. Like the details of Aeneas' rite itself, the serpent mediates the connection between Aeneas and Anchises through a larger religious structure. Whatever the exact identity of this particular snake, the animal was very much a part of the legitimate religious symbol-system at Rome.[43] Aeneas' acceptance of the serpent's ambiguity suggests his acknowledgment of the distance between the living and the dead. His recourse to further sacrifices (94–103) again turns our attention to a legitimate religious system.

In addition to its religious implications, the representation of Aeneas' unmediated access, in his public role, to Anchises' spirit would have had political implications. In order to have his *aetion* of *parentatio* seem appropriate to an Augustan context, Vergil must be careful not give the appearance that Aeneas performs the ritual in the service of a competitive arrogation of ancestral honor to himself and his line. The public evocation of the dead was strongly redolent of republican power politics. Cicero, for example, concludes the *Pro Scauro* with a pathos-laden claim to have had a vision of his client's dead father, and, in the same breath, calls upon the dead Scaurus to appear to the audience (Cic. *Scaur.* 49). Similar uses of the topos *mortuos excitare* are a recurring feature of republican oratory (cf. chapter 1). Thus Vergil keeps the good of the community constantly before Aeneas'—and our—eyes. Aeneas is sure to pray for favorable winds (Verg. *A.* 5.59) and Anchises' blessing on the whole Trojan endeavor (60).

While a vision of Anchises does appear to Aeneas in Book 5, it is in very different circumstances. After the commencement of the games and their interruption by maddened Trojan women's burning of the ships, Aeneas is overcome with despair and doubt that not even the counsels of his long-time friend Nautes can resolve. In this anxious state, he is visited by an image of Anchises, who claims to have come *imperio Iovis* (by the command of Jupiter) (726) and, accordingly, seems to descend to Aeneas from the heavens (722). Anchises identifies himself, however, as an inhabitant of a subterranean Elysium: a ghost, although one who has escaped the fate of the *tristes umbrae* (sad shades) in Tartarus (733–35). And yet the explicit specification of Jupiter's agency behind Anchises' arrival leaves no doubt that Aeneas himself has not conjured Anchises, but rather has been sent a vision in accordance with Jupiter's plan. Anchises visits Aeneas at a moment of private uncertainty to give him specific directions about the progress of his journey, rather than at a moment of public visibility and leadership. Further access to Anchises will necessitate the symbolic conquest of death itself: Aeneas is to proceed to the underworld and converse with the ghost of his father.

Anchises and the Idealization of Philosophical Dialogue

The philosophical coloring of Anchises' words in *Aeneid* 6 has long elicited attention, with Vergil's adaptation of the "*Somnium Scipionis*" episode from Cicero's *De re publica* a centerpiece of scholarly inquiry.[44] Thus we are now well-informed about the conceptual relationship between Vergil's text and Cicero's, its major precedent for a dialogue between a hero of the past and the spirit of his illustrious forbear. Yet in spite of the perennial interest in the relationship between the two texts, we still lack a complete understanding of them as successive idealizations of philosophical dialogue itself, a performance tradition taking its major impetus from Plato's "Myth of Er" in *Republic*, Book 10. Both Cicero and Vergil, imitating Plato, idealize philosophical dialogue by staging it in the *sedes beati* (abode of the blessed souls), a place of far greater access to, and so ideal for the discussion of, the arcane matters their interlocutors consider.[45] But while Cicero expresses discontent with republican politics, Vergil makes his ideal dialogue, in its content, form, and setting, appropriate to Augustan rather than republican Rome—and, through allusion to Cicero, calls attention to the fact that he is doing so.

Anchises' entire revelation of cosmic order revises and expands what in Cicero is merely a passing moment of discussion between the younger and the elder Scipios. Cicero has the younger Scipio, after being told of the blessed souls' celestial existence, ask his ancestor why he should continue living. He receives the immediate reply that suicide is prohibited by divine will (Cic. *Rep.* 6.15). The question is then dropped: the elder Scipio turns instead to an account of the universe so as to inspire his descendant to virtuous acts while belittling human fame from the perspective of the eternal. Vergil's Aeneas, by contrast, asks why the souls he sees before him in Elysium seem so eager to revisit the upper world (Verg. *A.* 6.721). Anchises' answer is postponed until he has first elucidated the universe's animation by a rational spirit and the process whereby certain souls are purified of corporeal taints, pass time in Elysium, and then drink from the waters of Lethe (724–51). By means of a delay between question and answer, Vergil suggests that the reasons for the soul's return to life require the process of dialogue to appreciate and internalize.

In this way Vergil assimilates the dialogue form itself to the therapeutic restoration of Rome. The ideal dialogue of *Aeneid* 6, that is, leads Aeneas symbolically through the experience of Augustan Romans faced with the problem of a return to life after the death and destruction of the civil wars. Faced, analogously, with the problem of the soul's desire for rebirth, Aeneas is encouraged by his father to embrace optimism about a future existence. This is a gradual process, requiring the instruction of a mentor attuned to principles of regeneration according to the workings of a divine *mens*. Anchises, not unlike the farmer of Vergil's *Georgics*, here stands for Octavian/Augustus as a leader apparently in touch with the workings of the cosmos. Just as Aeneas' reemergence from the underworld follows Anchises' discussion with his son, so, Rome may dare to hope, its own rebirth will be the effect of Augustus' guidance.

In Cicero's idealized dialogue, by contrast, the younger Scipio is assured immediately of an absolute law prohibiting suicide, although the basis of this law remains obscurely identified with divine will. No further discussion of the subject is called for, because in fact none is possible. Like other aspects of *De re publica,* this feature grounds the text in Cicero's own misfortunes as a member of the late-republican elite, excluded from politics, disillusioned with the pursuit of public life, and in search of an antidote to utter despair. So it is, for example, that we hear Cicero speaking through the younger Scipio's confession to a fear of betrayal by his peers or the elder Scipio's assessment, *vestra vita mors est* (what you call life is death) (Cic. *Rep.* 6.14).[46]

For Vergil, not only the form and content, but also the setting of his dialogue becomes a means of remaking Cicero. Far from the celestial realm that is the final destination of virtuous souls in Cicero's "*Somnium Scipionis*," Vergil fashions his Elysium as a subterranean paradise strongly reminiscent of earthly existence. This allows him, ultimately, to display Rome's future heroes in all their mortal specificity. There is far less distance, that is, both physically and conceptually, from Vergil's subterranean Elysium to Augustan Rome than there is from Cicero's heavens to the late-republican earth, and Vergil underscores this fact as he revises the Ciceronian tableau. Vergil's *sedes beatae* have their own *lumen, sol,* and *sidera* (Verg. *A.* 6.640–41): all terms that figure prominently in Cicero's description of the celestial home of the *beati,* but there function as signs of the vast distance separating earth from the heavens (Cic. *Rep.* 16–17). Not so for Vergil, whose next image after the subterranean constellations is that of blessed souls exerting themselves in exercise on "grassy wrestling-floors" and "yellow sand" (Verg. *A.* 6.642–43). Cicero in fact moves directly from the initial scene of meeting between the elder and younger Scipios to a vista of cosmic space opening up between the location of the speakers and the earth below. The elder Scipio points out Carthage, and in the same breath Cicero has his narrator explain that they are looking down "from a high place, one full of stars, bright and clear" (Cic. *Rep.* 6.11). Vergil takes pains to collapse the distance between paradise and earth at the opening of his dialogue, exactly where Cicero emphasizes this distance.

The physicality of Vergil's Elysium allows him to *show,* where Cicero has the elder Scipio only *tell,* his protagonist about the *sedes beati.* This helps Vergil use the coming dialogue between Anchises and Aeneas to describe not merely a destination for disembodied souls but a staging-ground for human existence. Vergil focuses on the signs of success in human endeavor, while Cicero has Scipio say little more about the actual dwelling place of the *beati* than that *certum esse in caelo definitum locum* (there is a fixed and definite place in the heavens) (Cic. *Rep.* 6.13) for each soul. Compare the words of Vergil's Musaeus: *nulli certa domus . . .* (no one has a definite home . . .), etc. (Verg. *A.* 6.673–75). Musaeus' words, anticipating the idea of reincarnation, emphasize as well the fact that Elysium is a place where human-like events occur, where there is corporeal motion in familiar terrestrial locales, including groves, river banks, meadows, and streams (673–74: *lucis . . . riparum . . . prata . . . rivis*). Musaeus thus facilitates the outcome of the dialogue between Aeneas and Anchises, which, proceeding before the backdrop of an ideal but corporeal existence, leads its interlocutors to a discussion of the world of the living and, ultimately, to Augustan Rome. Cicero's *sedes beati* are an abstraction, requiring a philosophical explanation from Scipio (only the first, in fact, of a series of abstract disquisitions touching upon the order of the universe), while abstract matters play a far less prominent role in Vergil's dialogue, in part because of what Vergil has shown us. So, for example, where Cicero's Scipio explains the music of the spheres (Cic. *Rep.* 6.18–19), Vergil's audience sees the legendary poets as it hears their song (Verg. *A.* 6.644–47, 657, 662–78). Their music is otherworldly, to be sure, and yet the poets of Vergil's Elysium are a familiar reminder of life on earth, a self-referential gesture, in fact, to Vergil's own performance of the *Aeneid.*

Vergil, of course, does far more in the latter part of *Aeneid* 6 than merely revise Cicero's "*Somnium Scipionis.*" He also adds to it, foregrounding the dream motif itself through the famous allusion, at *Aeneid* 6.893–96, to the Homeric gates of dreams at *Odyssey* 19.562–67. Aeneas' exit from the underworld through the gate of false dreams (Verg. *A.* 6.897–99) has done more to cast doubt on the status of what he has seen than any other detail in Book 6.[47] By my reading of Vergil's text, I do not mean to diminish the importance of questioning his pose with respect to Augustan ideology. Yet Vergil at least puts forward the possibility of philosophical discussion that would reveal the order behind Augustan Rome *rather than* the futility of republican politics. Ultimately, the choice remains with Vergil's audience whether to believe in this possibility—and in the Augustan ideal—or not. However "false" a Roman audience might have found Vergil's underworld as a mimesis of Augustan realities, the *Aeneid* nevertheless prompts such an audience (particularly that of the imperial court) to think through the broadest implications of the new regime.

Anchises and the Aristocratic Funeral

Aeneid 6 concludes with a procession of spirits, the famous "Review of Heroes," whose cultural resonance has now for some time been appreciated alongside its political import. With its emphasis on familial lineage, insignia, and *fama,* Vergil's procession recalls the *pompa* of the aristocratic funeral, a reminiscence sure to magnify the impact of the scene on Vergil's contemporaries.[48]

The funereal *pompa,* a central means of self-promotion for the aristocratic *gentes* of the Republic, continued to be practiced under Augustus, although its function as a type of political self-advertisement for *gentes* except the Julii would now be greatly diminished. The most lavish display of political preeminence became the exclusive right of the Princeps and his family.[49] In his underworld *pompa funebris,* Vergil bestows preeminence on Augustus through Anchises' praise for his yet-to be-born spirit (791–805). But rather than simply reflect cultural tradition for the sake of propaganda, Vergil, here again, transforms cultural tradition—and focuses his audience's attention on this gesture—by suggesting that the competing interests of republican *gentes* exist in conflict with true purpose of the prototypical *pompa funebris,* the procession that Vergil's epic recounts and effectively becomes. This purpose, the representation of the *Roman* family's progress from its origins through the rule of Augustus, is only achieved, Vergil suggests, by understanding the *pompae* of individual *gentes* as discrete parts of the larger whole that Vergil envisions. The *Aeneid* describes, and Vergil performs, this larger whole, at once the source and the *telos* of the republican *pompae* that might seem only to have aggravated the political strife of the Republic.[50]

Vergil's transformation of the *pompa funebris* takes place gradually and is the effect of Anchises' entire account of the underworld procession. It begins to gather force, however, in the most striking image of the account's first movement, that of Rome as the Magna Mater (781–87). To this point, Vergil has reproduced the strictly gentilitian orientation of the traditional *pompa funebris* in following the progress of Aeneas' line. With the mention of Rome's "offspring" in verse 784, however, Vergil's procession starts to become something very different. Rome, Anchises declares, will be *felix prole virum* (happy in her offspring of men) (784), just as the Magna Mater is happy in her divine offspring, her "hundred grandchildren" (786). This comparison is the basis for Anchises' inclusion of Romans other than those of the Julian line in his subsequent account. Because Aeneas' descendant, Romulus, will produce Rome, the Romans can claim to be *proles* of Aeneas' blood-line (cf. 756). The display enacted by the souls whom Anchises now describes points back to this unifying moment of origin: their "birth" from a common mother, Rome.

Anchises interprets the gestures and insignia of Rome's kings and republican *gentes* through their common participation in the Roman project symbolized by the procession itself. Indeed, in Vergil's depiction of Numa, the first soul described after his elaborate praise for Augustus, we are already presented with the idea that the procession only achieves its full meaning from the perspective of the Augustan regime. The sight of Augustus' soul prompts Anchises to ask the freighted question "And do we hesitate henceforth to extend valor through our deeds, or will fear prevent us from settling on Ausonian land?" (806–7). His inquiry applies simultaneously to Aeneas and to the subjects of Augustus, hopeful, after years of war, for deliverance from fear in the form of a lasting peace. Its answer, as it were, emerges in the next spirit to whom Anchises' directs his son's attention: Numa, Rome's second king, displaying the olive branch (808–12). The importance of Numa's achievement in bringing peace to early Rome appears, as a consequence, to lie first and foremost in its capacity to recall the possibility of peace to the subjects of Augustus.

While Numa, however, poses few problems to an audience watching for signs of Roman *virtus* and the possibility of social renewal, the same cannot easily be said of other souls described after him. Brutus the tyrannicide (817–23), for example, who inevitably recalls his descendant, the slayer of Julius Caesar, is obviously a problematic addition to a performance designed for an Augustan audience.[51] Likewise, the Drusi, Gracchi, and Scipiones are difficult to identify unequivocally as heroes and add a note of ambivalence to the passage's triumphalism.[52] But when these personages are considered as part of Vergil's effort to transform a practice of gentilitian self-advertisement into a prototypical display of the Roman family, such difficulty actually helps lend this section of the *Aeneid* its full cultural force. Viewed simply from the perspective of the *gens Iulia* in competition with other *gentes* for political preeminence, a figure such as Brutus is only a liability and a threat. But if Vergil is understood to be revealing a larger purpose behind the display of these men's images, the very strife they recall becomes merely a foil for the good qualities they also embody. Earlier Romans lived, after all, at a time before Rome's true hope for peace, Augustus, existed on the earth. Indeed, the more problematic the individuals in question, the more powerful the act of cultural restoration that recovers their images as symbols of the larger Roman project. The dissonance, as it were, that they introduce into the song of Rome potentially makes the new, Vergilian performance of it all the more gripping as a cultural gesture.[53]

Such is true in the highest degree of the final, great dissonance in Book 6's parade, Vergil's recollection of the recent death of Augustus' heir, the young Marcellus (860–86). Despair and hope are as densely intermingled in this passage as at any other point in the *Aeneid*.[54] Vergil leaves much to his audience's chosen outlook on the Augustan regime. But we need not rely solely on politically optimistic or pessimistic interpretations of the passage as a guide to Vergil's aims and achievement here. This is not only to say that Vergil is both optimistic and pessimistic at once (although he certainly is), but also to recognize his accommodation of Marcellus' death in the very act of cultural renewal.

We must remind ourselves that the occasion of Vergil's *pompa* is not actually the death of Marcellus or the funeral itself, but a moment of cultural production, the performance of an epic poem. Vergil's performance is not *a* funeral procession but *the* funeral procession: it possesses what no real *pompa funebris* does, its iterability. The *pompa* of Book 6, so Vergil's audience is encouraged to believe, is not grounded in political ambition, competition, and self-advertisement, but rather in the progress of the Roman family, the perpetuation of a whole Roman way of life. Vergil here insists on the *Aeneid* as supplanting the republican ceremony so as to perpetuate Roman culture. There is no better way to gauge Vergil's cultural ambitions for his epic than to remark how he looks straight at the one event most disruptive to political succession, Marcellus' death, while making this bold claim.

Conclusion: The Song of the Roman Dead

Vergil's interest in the evocation of the dead does not end with *Aeneid* 6; the poem bears further inquiry from the perspective advanced here, and holds the promise of still more varied results. Vergil's reference, for example, to Heracles' death-as-deification in Book 8 allows him, as Dennis Feeney has observed, to pose afresh the problem of transition from mortal to divine existence that had come to the fore in a virtually unprecedented fashion during the dictatorship of Julius Caesar and the period following Caesar's death.[55] The arrival of a Fury, Allecto, from the world of the dead in Book 7 contributes to a political critique of the late Republic as a tragic era, a gesture that echoes in turn the tropes of republican oratory (cf. chapter 2). The dead's wide-ranging "imitation" of the living, however, in Books 1–6, and the culmination of these books in a vision of Augustan Rome as heir of the Republic, makes them a fitting subject for the final chapter of this book.

Here, through the lens of myth, Vergil looks retrospectively at the Republic as a time of imperfect interactions between the living and the dead: imperfect in the sense that the cultural practices governing them are in need of revision. Vergil's orature, his self-conscious restoration of behavior, addresses this need in order to call attention to the *Aeneid* as a cultural gesture appropriate to Augustan society. In the person who recites the poem, the listener seems both to hear and to see Aeneas piously carrying out mortuary rites, engaging in philosophical dialogue with his father, then exclaiming in wonder as that ghostly father describes an infernal *pompa funebris*. The same performer calls up the dead Hector, bearer of Troy's legacy, and deploys, in Dido's persona, magical rituals from which Aeneas and Rome must distance themselves. The performance of Vergil's epic puts corporeal signs of social change before a listener's eyes at the same time as it offers a new, Augustan discourse to the ears. Through the *Aeneid*, the ghosts of a past at once Trojan and republican return to haunt—and yet to inform—the Augustan present.

The Living as the Dead

L OOKING FROM Cicero, Propertius, and Vergil to their successors, we are struck at once by the change in the Roman literary imagi- nation where the dead are concerned. Where the earlier authors portray the "imitation" of the living on which this book has focused, later writers have a greater tendency to depict the living's imitation of the dead—not the noble emulation of ancestral achievement denoted by the phrase *imitatio maiorum,* but a more sinister kind of mimesis we might term *imitatio mortuorum:* imitation of the dead *as* the dead. The descrip- tion of such behavior centers on the notion of an ancestral curse, a phe- nomenon we have seen operative previously but which is now portrayed as irresistible and all-consuming. Lucan, for example, frames the civil war between Caesar and Pompeius, a conflict that engulfs the Roman world, as a regression into a pattern of hostility set out by Romulus and Remus but anticipated more directly by Sulla and Marius, whose ghosts appear near the outset of Lucan's narrative to warn of the coming disaster (Luc. 1.580–83). At the opening of Seneca's *Thyestes,* a Fury drives the ghost of Tantalus to curse his descendants with madness that will assure they imitate his crimes (1–121). In *Agamemnon,* the spirit of Thyestes expresses his desire for ven- geance on the line of his brother, Atreus. Here, the ghost looks forward to the killing of Atreus' son, Agamemnon, by Clytemnestra and Aegisthus, whose murderous act, the basis of the plot, marks the fulfillment of vengeance (1–56). In Statius' *Thebaid,* the ghost of Oedipus' father, Laius, inflicts the curse of intrafamilial conflict upon his grandchildren, Eteocles and Poly- nices (2.102–24), while Oedipus himself, hovering in a living death, likewise curses his sons (1.56–87). Later, in the midst of war between the brothers, the prophet Amphiaraus makes a violent descent while still living into the underworld, whose inhabitants are amazed at his having become one of the dead before actually dying (7.818–23; 8.1–20). "Silver Age" works provide still other instances of this inverse phenomenon to add to those we have seen in their "golden" precursors.[1]

What has changed in Roman society to account for this transformation of literary fantasy? At least part of the answer lies in the consolidation of the political and cultural order around the figure of the emperor. With the firm establishment of the Principate, Rome's republican past becomes less a source of traditions to be transformed than a reified set of institutions through which to assess the imperial present. And assess it Romans did, for good or ill. Tacitus' bitter insistence that the slavishness fostered by Augustus himself had destroyed the Roman character of old (*Ann.* 1.2.1; 4.1) can stand for the "Republican" strain in imperial political critique, while the younger Pliny's *Panygyricus* finds in Trajan's Rome an exemplary illustration of republican *libertas*.[2] Indeed, while the benefits of stable regimes were obvious to many, Romans remained perpetually wary of falling into the worst mistakes of the past, above all, the abuse of absolute power that had led to the civil strife of the late Republic. Hence imperial authors' obsession with curses, tyrants, war between kin, and living death. In these circumstances, the literary evocation of the dead becomes, more often than before, a way to warn about the possibility of such failure or to imply that it has already occurred. It presumes a ruinous collapse of the distance between past and present, the very distance presupposed by the culturally transformative gestures of earlier literature.

In the poetry of Ovid, a transitional figure in so many ways, we can watch the change from one attitude to the other taking place. Consider the approach to change itself in Ovid's *Metamorphoses*. While in the *Aeneid*, Vergil had stressed the possibility of rebirth out of death's finality and despair, Ovid emphasizes the theme of change that elides death altogether, a posture that helps him avoid, at least outwardly, some of the thornier problems surrounding the consolidation of Augustus' rule. This theme is important in a great many of Ovid's stories from Greek mythology, but it takes on a marked political charge when he begins to recount the history of Rome. Indeed, the whole concluding segment of the *Metamorphoses* represents an exposition, in Roman terms, of a dictum Ovid attributes to the philosopher Pythagoras, whose journey to archaic Rome he recounts in Book 15: *nihil interit* (nothing dies) (165). In the previous Book, Ovid had told of Aeneas' transformation into the god Indiges (14.581–608) and Romulus' deification as Quirinus (805–28). Shortly after Pythagoras' disquisition, Julius Caesar undergoes his own fabled deification (15.745–851), the basis for Augustus' reputation for divinity while he lived and precedent for the formal emperor worship established upon his death. It is significant that the ghosts of the *Aeneid,* symbols of loss and violence haunting the present, are all but absent from Ovid's brief version of Aeneas' wanderings (13.623–14.608). Still more telling is Remus' total absence from the story of Romulus (14.778–828), with whom, as with Aeneas, Augustus had identified himself. The contrast with Vergil's *Aeneid* could not be more evident: as we have seen, Vergil, who makes no secret of Remus, finds a cultural alternative to recent emphasis on Remus' curse in the transferral of a positive legacy from the ruined Troy to Rome. However much Ovid's silence about Remus might have helped him emphasize Augustus' strengths, Ovid nevertheless constructs an imperial mythology vulnerable to the criticisms of the past on charges of ideological amnesia.

In the *Fasti,* unfinished at the time of his exile in 8 CE, Ovid takes a different approach to the Remus story: he actually summons the ghost of Remus in a dream-appearance to Faustulus and Acca so as to have Remus deny that Romulus killed him (5.457–74). Could Ovid really have imagined that this outright denial of the legend's dominant version would have the force to erase its inconvenient details? Would contemporary audiences simply have applauded the blunt exculpation of Augustus' legendary counterpart? The obvious potential for failure inherent in Ovid's gesture has led scholars to suspect subversive intentions.[3] Indeed, Remus' account appears to be contradicted by the very words of reproach that Ovid, as narrator, has addressed to Romulus earlier in the *Fasti: te Remus incusat* (Remus accuses you) (2.143). At the least, the apparent self-reversal of Ovid's text sounds a note of uncertainty about the harmonious relationship of past and present, a sentiment that later authors would take up and magnify to a far greater pitch. Whatever Ovid's intentions, his very attempt to provide absolution for the Augustan regime carries the seeds of its own undoing.

In his poetry from exile, Ovid constructs his condition as a living death in which true death, while desired, nevertheless eludes him.[4] In *Tristia* 1.3.21–24, he portrays his departure into exile as a funeral. In *Tristia* 3.11, he describes himself as a ghost (*umbra*), his body already reduced to ashes and buried in a tomb (25–26), while in *Ex Ponto* 1.9.55–56, he exhorts his friend Maximus to number him with the dead. In *Tristia* 3.2.21–24 Ovid casts himself in the role of traditional erotic elegy's excluded lover (*exclusus amator*) knocking in vain on the door of death; in 3.3 he looks forward to death, since it will mean his longed-for return to Rome, once his wife has transferred his bones there (65–66). Ovid's exile poems are a testament to the consolidation of Augustus' power. Indeed, in their expressions of dependency on the Emperor's mercy and frank acknowledgment of his authority, they even provide a model of imperial subjecthood itself.[5] But the ghostly Ovid who speaks here also points to the possibility of the dead's indictment of tyranny. The closer Ovid gets to death, whether figurative or literal, the more he encourages his readers to weigh the gravity of his transgressions, which he never names outright, against the severity of his punishment. While Ovid himself cannot make accusations of despotism, his sepulchral voice is nevertheless a warning, an admonition to consider how the circumstances of tyranny might in fact be met. As a prophet (*vates*) now gone to his "death," the exiled Ovid prefigures the prophetic ghosts who populate later literature and decry tyrannical behavior on the part of absolute rulers.

As Ovid anticipates a change in the literary evocation of the dead, so his work also suggests avenues for future inquiry based on the methods of this study. To take the example just cited—Ovid's self-portrayal as a ghost—how, we might wonder, did the status of the *Tristia* and *Epistulae ex Ponto* as orature render this tactic all the more poignant and tension-prone? In the context of oral delivery at Rome, the poems would have recalled not only earlier Roman elegy as a literary tradition with which Ovid engaged in characteristically allusive play but also performance occasions when Ovid was a popular figure in the capital. An awareness of the distance that the physical manuscripts of the exile poems would have traveled in order to be read in Rome would have highlighted the contrast between these earlier occasions, when Ovid either performed himself or a reader intoned the verses of the Roman poet, and the experience of reciting poetry whose author could actually have died without news of the event having yet become common knowledge. Imagine the chill of reading aloud a poem such as *Ex Ponto* 1.9, with its concluding exhortation to consider Ovid as already dead, and wondering whether one were in fact reciting the words of a dead poet, lost now from the circumstances of living performance and yet also tenuously present in the poetry as performed. In becoming, momentarily, Ovid's ghost, was one also enacting a style of performance that was now only a historical throwback, its most illustrious—and notorious—*auctor* dead?

Passages in Ovid's poetry like those to which I have referred do not so much restage cultural traditions as suggest all but untenable distortions of them. For the living to become the dead means taking on behaviors that literally do not belong in the present; Ovid's distant voice is the echo of Ovidian erotic elegy excluded from Augustan Rome. Following up the implications of Ovid's later work, one might ask how subsequent authors, rather than emphasizing the socially regenerative effects of orature and restored behavior, focus instead on their disquieting counterpart: the sense of alienation or nostalgia arising from the reenactment of practices whose original social and political context is now a historical memory. Thus one might turn to a passage such as the reminiscence of the aristocratic *pompa funebris* following the death of Opheltes in Book 6 of Statius' *Thebaid* (268–95).[6]

Statius' description of the procession strikes a tone of reverence for ancestral glory, but the pitiful occasion of the funeral itself, the apparently random death of the infant Opheltes from a snake bite, undercuts deeply the sense of purposefulness that might arise from such display. Troubling, too, is the reminder of the enmity between the brothers Aegyptus and Danaus that accompanies the mention of their images (291–93). In a rite observed by the followers of Polynices, who are themselves engaged in a self-consuming war between brothers, the expectation of fraternal conflict that the images arouse stands unredeemed by immediate hope for resolution. Again, contrast Vergil, whose "Review of Heroes," the passage with which our study began, couches its anxiety over civil war in expressions of hope for the Augustan future. What does it mean for Statius to retroject the *pompa funebris* into a violent episode from the Greek mythological past, whereas Vergil had cast its prototype in Elysium? Statius' adaptation of the ritual under Domitian frames it in significantly different terms from those of the Augustan poet a century before.[7]

Latin literature both reflects and helps determine Rome's changing relationship with a past at once silent and speaking, bodiless and embodied, dead and living. Cicero's ghostly ancestors, murder victims, and war heroes, even as they point to a comforting and familiar sense of solidarity with the dead, unsettle any secure notion of history as a seamless progression of events. But their staging of practices threatened by disjuncture or reaffirmed through an emphasis on continuity functioned as a powerful political tool at a moment when the traditional structure of the Roman state was in fact breaking down and aristocratic clans vied ruthlessly for power. In the early Augustan Principate, literature had an important part in voicing both the hopes and anxieties of a new elite looking for revised models of subjecthood and citizenship. In Propertius and Vergil, the dead act out new versions of traditional roles, whether through the gender play of erotic elegy or epic's grand rediscovery of Roman prehistory. Thus in the first century BCE the forces acting on and through literary production at Rome resulted in something not seen to the same degree before or since: the culture of the living reenacted through the ghosts of the past.

NOTES

Introduction

1. As Paul Allen Miller has recently observed, Augustan literature, in contrast to its republican precursor, was less a form of self-assertion than a complex negotiation of categories such as *Romanitas* (Romanness) and *nobilitas* (nobility) under the circumstances of subordination to a single central authority (Miller 2004: 75 comparing Fear 236–37; Habinek 1998: 121; Wallace-Hadrill 22; Conte 251, etc.). In this book I respond to growing interests both in the relationship between literature and performance at Rome and in the changing political motivations behind Romans' literary and cultural relations to the dead. On Latin literature and performance culture see, e.g., Skinner 1993; Valette-Cagnac; Feldherr 1998; Gamel; Habinek 1998; Wachter; Wyke; Habinek 2005b. Further bibliography in Habinek 2005b: 261, n1. For recent perspectives on cultural aspects of the dead in Latin literature, see Feldherr 2000; Littlewood; Bernstein 2003, 2004, 2005. More examples of both scholarly trends are cited in the chapters to follow.

2. Roach 11–12 citing Ngugi 61. For the appropriateness of viewing ancient Rome as one such society, see Habinek 2005b: 261–62 n1, with bibliography.

3. Roach 2–3.

4. Ibid., 2.

5. Ibid., 12 citing Fliegelman 98, 192.

6. Ibid., citing James 87.

7. Schechner 1986: 7; cf. 1990: 43.

8. See Schechner 1985: 35–116, esp. 35–37.

9. An illuminating example of the phenomena on which Schechner bases his views is the recreation of the past involved in the "restored village" theme parks so popular in the United States (see Schechner 1985: 79–94). Here actors dressed in period costumes perform historically specific activities for the benefit of park visitors. The actors, in persona, even encourage the audience to engage in dialogue, often meant to call attention to the changes in social mores that mark the difference between an earlier time and the present. The total experience, however, is intended not only to highlight difference but also to show how people "back then" were in some ways very much "like us," a claim that may take on various sorts of resonance (humanistic, patriotic, aesthetic) depending on how it is made and who is listening.

10. Galinsky 65; cf. Wallace-Hadrill.

11. I say this fully aware that any discussion of "Roman performance" is no more than a further textual mediation of behaviors already highly mediated though ancient texts and material artifacts. That is, I knowingly deal in a "rhetoric of reality" like that described by Duncan Kennedy in his study of Roman erotic elegy (Kennedy 1993; cf. Edmonds 4 on Habinek 2005a). In my view, however, the careful implementation of such a rhetoric can have the salutary effect of undoing the historical tendency to treat Latin literature as a phenomenon isolated from the broader culture (see Habinek 1998: 23–33). But, although I think the historical record is sound, the degree to which we can trust its testimonia, which are heavily skewed to an elite perspective, ultimately matters less to me than the correspondences between the Romans' perceptions of various performance traditions and aspects of their literature.

12. Readers will find full citation of sources and scholarship on the Roman practices discussed here in the individual chapters below.

13. Cf. Wiseman 1998: 52. There were numerous other occasions, besides funerals, available for the performance of *praetextae*. By the Augustan period, the Roman calendar included fifty-six days set aside for *ludi scaenici* (theatrical games) (Wiseman 1998: 17).

14. On Greek tragedy's "fascination with the dead," see Johnston 23–30.

15. So Wiseman 1995. See chapter 5 below.

16. A focus on *prosopopoeia* has helped me to narrow down what might otherwise be an ungovernably large mass of material. It might be argued, for example, that the entire genre of historiography constitutes a series of "evocations of the dead." In fact, most ancient rhetoricians distinguished between *prosopopoeia*, which could be used to have the dead speak *as* the dead (in which case it was sometimes called *eidolopoeia* ["ghost-making"]), and *ethopoeia* or *sermocinatio*, the technique for introducing the speech of natural persons. See Lausberg 370.

17. See Skutsch 164–65.

18. See, e.g., Skutsch 1–2, 501–502, 552, 569–70, 572–74.

19. Ennius used the technique at least once more in the *Annales*, in Aeneas's appearance to the dreaming Ilia (44–46 Vahlen; although the dead Aeneas was, by this time, a god).

Chapter One

1. Lysias asserts that the dead are listening to the court proceedings, will recognize the jurors when they cast their ballots, and will consider the extraction of justice to have been carried out on their behalf (Lys. 12.100). Andocides asks his audience to envision his own ancestors pleading for him (And. 1.148). Isocrates asks the audience to imagine that the dead perceive what is happening in the world of the living; the possibility, however, is hypothetical (Isoc. 14.61; 5.105, 137; 6.110). Demosthenes uses a similar formulation (see Jost 231 on D. 19.66; 20.87; 23.210; cf. Jost 152–53). Antiphon's *Tetralogies* refer to the avengers of the dead (see the following chapter).

2. On the topos *mortuos* [or *defunctos*] *ab inferis excitare*, see Cic. *de Orat.* 1.245; *Orat.* 85; *Top.* 45; Quint. *Inst.* 4.1.28, 9.2.31, 12.10.61; Rutilius Lupus 2.6; Aquila Romanus 3; cf. Quint. *Inst.* 9.2.36.

3. Cic. *de Orat.* 1.245 (Antonius to Crassus): *patrem eius, ut soles, dicendo a mortuis excitasses; statuisses ante oculos; complexus esset filium, flensque eum centumviris com-*

mendasset (through your eloquence, as you are accustomed, you would have conjured his father up from the underworld, you would have set him before the eyes of all; he would have embraced his son and, weeping, have commended him to the *centumviri*). Cf. Cic. *Scaur.* 49 and the performance Cicero ascribes to his colleague P. Servilius Vatia Isauricus at *Red. Sen.* 25–26 and *Sest.* 130–31 (passages discussed in detail below). Note that at *Brutus* 322, Cicero implies that no other orator used the technique the way he did.

4. On the relation of Cicero's published speeches to those he actually delivered, see Humbert; Stroh 1975: 31–54; Narducci 157–73; Powell and Patterson 52–57. In what follows, I assume that the published speeches, whatever the extent to which they actually reproduce Cicero's words on a given occasion, approximate the conventions of live speech closely enough to be regarded as records and/or models of actual oratory.

5. Cf. the poetic description of Lake Avernus Cicero quotes at Cic. *Tusc.* 1.37 (*Inc. trag.* 76–77 Ribbeck): *unde animae excitantur obscura umbra opertae ex ostio / Altae Acheruntis, salso sanguine* (whence spirits, shrouded in dark shadow, are summoned up from the blood-spattered portal of deep Acheron). For more on the ancient association of rhetoric with magic, see De Romilly; Covino.

6. On ancient necromancy, see Ogden; cf. Dickie 22, 78, 138, 149, 214, 237–39, 254. Many other studies of ancient magic are now available, e.g., Faraone; Johnston *passim;* Graf; Gager; Faraone and Obbink. On the political significance of magic directed toward the dead in Rome, see Habinek 2005b: 220–56.

7. For the individual charges and their division among Cicero and M. Licinius Crassus, Caelius' other *patronus,* see Austin 152–54. On the case for the prosecution, see Alexander 218–43. On Cicero's response to the general charge of *vis,* cf. Riggsby 97–105.

8. Craig 108–9 provides a useful summary of, and a balanced solution to, the debate. As also noted there, Heinze 1925: 228, 245–48 and Stroh 1975: 269–73 argue for and against general knowledge of the affair respectively, while Reitzenstein 1925: 32 and Austin 86 maintain that Cicero could not have been the first to mention in court a circumstance as potentially damaging to Caelius' standing (cf. Drexler 25; Classen 1973: 76 n74; Wiseman 1985: 74). Craig sees Cicero playing to both informed and uninformed members of the audience, although he admits that embracing either perspective on Cicero's persuasiveness requires a "leap of faith" (Craig 109).

9. For Cicero's manipulation of female stereotypes, see Geffcken 27–43; Lefkowitz 32–40; Skinner 1983.

10. So already Heinze 1925: 232.

11. See Geffcken 18–19, 34; Vasaly 172–90, esp. 174–75, 181. Scholars following Geffcken's emphasis on humor include Skinner 1983, May 105–16; Riggsby 97–105 (but cf. Wiseman 1985: 84; May 116). For more on comedy in the *Pro Caelio,* see Leigh. While I depart from the current tendency to describe the Appius passage's dramatic effects primarily in comic and/or trivializing terms, I certainly do not mean to deny the comic qualities of the speech, but rather to follow in a direction suggested by Salzman, for whom the speech's evocation of drama functions also as an attack upon the unconventional religious behavior of the Clodii (a further subject of gossip behind those I discuss here). The broad civic context recalled by Salzman suggests the benefits of widening the horizons of our interpretation beyond the specific festival circumstances of the *Ludi Megalenses.*

12. Here "system" suggests the organized, even ritual *process* of information transmission in the judicial context, while "network" refers to a *set of interrelations* not necessarily defined by such organization (although, admittedly, views of the informality of gossip

differ [cf. Haviland 48–66; Spacks 13; Bergmann 139–53]). I assume a common definition of "gossip" as "idle talk; trifling or groundless rumour" (*OED*) and so do not adopt
a binding distinction between gossip and rumor (cf. Rosnow and Fine 81–93; Bergmann
70). I am further indebted to Reumaux for my understanding of gossip and rumor as
social phenomena and topics of critical concern. Discussions of Roman gossip are few.
Laurence documents the importance of rumor to the overall functioning of the Roman
political system. Millar 13–48 discusses a key Roman information network in examining the crowd's experience of the judicio-political system in the Roman Forum. Richlin
81–104 describes interchange among the informal discourses of graffiti, gossip, lam-
poons, and rhetorical invective (hardly institutionalized in the manner of judicial oratory). For the ethical basis of Roman political invective and its associations with slander,
see Corbeill *passim*. It is worth noting that the social aspects of gossip often emphasized
by scholars of Greco-Roman antiquity—namely, the definition and enforcement of societal norms (cf. Hunter 96–119 with bibliography)—are not the only ones relevant to a
full appreciation of the *Pro Caelio* in its socio-cultural context. While helping to police
society in this way, gossip may also have a more creative function, in that formal societal
institutions such as judicial oratory feed off informal practices and draw their strength
partly from their ability to co-opt them without seeming to. Indeed, for John Schotter,
"humanly *adequate* social orders . . . can only be created, sustained, and transformed" by
"drawing upon" activities such as gossip, "usually dismissed as a waste of time" (Schotter
150). Formal institutions, in other words, may explicitly deny the power of the informal
practices they co-opt; they betray, however, their dependence on the informal in their
attempt to redefine practices such as gossip into a shape that is amenable to their own
ends, namely, the support of the existing power structure. Both Schotter and Lorraine
Code have called our attention to the way that informal, disorderly social activities are
not only threatening but also valuable because of their "resistance to paradigmatic sum-
ming-up," their disassociation from an answerable source (Code 104; cf. Schotter 150). It
is this very resistance that allows Cicero to benefit from the "creative" potential of gossip
to such a remarkable degree in the *Pro Caelio*. In the place of an anonymous *vox populi*,
Cicero easily substitutes Appius Claudius Caecus, an arresting figure from Rome's public
world of traditional aristocratic spectacle and display.

13. On the centrality of elite-sponsored spectacle within Roman society, cf. Dupont
1985; Feldherr 1998; Kyle. The ambiguity of the Latin term *fama* suggests that evocation
of the illustrious dead was an especially effective way to manage gossip at Rome. *Sermo*
and *rumor* regularly signify gossip as a means of information transmission as well as
specific topics gossiped about (*OLD sermo* 4, 5; *rumor* 2); *opinio* and *fama* commonly
refer to reputation, with *fama* used in particular for rumor, hearsay, and public opinion
(*OLD opinio* 5; *fama* 2, 4, 5, 6). *Fama* however, can also be synonymous with *gloria*, and
so stands at once for the vagaries of informal speech and its transformation into the
institutionalized reputation of the dead (*OLD fama* 7). As does Cicero's Appius Claudius
Caecus.

14. On the importance of *Pro Caelio* 6 for our understanding of republican political
invective, see Corbeill 17–18.

15. Cicero's claim may strike us as odd in light of the fact that the republican judicial
system did not have formal rules of evidence (Zumpt 245–46 ; Greenidge 274; Strachan-
Davidson 121–24). Rhetorical topoi governing Cicero's claim are discussed below.

16. *Rhet. Her.* 2.12: *Contra rumores dicemus . . . si . . . aut iniquos nostros aut homines
natura malivolos et maledicos confinxisse dicemus . . . aut verum rumorem proferemus qui*

[s.c. *adversariis*] *aliquid turpitudinis adferat, neque tamen ei rumori nos fidem habere dicemus, ideo quod quivis unus homo possit quamvis turpem de quolibet rumorem proferre et confictam fabulam dissipare* (We will speak against rumors . . . if . . . we say that our enemies or men by nature malevolent and slanderous invented them . . . or produce a true report carrying some disgrace [to our adversaries] and yet say that we have no faith in it because any person at all can produce and spread any disgraceful rumor or fictitious story about any other person). The same passage offers arguments for *rumores* in separate circumstances. See further Quint. *Inst.* 5ḃ.1.1, which locates *rumores* among the proofs not invented by the orator (cf. A. *Rh.* 1355ᵇ 35–38). *Rhet. Her.* 4.47 describes the duty of a witness as to say "what he knows or what he has heard" and *opinio* is one of the *adiuncta* to the trial that can be useful as a prooimial *locus* (Quint. *Inst.* 4.1.31 referencing Cic. *Ver.* 1). Cicero frequently claims to reproduce the common gossip about individuals as a means of stigmatizing his enemies and opponents (above all, Clodius); cf. Richlin 83–86; Laurence 64. For my discussion of rhetorical theory I have relied especially on Lausberg.

17. Cicero admits to having himself been taken in by Catiline before he achieved an unobstructed perception of Catiline's true nature—before he could rely, that is, on his own eyes to confirm the *opinio* surrounding Catiline's acts (*Cael.* 14). On the importance of a young man's public associations, cf. Vasaly 184.

18. Indeed, in a notorious sexual double standard, the example of Roman public figures helps Cicero excuse Caelius' involvement in the affair with Clodia while holding Clodia morally accountable for the same affair. Many, Cicero insists, of the most illustrious Roman men, even in the times of the ancestors, fell victim to *cupiditas* and *libido* in youth, only to have their *virtus* emerge in full force during their careers as adults (43). Clodia's virtue as a woman is not subject to a similar recuperation once undermined.

19. Geffcken 18.

20. Stroh 1975: 281.

21. Although he first asks whether she has not *seen* that her father was a consul (*Cael.* 33).

22. On the scurrilous connotations of Clodia's "unchaste" use of water, see Butrica and Bruun.

23. On Appius and the Via Appia, see MacBain.

24. Cf. Ogden xxix, 61, 76, 254, 256. For Laberius, see Ribbeck, vol. 2: 349–51; for comic ghosts cf. Riggsby 101; Plaut. *Most.* 454–531.

25. Cf. Johnston 85 and Ogden xxvi–xxvii and *passim* on tragic necromancy.

26. On Lake Avernus as a *nekuomanteion*, see Ogden 61–74.

27. Direct reference to tragedy also has a place in Cicero's denunciation of Clodia, since it is very much in keeping with the nature of Roman moralizing to treat the chastisement of an errant member of the *familia* as a solemn event, worthy of the pathos of tragedy even if open to the humor intrinsic in blame and invective. The *Pro Caelio* as a whole is not without serious, even tragic, effects, as memorably in Cicero's digression on the death of Q. Caecilius Metellus (*Cael.* 59).

28. Cf. Gaffney 428. On Cicero's use of the prosecution's arguments more generally, see Gotoff. Appius shields Cicero from the kind of criticisms Cicero directs at Herennius because Cicero can thereby transfer some of the responsibility for what he says to Appius (cf. *Cael.* 33, where Cicero ironically suggests that Appius will speak for him so that Clodia won't become angry with him). Part of Cicero's effectiveness is in distinguishing between those who act like stern fathers in disciplining someone else's child (i.e., the prosecution) and paternal figures who appropriately discipline their own offspring

(Appius, and the *lenis* father from comedy in *Cael.* 38) or someone for whom they have a responsibility (Cicero himself as he disciplines Caelius in *Cael.* 37).

29. Vasaly 181 n39.

30. For the identification of these persons as Stoics, see Austin 104. The passage as a whole divides attitudes toward pleasure into Epicurean, Academic/Peripatetic, and Stoic camps.

31. Gossiping old men, we may observe, are a paradigmatic butt of Greco-Roman comedy generally.

32. Nicolet treats the various formal and informal venues, including the theater, funerals, *contiones,* and more casual meeting-places, available for the expression of popular opinion at the close of the Republic. See especially "Escorts and demonstrations" (356–61), "Games, festivals, and theatres" (361–73, detailing Cicero's sensitivity to the responses of theater crowds), and "Trials and lawsuits" (373–81).

33. On the *imagines* and the *pompa funebris,* see Drerup; Lahusen; Lucrezi; Dupont 1987; Flower 1996; Walter 89–112. The ancient *locus classicus* is Plb. 6.52–54.

34. Diodorus Siculus (31.25.2) suggests the actors' imitation of the dead's bearing and appearance, but neither he nor any of our other sources mention verbal imitations as a part of the republican *pompa.* But cf. Flower 1996: 104 on the speaking actor who played the part of the emperor Vespasian at the latter's funeral.

35. Cf. Flower 1996: 129 n5, who observes that it is possible to interpret Appius' address as "a reversal of the dramatic action of the eulogy," in which a family member addressed an audience of actors wearing the *imagines.*

36. On the *laudatio funebris,* see Vollmer; Durry; Kierdorf; Flower 1996: 128–50.

37. Cicero himself doubted the credibility of Roman *laudationes* (Cic. *Brut.* 62). His vehement expression of such doubt, however, suggests the extent to which funeral eulogy *was* in fact regarded as truth.

38. Cf. Cic. *Tusc.* 4.4 and [Sall.] *Rep.* 1.1.2. On the fragments of Appius' *carmina,* see below.

39. Ancient texts were commonly meant to be read aloud, but the stylistic features of many *carmina,* including alliteration, assonance, and *figura etymologica,* made them particularly suitable for oral delivery (see Williams 1968: 693). On *carmen* and performance more broadly, see Habinek 2005b. The association of epitaphs with performed *carmina* is underscored by their early adoption of the Saturnian verse form, used likewise for hymns and epic poetry. On the scope of Saturnians, cf. West 1973: 175. On the association of epitaphs and *laudationes,* see Flower 1996 *passim.*

40. Appius Claudius Caecus, fr. 1–3 Blänsdorf. For interpretation and commentary, including the metrical debate, cf. Ballaira; Tar; Giardina; Stoessl; Marini.

41. Fest. p. 48 in Lindsay's Teubner edition. We do not know, of course, whether Appius' work was actually performed in public. Performance, however, attaches to him as a public figure and author of *carmina* (cf. Habinek 2005b: 49). Appius' reputation as a persuasive orator adds further to the authority he is able to bestow on Cicero's own speech. The *Pro Caelio* alludes to a specific speech of Appius, his argument against the peace with Pyrrhus, that helped establish Appius' reputation as a persuasive public speaker (cf. *Cael.* 34). A version of this speech was circulating in Cicero's day and available for him to consult. In spite of his skepticism about the charm of Appius' oratory, Cicero concludes that Appius must have been *disertus* (a ready speaker) because he was able to sway the opinion of a senate leaning toward peace (cf. Cic. *Brut.* 55, 61; *Sen.* 16).

42. On the *praetexta* see Zehnacker; Manuwald; Feldherr 1998: 172; Wiseman 1998;

Walter 75–83. The frequency which these plays were actually produced is debated by scholars. For the controversy, see Flower 1995; Wiseman 1998: 1–16.

43. Cic. *Brut.* 322 recommends a knowledge of Roman history, *ex qua . . .* [sc. *orator*] *ab inferis locupletissimos testis excitaret* (from which . . . [the orator] may call up the most reliable witnesses from the underworld).

44. Cf. Geffcken 17 following Austin 94–95.

45. Cf., e.g., Geffcken 17–18 on Quint. *Inst.* 11.1.39.

46. Cf. Salzman 301.

47. Cf. Prop. 4.11.51–52; Ov. *Fast.* 4.326; Bömer 1964; Wiseman 1985: 36. Wiseman 1998: 3 adds this play to the list of *fabulae praetextae* in Ribbeck's catalogue of the remains of Roman drama (Ribbeck, vol. 1, 319–31, 335); cf. Flower 1995: 175. Salzman 302–3 reveals further how the myth of the Great Mother and her consort Attis humorously informs Cicero's portrayal of Clodia and her lover, Caelius.

48. For the topos, see above, n2. It is possible that the necromancy apparently practiced by Clodia's other brother, Appius Claudius Pulcher, somehow lies behind Cicero's use of *mortuos excitare* in the *Pro Caelio* (cf. Ogden 150–51). Cicero and Appius Claudius Pulcher were not always on good terms, although Appius receives a favorable mention at *Pro Milone* 75 (another speech, interestingly, in which Cicero uses *mortuos excitare* to attack Clodius: see below).

49. The conventional emphasis also seems to have been on those who had died fairly recently (but cf. Cicero's suggestion that P. Servilius Vatia Isauricus evoked long-dead Metelli [*Red. Sen.* 25; *Sest.* 130]).

50. Cic. *Red. Sen.* 25; cf. Cic. *Sest.* 130.

51. V. Max. 6.2.8. On the incident, see Gruen 1974: 314.

52. In the circumstances of Caelius' trial, Cicero's unconventional, self-conscious exploitation of the topos could also generate a useful ambivalence. If the audience regards Cicero as an experienced orator employing a rhetorical topos in its known form, this will help them view Appius as a feature of oratorical *gravitas* and institutional "truth." If, however, the audience is listening more closely for rhetorical parody (Cicero has by this point already described Caelius' accusers as overly 'censorious'), then Cicero's signaling of Appius as an irregular example of the topos adds to the sense of parody in his remarks. Of course, both effects are simultaneously possible and beneficial to Cicero's case. Given Cicero's use of the topos elsewhere in his speeches, we may even hear mild self-parody in his introduction of Appius as *ab inferis excitandus*. The benefit of such self-parody would be further to distance Cicero from his opponents' type of censure, delivered in full seriousness (and, apparently, *in propria persona*) against Caelius.

53. Cicero had previously compared Clodius to Appius Claudius Caecus in his invective *In Clodium et Curionem*. For attestations, fragments, and commentary, see Geffcken 57–89; Crawford 1994: 227–63. Crawford 1994: 261 also compares Cic. *Dom.* 105.

54. Most scholars have assumed a considerable gap between the spoken and published versions of the *Pro Milone*. See Humbert 189–97; Lintott 1974: 74; Stone; Crawford 1984: 210–218; Marshall; Dyck 2002; Powell and Paterson 55. Settle, however, dismisses the evidence for a major discrepancy as inconclusive. In what follows I will assume that the extant *Pro Milone*, whatever the differences between it and the speech Cicero actually delivered, can and should be read as a response to the actual circumstances of the trial. Asconius himself may be suggesting as much in saying *scripsit vero hanc quam legimus ita perfecte ut iure prima haberi possit* (Yet he wrote this [speech] which we read so perfectly that it can deservedly be considered the original) (Asc.p. 42 in Clark's Oxford

edition) and Milo's ironic remark (D.C. 40.54.3) that he would not be eating the mullets of Massilia, his place of exile, had Cicero delivered the speech in its published form, points to a similar understanding of the text. A speech with little relation to the original circumstances would have undermined any benefits of publishing the *Pro Milone* for an audience familiar with events.

55. Many accounts of the period are available. For a concise chronology of events leading up to the trial see Ruebel; cf. Gruen 1974: 233–39.

56. Milo had been instrumental in Cicero's recall from exile in 57 BCE and the two had collaborated in political trials in 56. For the history of their relations see Lintott 1974.

57. On Milo's own history of violence, including his organization and deployment of armed gangs, see Lintott 1999: 60 ff., 83–85, and *passim*.

58. Asc. pp. 40–41 in Clark's Oxford edition. Cf. Cic. *Mil.* 3.

59. See above, n53.

60. Plu. *Cic.* 35.4.

61. Ancient rhetorical theory recognized the *constitutio adsumptiva*, of which sections 72–91 of the *Pro Milone* are a clear example, as the shoring up of a weak argument through the insertion of material not strictly relevant to the case. *Rhet. Her.* 1.24: *Adsumptiva pars est cum per se defensio infirma est, adsumpta extraria re conprobatur* (The assumptive issue is when the defense is weak in itself but is proven by the introduction of extraneous matter); cf. Quint. *Inst.* 7.4.7. The designation *extra causam* comes from Cicero's own words in *Mil.* 92: *Sed iam satis multa de causa, extra causam etiam nimis fortasse multa* (But now I have said a sufficiently great amount concerning the case, and even perhaps too much outside the limits of the case). Cf. Stone 95–96.

62. It is tempting to see (with Stone 96–97) a jab at Pompeius lurking in this passage. Cicero may be suggesting that it is hypocritical of Pompeius to have ordered a special inquiry into Clodius' death when even he would not wish Clodius to return to life. The question remains open as to whether Cicero actually risked making this suggestion at Milo's trial. For the argument that he did not, see Stone 98ff.

63. Cf. Cic. *Phil.* 2.91: *tu . . . illas faces incendisti . . . quibus semustilatus ille est* (you [Antonius] . . . kindled those torches . . . with which that man [Julius Caesar] was scorched).

64. For animate corpses, cf. Plin. *Nat.* 7.52.178–79 on Gabienus, the Caesarian soldier who returned to life after being beheaded by order of Sex. Pompeius. Bodies magically reanimated appear both in the Erictho episode of Lucan's *Bellum Civile* (6.667–821), as well as in Apul. *Met.* 2.29–30. Ar. *Ra.* 173–177 portrays a corpse who engages in dialogue from its bier. Cf. Ogden 202–16.

65. Elsewhere, Sallust, Livy, and Cicero himself express similar views. Sallust, for example, describes how the *gloria* of figures from the past incites outstanding men to achieve a similar renown (Sal. *Jug.* 4.6; cf. *Cat.* 11.2). Livy reports the zeal with which the heroic M. Valerius sought to emulate the *gloria* of his house by killing the young T. Tarquinius, son of L. Tarquinius Superbus, the last king of Rome (Liv. 2.20.1). Cicero declares that the Romans surpass other nations in their desire for *gloria* (Cic. *Man.* 7; cf. *Tusc.* 1.91). Further parallels in Knoche and Leeman.

66. Cf. esp. Cic. *Tusc.* 1.40, 51; *Rep.* 6.25.

67. Cic. *Tusc.* 1.37.

68. For Cicero's reactions to Clodius' adoption, cf. Cic. *Att.* 2.7.2; 2.9.1; 2.12.1–2; 8.3.3; *Dom.* 34–42; *Har.* 44–45. Clodius arranged the adoption in order to stand for the office of Tribune for 58 BCE, to which he was elected.

69. See above, n2.

70. See Flower 1996: 223–55.

71. See D.C. 49.43.5 on Agrippa's bill expelling astrologers and witches from the city (cf. 52.36.1–3; Dickie 155, 192). For more on constraints against magicians in Rome, see Dickie 142–61.

72. Cf. Kennedy 1972: 303.

73. Suet. *Aug.* 33.1 relates that Augustus tired to help an accused man avoid punishment in the *culleus* (sack) by asking him a leading question. The Romans traditionally punished condemned parricides by first enclosing them in the *culleus* with a dog, a cock, a snake, and a monkey, then throwing them into a river or the sea.

Chapter Two

1. Verg. *A.* 4.173–97; X. *Mem.* 2.1. The passage from Ennius is lost. Cf. Lausberg 371.

2. Cicero professes disbelief in the Furies of myth and interprets them in psychological and symbolic terms (Cic. *Leg.* 1.40; cf. *Rosc. Am.* 67; *Pis.* 46). Thus they are appropriately viewed as instances of descriptive *prosopopoeia* in his oratory. Greek oratory suggests, on the one hand, efforts to engage with traditional beliefs in the Erinyes as actual divinities (see Gagarin 23 on Antiphon's *Tetralogies*) and, on the other hand, signs of a similar skepticism (Aeschin. *Tim.* 190–91).

3. Cicero's technique reflects the politicization of Roman tragedy itself, on which see Nicolet 366–73; Gruen 1992: 183–222.

4. For Cicero's discussion of pathetic techniques in oratory, see esp. *de Orat.* 1.17, 53, 60, 2.178, 215; *Brut.* 276, 279, 322; *Orat.* 69, 128; cf., e.g., Quint. *Inst.* 6.2.8 and esp. 6.2.20: πάθος... *tragoediae magis simile* (*pathos* ... is more similar to tragedy).

5. For the pathetic display routinely engaged in by the accused in Roman lawsuit, who appeared in mourning garb, see Dyck 2001: 120.

6. For fear and pity as the emotions appropriate to tragedy, the *locus classicus* is Arist. *Po.* $1449^{b}24$–28.

7. By contrast, *Rosc. Am.* 45–51 portrays the young Roscius as a paragon of old-time Roman virtue and familial piety. On Cicero's *bonus rusticus* stereotype, see Vasaly 157–72.

8. The political argument of the *Pro Sex. Roscio Amerino* has been a subject of considerable interest and debate; I do not seek to offer new insight into this problem *per se*. In general, I agree with Gruen 1968: 265–71 that the speech we possess constitutes a harsh critique of the Sullan regime but was probably modified somewhat for publication. Cf., e.g., Kinsey 1975 and 1982; Seager. The problem of the two versions was phrased in extreme terms by Humbert 100–11. Subsequent critics have not shared his views. Buchheit 1975b provides a good introduction to the indirect and ironic means through which Cicero makes his criticisms felt.

9. On the rhetorical importance of this section to the overall effect of the speech, see esp. Stroh 1975: 55–79.

10. Aeschines insists that the origins of misfortune are not only to be found in the gods' actions but also in mankind's own depraved nature. It is not the case, he suggests, that those who have committed impiety are hounded by the Furies as in plays, but rather that men's own licentiousness and insatiability are the Furies that drive them to commit criminal acts (Aeschin. *Tim.* 190–91).

11. The *Pro Roscio Amerino* is notable for its dramatic reversal of the charges onto parties linked to the prosecution. For the *remotio criminis* as a technique, see Cic. *Inv.* 1.15, 2.71, 86–94. On Cicero's handling of the charges in general, see Butler 14–23. On the details of the case and the possibility that Roscius may in fact have been guilty, see Kinsey 1980 and 1985; Alexander 149–72; Dyck 2003.

12. For more on Cicero's portrayal of Chrysogonus and use of *ethos* in the *Pro Roscio Amerino*, see Buchheit 1975a; May 21–31.

13. Still further correspondences emerge between Cicero's descriptions of Roscius' accusers and his portrait of the parricide in general. The parricide outdoes the wild beasts in his *immanitas* (savageness) (63). So, too, Chrysogonus displays a worse than bestial *immanitas* in his relentless pursuit of Roscius' life (150). The parricide has polluted all human and divine laws (65). Chrysogonus has committed ritual pollution in breaking the sacred bond of *fides* incurred by an embassy, while T. Roscius Capito has contaminated himself with every imaginable *maleficium* (112–13, 116). The parricide is permanently stained by the parental blood he sheds and harried night and day by the consciousness of his crimes (66–67); Roscius' persecutors are perpetually involved in bloodshed and are guilty of untold murders (81: note the repetition of the phrase *dies noctesque* here and at 6 and 67).

14. Cf. Lenaghan 156 and below on Cicero's characterization of Clodius as a Fury in the *De haruspicum responso*.

15. On the Erinyes and blood, see Moreau 72 and *passim*. Cf. Cicero's characterization of Sex. Naevius in the *Pro Quinctio* (39: *sanguinem vitamque*; 46: *vitam et sanguinem*).

16. This is Madvig's emendation, adapted in Clark's Oxford text, of a slightly different wording in the manuscripts.

17. E.g., at A. *Eu.* 304–5.

18. On the exordium of the *Pro Sex. Roscio Amerino*, see Loutsch 127–74 and Cerutti 49–82. On the conventions of Ciceronian perorations, see Winterbottom.

19. Cicero here goes well beyond the narrow technical sense of the word *periculum* as a "danger" incurred by a defendant or plaintiff (*OLD* 3).

20. See *OLD*, s.v. *domesticus*.

21. Dramatic tradition anticipates Cicero's configuration of the Furies, *crudelitas*, and *nefas*. The connection between the Furies and *crudelitas* finds a close parallel in Euripides' *Orestes*. Here, the Furies are described as both divinities susceptible to prayer and figments of Orestes' fevered imagination. The Chorus, for example, prays devoutly to the Eumenides to cease their torments of Agamemnon's son and heir, while Electra tries to convince her brother that he sees none of the things he thinks he sees (E. *Or.* 259). In response to Menelaus' question, "What sickness (νόσος) is destroying you?" Orestes responds, "Conscience, for I am conscious of having committed terrible acts" (395–96). The figuration of Orestes' guilty conscious as a νόσος recalls an earlier passage in which Electra describes her brother as ἀγρίᾳ συντακεὶς νόσῳ (wasted by savage illness) (34). Orestes' ἄγρια νόσος makes him like a beast—a colt—who chafes at going under the yoke. Indeed, the adjective ἄγριος suggests life in the fields, that is to say, at the opposite topographical extreme from civilized, law-abiding life of the polis. In its savageness, Orestes' illness is thus locatable in a tradition of ancient medico-political discourse, from which the *crudelitas* of Cicero's *Pro Sex. Roscio Amerino* also draws. Should *crudelitas*, Cicero insists, afflict the minds of Cicero's jury, *inter feras*, he insists, *satius est aetatem degere quam in hac tanta immanitate versari* (it would be better to live among the wild beasts than to be in the midst of such great brutality as this) (150). The roots of

Cicero's imagery extend still further back to Euripides' own paradigm, the *Eumenides* of Aeschylus. Aeschylus repeatedly likens the Erinyes to savage beasts and wild animals (A. *Eu.* 131–32, 193–94, 644; etc.). They are described as δυσπαρήγοροι (hard to appease) (384) and, before being forced by Athena to accept their new cult status, they threaten to let loose "every kind of death" and to disregard the claims of parents against murderous children (502, 508–516). Athena warns them not to "establish in my citizens war among kin, its insolence directed toward one another," a condition that she likens to the spirit of fighting cocks (861–863; cf. 976–87). Once their change has been effected, the Eumenides pray that insatiable stasis not βρέμειν (thunder) in the polis (976–79). Cf. Cicero's fear that *crudelitas* harden the minds of the jury and wipe out their *misericordia* (pity), a condition that would make them impervious to appeasement and so renew civil strife (Cic. *Rosc. Am.* 150). Men's insolent desires, Cicero warns, may *prorumpere* (burst forth) to such a degree that murders will be committed among the very benches of the court (12). *Crudelitas* has within it the evil that has destroyed so many citizens (154). The animal, bloodthirsty desires of Roscius foes are virtually insatiable (150).

22. See chapter 1, n73.

23. Similarly, although with somewhat less irony, Cicero concludes that the victory of the *nobiles* in the recent civil war was achieved *deorum voluntate, studio populi Romani, consilio et imperio et felicitate L. Sullae* (by the will of the gods, with the enthusiasm of the Roman people, and through the planning, the command, and the good fortune of Lucius Sulla) (136).

24. Although Cicero names Sulla *honoris causa* (with honor), and later insists that Sulla was ignorant of Chrysogonus' actions (6, 25, 131–132), the doubts about their relations are a part of the speech's overall strategy, and Cicero's claims that Sulla was unaware have been read as ironic (e.g., Buchheit 1975b: 588).

25. For the trial and its context, see Gruen 1974: 283–85; Berry 14–42.

26. Catiline himself had killed M. Marius Gratidianus at the tomb of Q. Lutatius Catulus during Sulla's march on Rome in 82 BCE.

27. On the exile of Q. Caecilius Metellus Numidicus (cos. 109 BCE), cf. *Red. Sen.* 25 and *Sest.* 130–31. P. Servilius Vatia Isauricus, Cicero reports, spoke forcefully for Cicero's recall by "calling up" the dead Metelli from the underworld (cf. chapter 1, p. 28).

28. This is especially so since a "tragic" styling of Clodius' killing seems to have occurred to others involved in Milo's trial: at one point Cicero professes to be astounded that Clodius' death on the Via Appia, the road built by his ancestor Appius Claudius Caecus, has stirred up such *tragoedias* (tragedies) among those on the opposing side (18). More significant, Cicero maintains, is the fact that Clodius fell near Mount Alba in Latium, an area he had defiled (85). It is also appropriate that the killing took place near a temple of the Bona Dea, whose rites Clodius had desecrated (86). Such details prove, for Cicero, that Clodius' death was actually ordained by a divine force acting for the good of Rome. Anthony Corbeill suggests to me the interesting possibility that the Clodians might actually have styled *themselves* as Furies (through dress, props, etc.).

29. Dyck 1998.

30. See Clark and Ruebel and chapter 1.

31. On manipulation of the legal system as a feature of tyrants, see Clark and Ruebel 64.

32. The corresponding identification of Clodius with the dead Clytemnestra seems less surprising the more we take into account Cicero's overall feminization of Clodius in his invective. See Dyck 2001: 126–27; Leach. The story of Orestes, who killed his mother

to avenge his father, has an added relevance to Milo's defense insofar as Milo's accusers emphasized that his killing of Clodius on the Via Appia was an affront to the Claudian *gens*. Through the figure of Orestes, Cicero compares Milo to one who upheld familial traditions while appearing to disrupt them. Cicero thus opens the door to seeing Milo as a champion of a cause the Claudii themselves might embrace, namely, patriotism in service of a familial legacy. Clytemnestra, of course, undermined the illustrious house into which she married through murder and adultery. Clodius, Cicero insists, was likewise unworthy of the illustrious family into which he was born, while Milo is actually more worthy to be associated with the good name of the Claudii. Cicero is careful to point out that Clodius' own brother, Appius Claudius Pulcher, shares with Milo his victimization at the destructive Clodius' hands (75).

33. Brunt 63.

34. Braden 13–15.

35. Boyle 128 on Sen. *Med.* 369–79.

36. The passage in fact echoes Verg. *A.* 7.299–303, where Juno, about to summon the Fury Allecto from the underworld, complains that the Syrtes, Scylla, and Charybdis have failed to stop the Trojans in their journey (another mythical prototype for Roman imperial expansion).

37. For more on Cicero's rhetorical representation of Romans in the provinces, see Steel 21–74.

38. The second *actio* of the trial of Verres never took place due to Verres' flight into exile. Cicero retains, nevertheless, a semblance of oral performance in the material he published as his "speech." See Narducci 169–71; Butler 61–84.

39. Cicero distinguishes here between the avengers of the innocent dead, the *Poenae*, and those of the damned, the *Furiae*; cf. Cic. *Clu.* 171; *Pis.* 91.

40. See Dugan 55–74 for a recent discussion of *In Pisonem* as "a literary intervention into the political realm" (61). For more on the tragic qualities of Piso's madness, see Kubiak.

41. Suet. *Aug.* 33.1. [Longin.] *Subl.* 15.8, however, suggests that the motif persisted in some form in imperial delamation. Cf. Petr.1. On the disappearance, under Augustus, of publicly performed tragedy itself, see Coffey; Goldberg.

42. Mankin 109, 301. Cf. below, chapter 5, p. 103.

Chapter Three

1. Cf., conveniently, the inscriptions included in Appendix B of Flower 1996 (326–30): *ILLRP* 309 = *ILS* 1; *ILLRP* 310 = *ILS* 2 & 3; *ILLRP* 311 = *ILS* 4; *ILLRP* 316 = *ILS* 6; etc. On the *laudatio funebris* in general, see chapter 1.

2. Plin. *Nat.* 7.43.140 (= *ORF*[4] no. 6 fr.2): *voluisse enim primarium bellatorum esse, optimum oratorem, fortissimum imperatorem, auspicio suo maximas res geri, maximo honore uti, summa sapientia esse, summum senatorum haberi, pecuniam magnam bono modo invenire, multos liberos relinquere et clarissimum in civitate esse. Haec contigisse ei nec ulli alii post Romam conditam* (for [Q. Metellus said that] he wanted to be the most outstanding of warriors, the best orator, the bravest commander; he desired the greatest deeds to be accomplished under his auspices, and he himself to enjoy the greatest honor, to possess the utmost wisdom, to be considered the leading senator, to acquire great wealth by honest means, to leave behind many children, to be the most eminent man in

the state. These things *he* attained and not any other man in Rome's history). Metellus' eulogy was delivered in 221 BCE.

3. Most obvious is the asyndeton that marks Cicero's catalogue of Caesar's virtues and achievements. Metellus' list of his father's achievements, for example, almost entirely lacks connectives, as do many similar passages in the inscriptions associated with the tomb of the Scipios as well as the later *"Laudatio Turiae"* and *Laudatio Murdiae.* With the alliteration and cumulative structure of *Phil.* 2.116 cf. esp. *Laudatio Murdiae* (*CIL* VI 10230 = *ILS* 8394, lines 27–30. The abstracts *cogitatio* and *diligentia* recall the funereal emphasis on *sapientia,* while *ingenium* is a term applied to the Scipios and others. The repetition of the adjective *magnus* echoes its repetition (often in the superlative) in the Metellan *laudatio.* Finally, even the very phrase with which Cicero begins his praise of Caesar, *Fuit in illo,* suggests funereal texts such as the Scipionic inscriptions for the prominence of the perfect form of *esse* and the close conjunction of this verb with the demonstrative pronoun (*ILLRP* 310 = *ILS* 3, lines 2, 4: *duonoro optumo fuise viro / . . . consol, censor, aidilis hic fuet a[pud vos]; ILLRP* 309 = *ILS 1,* lines 2–4: *fortis vir sapiensque, / quoius forma virtutei parisuma fuit; / consol, censor, aidilis quei fuit apud vos;* cf. the epitaph of A. Atilius Caiatinus, which Cicero himself quotes in another context: *hunc unum plurimae consentiunt gentes populi primarium fuisse virum* [Cic. *Sen.* 61; cf. *Fin.* 2.116; *Tusc.* 1.13]). In general, the economy of expression demonstrated by Cicero's praise of Caesar in the *Second Philippic* is in keeping with Cicero's own prescriptions for the Roman *laudatio:* delivered in the forum as a testimony to character, it has *brevitationem . . . nudam atque inornatam* (a bare and unadorned brevity); composed specifically as a funeral speech, it is *ad orationis laudem minime accomodata* (least suited to a display of oratorical excellence) (Cic. *de Orat.* 2.341).

4. For Cicero's attitudes, see, e.g., Mitchell 252–66.

5. Cf. Dugan, who argues for Cicero's *Pro Archia* as a "pre-mortem *laudatio funebris*" for Cicero himself, allowing "Cicero's self-presentation . . . to assume the perspective of ultimate monumentality and the authority of a narrative that has reached its final conclusion" (43) especially in contrast to the narrative of illegiticmacy and failure he uses to characterize L. Calpurnius Piso Caesoninus in *In Pisonem* (cf. my discussion of similar aspects of this speech in chapter 2 and cf. chapter 1 on the adaptation of *laudatio funebris* in the *Pro Caelio*). For another recollection of *laudatio funebris* earlier in the *Second Philippic,* see below on *Phil.* 2.69 and, for Antonius' devotion to Caesar's *species,* on Cic. *Phil.* 13.46.

6. On Cicero's expressed reasons for silence, and his circulation of the written text, first to Atticus and then to a wider audience, see Ramsey 158–59; Shackleton Bailey 1986: 31. There has been some debate over the *Second Philippic's* exact date of "publication"; however, as Ramsey observes, the prevailing theory is the most likely: the speech, which had already been sent to Atticus for comment and accordingly revised (cf. Cic. *Att.* 16.11), "was put into circulation not long after Antony left Rome for Cisaline Gaul on the night of 28/29 Nov." (158). The threat posed by force of arms to the practice of free oratory had been among Cicero's preoccupations during his withdrawal from politics under Caesar's dictatorship, and a belief in the impossibility of oratory as he had known it was responsible in part for his return to study, and the burst of creative activity that produced the rhetorical works *Brutus* and *Orator* in 46 BCE. In the *Brutus,* Cicero recalls it as one of his great disappointments that at a time (the outbreak of the civil war) when the authority and oratory of a good citizen could have wrenched the weapons from the hands of irate citizens, men's error or fear made the advocacy of peaceful measures impossible (7).

A similar theme recurs in the *Second Philippic* itself, as at section 108, near the speech's conclusion, when Cicero recalls that already on the Kalends of June, 44 BCE, the Senate was prevented from meeting by Antonius' show of arms.

7. On the *Second Philippic* as a *contentio dicendi*, see Craig 154; cf. Butler 117–23, who rightly points out that Cicero is also aware of the text of the *Second Philippic* as a document for posterity.

8. For Bourdieu's theory of "objectification" and "embodiment," see n27 below.

9. For a full account of the events pertaining to Caesar's divinization see, above all, Weinstock, with the review by North. See further Taylor; Dobesch; Gesche; Alföldi 1973 and 1985.

10. For the divine qualities of the illustrious dead, cf., e.g., Cic. *Scaur.* 50 (on Scaurus' *animus* [spirit]); Cic. *Rab. Perd.* 29–30 (on great men's *mentes* [minds]); etc.

11. On the cult and the temple, see Weinstock 385–410.

12. On his identity, see Meijer. His activities are the source of much uncertainty. Cicero's suggestion of a funeral monument accompanied by a column must be taken together with the indication of an *ara* (altar), apparently described by Brutus and Cassius in a letter complaining to Antonius that Caesar's veterans planned to rebuild it. See Weinstock 364 on Cic. *Phil.* 1.5; 1.30; 2.107; *Att.* 14.15.1; 14.16.2; *Fam.* 9.14.1; 12.1.1; Lactantius, *Divinae institutiones* 1.15.30. D.C. 44.51.1 refers to a βωμός (altar) and Appian actually ascribes the erection of a βωμός to Pseudo-Marius (see App. *BC* 2.148.616, 3.2.3, 3.3.7). Suet. *Jul.* 85 reports that sacrifice at a *columna* went on "for a long time"; Weinstock 365 assumes this to be a column set up by Octavian after Dolabella's destruction of Amatius' monument. Weinstock understands Cic. *Phil.* 2.107 to suggest "that there was no column in September or that there was a different one with which Antonius was not connected" and proposes that Amatius began building an altar that remained unfinished and unused before being destroyed by Dolabella and later restored by Octavian (365).

13. Weinstock 272–73, 281–84, 367–68.

14. This is the title by which scholars have assumed the games were known in 44, their name having been altered from *ludi Veneris Genetricis;* reassessing the evidence, however, Ramsey and Licht argue that "the festival is likely to have continued to be called the *ludi Veneris Genetricis* for some years after [July of 44], becoming only later, in the early Augustan age, the *ludi Victoriae Caesaris*" (8).

15. Although we are also told by Pliny (*Nat.* 23.94) that he privately interpreted the comet as "born for his own sake and himself as born in it." Gurval 1997: 41–42 convincingly maintains that the comet "may be better understood as a construction of Augustan politics, an ideological myth whose origins and development are more complex than an immediate and full embrace of an astronomical phenomenon and may, in fact, belong to a period significantly later than the games in July of 44."

16. For discussion and bibliography on the *sidus Iulium* or *Caesaris astrum* motif, see esp. Zanker 33–37; cf. Weinstock 370–384.

17. Weinstock 365.

18. See Weinstock 385; but cf. Gesche 74–79. On *supplicationes*, see Halkin and following note.

19. Weinstock 385.

20. In each reference to Caesar in the dative (through the repeated noun *mortuo* and then through the pronoun *ei*) Cicero introduces ambiguity, still unresolved in modern discussions, as to whether the ceremonies in question would simply be in Caesar's honor, actually take him as their object, or, still more remarkably, identify him with the high

gods (*cum deorum immortalium religione*). Gesche 74–78, for instance, differentiating between "normal" *supplicationes* and those proposed for the dead Caesar, suggests that the *supplicationes* were directed *to* Caesar as a god, but that Antonius himself did not, in fact, propose them. Weinstock 385, however, speaks of supplications "for" Caesar; cf. Ker 33; Alföldi 1973: 114; Lacey 238; Shackleton Bailey 1986: 13 n23. *Supplicationes* could be offered *in honor* of a living man, as they had been for Caesar, Cicero, and others and would be later for Antonius and Octavian (see Halkin 15–76; for Cicero's pride in this honor, see esp. Cic. *Cat.* 3.15ff.). In fact, Cicero's words allow for more than one possibility. The very addition, for instance, of a day in honor of Caesar could be construed as admitting "religious taints" into the state and associating a dead man with the worship of the gods (cf. Ramsey 110). On the other hand, one could understand Cicero's words to mean that Caesar was to be numbered among the "immortal gods" as a recipient of *supplicationes*. What we can reconstruct of Antonius' own actions exacerbates rather than relieves our doubt. Antonius pursued a cautious policy with regard to Caesar's divinity (see above, pp. 58–59). At the time of the delivery of the *Second Philippic,* he had not yet put into effect all of the measures glorifying Caesar with apparently divine honors, an omission that Cicero regards as inconsistency.

21. As Ramsey notes, Cicero "seems to be thinking of the lesson to be learned from putting too much trust in Caesar. Caesar's success in imposing tyranny should cause the Roman people to be on their guard against all future politicians who pursue the path taken by Caesar and who have charisma" (334).

22. Somewhat contradictory reports survive as to the exact nature of Antonius' eulogy for Caesar. Appian's account has Antonius reading the honors decreed for Caesar and the oaths sworn for his safety, then gesturing to the temple of Jupiter on the Capitoline and stating that he was ready to avenge him; after the oration proper, Antonius intones a hymn to Caesar, recites his achievements, and weeps, then uncovers Caesar's body and engages in a choral lament with the audience. However many of the details of Appian's account they accept, scholars are in general agreement that the ceremony was "not . . . a traditional Roman funeral laudation" (Kennedy 1968: 105; cf. Kierdorf 153; Weinstock 352). Even for Antonius, as consul, to deliver it, was an innovation, since a family member was the normal choice. Cicero certainly expresses doubt about the legitimacy of Caesar's funeral as a whole: *si illud funus fuit* (if funeral it was), he remarks (*Phil.* 2.90).

23. It is of interest that the new senators appointed by Antonius on the basis of Caesar's purported documents were known popularly as *orcivi* or perhaps *orcini,* the epithet used for slaves set free "thanks to Orcus," i.e., by the terms of their masters' wills (Suet. *Aug.* 35.1; cf. Plu. *Ant.* 15.3). Not unrelated in theme are Cicero's repeated references to Caesar's own entourage of disreputable politicians as νέκυια (conjuring of the dead) (*Att.* 9.10.7; 11.2; 18.2; cf. Powell 85).

24. Metellus' son praised his dead father for being a great orator and a great general as well as for leaving behind many children (see above, n2).

25. A famous example is the epitaph of A. Atilius Caiatinus, which Cicero himself quotes in another context (see above n3); cf. *ILLRP* 310 = *ILS* 3, line 1: *Honc oino ploirume consentiont . . .*). In a related manner, the *Laudatio Murdiae* declares, *constitit . . . ergo in hoc sibi ipsa ut . . . post decessum consensu civium laudaretur* (She was self-consistent, with the result that . . . after death she was praised by consensus of the citizens) (*CIL* VI 10230 = *ILS* 8394, lines 14–17). The *laudator* of L. Caecilius Metellus recognizes public opinion in a different way by stating that the deceased wanted *summum senatorem haberi* (to be thought the most eminent senator) (see above, n2).

26. *ILLRP* 310 = *ILS* 3, line 2: *duonoro optumo fuise viro;* cf. the epitaph of A. Atilius Caiatinus quoted above, n3.

27. On "objectification" and "embodiment," see Bourdieu 1977: 87–95; cf. Bourdieu 1990: 52–65.

28. Bourdieu 1977: 72.

29. Ibid., 170.

30. On Cicero's discussion of honors for Sulpicius in this speech and its connection to his defense of the *res publica,* see Kröner.

31. It is significant that Cicero probably alludes here to the gilded statue of Octavian on horseback that was voted to him on January 2 of 43 BCE (on the image, see Zanker 37–39).

32. Liv. fr. 120 draws the connection between the display of Cicero's hands and head and his writings and speeches against Antonius.

33. On the Greek character of Cicero's proposed eulogy, see Loraux 384 n. 96 and Sordi, who likewise argues for Cicero's innovation in this regard. Cicero envisions an elaborate public funeral and a common grave that would be, in effect, an altar to *Virtus* (Cic. *Phil.* 14.34).

34. Allowing the state to "speak" for itself is, we may observe, a quintessentially republican act. Cicero had introduced a *prosopopoeia* of the *res publica* in the conclusion of *In Catilinam I* to magnify the sense of the danger posed by Catiline and his followers (*Cat.* 1.27–29).

35. On the much-studied question of Demosthenic influence, see Weische 100–104, 166–94, and *passim;* Stroh 1982 and 1983; Wooten; Schäublin.

36. Cf. Mitchell 289–326.

37. Cf, e.g., Galinsky 45–47, 73–74 with bibliography. Galinsky rightly points out the naïveté of the traditional picture "of the young Octavian learning about the value of republican principles at Cicero's knees in 44–43 B.C." (73).

38. Spengler, vol. 2: 433.

39. Baehr 260 on Riencout 269–91.

40. Cf. Habinek and Schiesaro xv–xvi. As they point out, the change of this period is hardly "revolution" from a Marxist standpoint in that it did nothing to alter the agrarian, slave-dependent economic base of Roman society. Syme's view bears a superficial resemblance to Marxism, however, in interpreting culture as secondary to more basic shifts in power.

41. Cf., e.g., Galinsky 9. The distinctive aspect of Augustan culture, in Galinsky's view, is its gradual inspiration by ideas, ideals, and values that found expression across a wide range of cultural activity.

42. E.g., at *Phil.* 2.108.

Chapter Four

1. For recent bibliographies of both Prop. 4.7 and 4.11, see Janan 100–13, 146–63. I make no attempt here to provide an exhaustive account of the vast scholarship on these two famous poems. For the purposes of this chapter, seminal studies include (on 4.7) Yardley and Warden; (on 4.11) Williams 1968: 387–400; Reitzenstein 1969; Hallett 1985; (on the two poems together) Hallett 1973; Lange; Janan; Wyke 78–114; cf. the commentaries of Camps and Richardson. Additional works cited in the individual analyses of the poems below.

2. Flower 1996: 223–55.

3. The Augustan aristocracy was very different in composition from that of the Republic, many members of old families having died in the civil wars of the 40s and 30s BCE, and a new elite drawn from the Italian municipalities predominant by 19 BCE. This new elite prided itself to some extent upon inherent *virtus* and *industria* rather than the privilege inherited from old *nobilitas*. And yet fascination with claims of exemplary ancestry, and the practices through which these claims became public knowledge, remained.

4. The declaimers' topics included the questions of whether Cicero should seek absolution from Antonius (Sen. *Suas.* 6), whether he should burn his books in exchange for Antonius' sparing of his life (*Suas.* 7), and whether Cicero's purported killer, Popillius, had acted wrongly in view of the fact that Cicero had once successfully defended him on a charge of parricide (*Controv.* 7.2). The social, cultural, and political implications of imperial declamation are a topic of growing interest among scholars. See Bloomer; Beard; Kaster; Gunderson. On the Cicero declamations, see recently Dugan 70–74, esp. 71: "The *suasoriae* re-stage Cicero's death and, by extension, the republican oratorical traditions that disappeared with him, with a compulsiveness that indicates the trauma of this event, as they seek to achieve mastery over this original loss." Further bibliography in Gunderson 1–25.

5. See chapter 1, n2.

6. Wyke 182.

7. Cf. Dupont 1997. For more on imperial *recitationes,* see Pennacini 254–67; Valette-Cagnac 111–69.

8. See esp. Gold 1993a; Miller 1999; Janan; Miller 2004.

9. Performance has been little emphasized, until recently, in Propertian criticism, partly through the influence of views like that of Quinn 142: "the [Augustan] poet thinks of himself as a writer rather than a performer." Ovid, however, recalls that Propertius "was accustomed often to recite his fiery loves / according to the obligation of fellowship that joined him to me" (*saepe suos solitus recitare . . . ignes / iure sodalicii, quo mihi iunctus erat* [Ov. *Tr.* 4.10.45–46]) and even Quinn admits that "the written text continues to be felt as no more than the basis for a performance" with the "normal route of access to a work," usually "a private reading by the author to a small group" (Quinn 144–45), i.e., the *recitatio.* Interpretations of Propertian elegy in performance include Gamel and Wyke, both of whom focus on aspects of gender-representation. For Wyke, Propertian elegy, "as a form of poetry recited before an audience of the Roman elite, . . . was part of an institutionalized system of representation—a social technology—through which gender was performed and, therefore, constructed at Rome" (189). Gamel emphasizes the implications of performance for isolating the meaning of elegiac texts. Gamel 79: "A reader/performer invests more—physically, emotionally, and intellectually—in interpretive choices than a silent reader does. Selecting between alternatives makes a performer more conscious of choices: reading as performance makes those choices more precise and more vivid, and the implications—psychological, social, ethical—of such reading/performance become clearer to both performer and audience" (93–94). For more on Latin poetry in performance, see, e.g., Skinner 1993 on Catullus; Gold 1998, Reckford, and Walters on Roman satire; Markus on imperial epic; cf. chapter 5 with bibliography on Vergil's *Aeneid.*

10. This passage would have been well known to Propertius' elite audiences, for whom rhetorical training was a mainstay of education. For Cic. *Cael.* 33–34 as a textbook

example of *mortuos* [or *defunctos*] *excitare*, see Quint. *Inst.* 12.10.61; Aquila Romanus 3.

11. On the Homeric echoes of Prop. 4.7, see, e.g., Dimundo 27–39. For the poem's oratorical and legalistic cast, cf. Guillemin 190–91; Warden 37.

12. The preposition *sub* in line 95 also has "a legalistic flavor" (Richardson 462).

13. Cf. Warden 37; Guillemin 190–91. The familiarity of poisoning as a charge in rhetorical school declamation (on which see Krokowski 95; Warden 37) would have made it all the more likely for Propertius' audience to draw a connection between Prop. 4.7 and the republican oratorical tradition.

14. Warden 37. Yardley further ties Prop. 4.7 to a Roman context of commemoration through noting its echoes of the sepulchral epigram, while Janan 100–13 illuminates the affinities and tensions between the elegiac discourse of Prop. 4.7 and that surrounding the *mos maiorum* (custom of the ancestors). For Appius' monologue as *laudatio funebris*, see chapter 1, pp. 25–26.

15. Cf. Cicero's account of Servilius' evocation of the dead Metelli in *Red. Sen.* 25–26 and *Sest.* 130–31. V. Max. 6.2.8 describes Helvius Mancia Formianus' description of the illustrious Roman dead, victims of civil war, he claims to have seen in the underworld.

16. The reading of all MSS; for the translation, see Richardson 455. In spite of comparanda such as Hor. *Carm.* 2.1.17, I am unable to understand *murmur* as the sound of a trumpet here, and so cannot adopt, with Goold (356), *tubae* for *viae*. The whole point of Cynthia's complaint in verses 25–34 is that her funeral lacked the trappings of an elaborate ceremony (even a proper head-rest for her corpse [26]) that would have included musical accompaniment. Propertius' Cornelia, by contrast, was escorted to the grave with *tubae* (4.11.9). Cf. Dimundo 104–5.

17. Cf. the conventional address, *Siste, viator* (Halt, wayfarer), so prominent in the sepulcral tradition that likewise forms a background for Prop. 4.7 (Yardley 83–84).

18. Richardson 455.

19. Ibid.

20. Cf. Flaschenriem, who notes as well that Cynthia's grave is located "at a perceptible distance from the imaginative and aesthetic world regularly inhabited by the Propertian *amator*" (56).

21. On Propertian elegy as a dialogue of contesting voices, cf. Flaschenriem 63; Wyke 78–114. For more on the complexity of "Cynthia's" persona, see Gold 1993a and 1993b.

22. Gold 1993a: 88.

23. On Cynthia's programmatic qualities in Prop. 4.7 and 4.8 and her significance within the larger programmatic statement of Book 4, see esp. Wyke 99–108 with bibliography. Cf. Johnson 177–80.

24. Janan 100–113. Cf. Flaschenriem, who calls attention to the Cynthia of Prop. 4.7 as "a maker of 'texts' that emphasize her autonomy from the poet-lover" (49).

25. On the humor of Cynthia's tirade, cf. Johnson 177–78.

26. Cf. Flaschenriem's account of Cynthia as an "authorial figure" in Prop. 4.7: "like the Propertian lover, [Cynthia] too is preoccupied with the problem of constructing a poetic persona, and with how this 'self' will be perceived in the public realm" (55–56).

27. For oratory and funeral ritual in Prop. 4.11, see, e.g., Reitzenstein 1969; Williams 1968: 390–400; Hallett 1985; Janan 146–163; Wyke 109, 113.

28. As Hallett reminds us, Augustus had also honored Cornelia's ancestress, the daughter of Scipio Africanus the Elder, by placing a bronze statue of her in a colonnade honoring Augustus' own sister (Hallett 1985: 82–83 citing Plin. *Nat.* 34.14.31). Caesar's wife's father, we should recall, was not a Scipio, but L. Cornelius Cinna (cos. 87) (Cornelia's father is an unidentified Cornelius Scipio). On the Roman custom of *laudationes* for

women, and the extant "*Laudatio Turiae*" and *Laudatio Murdiae* (which probably belong to a context of private eulogy rather than the public one recalled in Prop. 4.11), see Durry; Kierdorf 112–16; Flower 131–32.

29. Quint. *Inst.* 12.6.1; Suet. *Aug.* 8.1; Nic. Dam. *FGrH* no. 90 fr. 127.

30. On Q. Claudia, see Bömer 1964 and Scheid 2001. The Vestal Virgin of Cicero *Cael.* 34 is another Claudia, while Prop. 4.11.53–54 is usually taken to refer to a certain Aemilia (cf. Camps and Richardson *ad loc.*), although Scheid 2001: 23 seems to suggest that this is also Claudia the Vestal.

31. Hallett 1989: 77 n39; cf. 76 n25.

32. Cf. Janan 163; Wyke 113.

33. For Augustus' close relationship to the Cornelii, see Hallett 1985: 82–83. Her reading of Prop. 4.11 as a precursor to and even influence on Augustus' *Res Gestae* illustrates all the more how the poem can be understood as belonging to an Augustan rather than a republican commemorative context.

34. See Richardson 485 for the possible criticism of Paullus' censorship at Prop. 4.11.41 (*me neque censurae legem mollisse* [that I did not cause the censor's law to be relaxed]). On Paullus' censorship itself, see Vell. 2.95.

35. For references, see Janan 210 n2.

36. La Penna 1951: 86–88; Hallett 1973; Hubbard 145–49; Sullivan 44; LaPenna 1977: 94–95. See Janan 147 for a useful summary of additional scholarship, including Stahl 1985: 262 (who finds in Prop. 4.11 a capitulation to Augustan ideology; cf. Wyke 111–12); Highet 98–105; Luck 1959: 115; and Reitzenstein 1969 (who read the poem as a tribute to marital virtues). For the intersection of Cornelia's virtues with Augustan moral ideology, see Williams 1968: 388–400.

37. Richardson 481; Janan 159–63.

38. Johnson 173–76.

39. Miller 1999: 198.

40. Except, that is, obliquely in v. 57: *laudor . . . urbisque querellis* (and I am praised . . . by the city's lamentations).

41. Cf. Kennedy 1972: 301–4, although I am less inclined than Kennedy to see Augustan oratory as imbued with a sense of inhibition, anxiety, or frustration (cf. Kennedy 1972: 303). Prop. 4.7 and 4.11 suggest the extent to which the vibrancy and popularity of imperial declamation and judicial oratory could be turned toward the inspired transformation of its republican heritage.

42. In Schechner's terminology, Prop. 4.7 and 4.11, somewhat like Japanese Noh drama (see Schechner 1985: 44–45), hover between the restoration of a historically verifiable "event" (e.g., the speech that Cicero's *Pro Caelio* supposedly records) and a "nonevent" (a reconstructed idea of republican oratory in general).

43. Janan 4. Janan 4–6 emphasizes the tensions and contradictions in aspects of the Forum's iconography, which would allow Augustan audiences to bring an "intensified awareness of their culture's internal contradictions to their reading of the Propertian corpus" (4). Zanker (*passim*) remains the fundamental discussion of the Forum's imagery. For an illuminating discussion of Propertius' poetic engagement with Augustan monuments, see Welch 2005.

44. From this perspective, we might group Propertius' poetic genealogies (e.g., 2.34.85–94, 3.1.1–4) together with Prop. 4.7 and 4.11 as products of a similar response to the Augustan context. Cf. below on Prop. 3.1.

45. The Appius passage of the *Pro Caelio* is only one among many places in Cicero's speeches where he promotes the imitation of the exemplary dead (*imitatio maiorum*)

as a practice in which all true Romans engage. Cf. Cic. *Clu.* 196; *Flac.* 101; *Red. Sen.* 25; *Sest.*130; *Phil.*1.13, 2.26, 3.25, 13.29; etc. On Cicero's conception of *imitatio maiorum,* see Cic. *Off.* 1.116, 121.

46. For a wider discussion of *exempla* and exemplarity in Propertius, see Gazich, who likewise suggests a connection between elegy and oratory in this respect.

47. Stahl 1985: 197, for example, calls Propertius' pose in Prop. 3.9 "cheeky"; cf. Sullivan 17. For the poem as a self-deprecatory celebration of Maecenas, see Bennett; Shackleton Bailey 1967: 165–66.

48. Although Propertius goes much further than Cicero in imagining himself declared a "god" (3.9.46).

49. On praise for the audience as a feature of the *prooemium* aimed at inducing *benevolentia,* see Cic. *Inv.* 1.22; Quint. *Inst.* 4.1.16; cf. Hor. *Carm.* 1.1.1 for Horace's address to Maecenas the scion of kings.

50. In rhetorical terms, Prop. 3.9.21–34 corresponds to orator's use of historical *exempla,* which are both plausible and true (cf. *Rhet. Her.* 1.13). Quintilian defines *exemplum* as *rei gestae aut ut gestae utilis ad persuadendum id quod intenderis commemoratio* (the recollection of a deed performed or as though performed for the purposes of persuading [the audience] of that which you are claiming) (Quint. *Inst.* 5.11.6).

51. On the relation of *mores* to *ethos* see Quint. *Inst.* 6.2.8.

52. For the *duplex ratio* of the peroration (*in rebus* and *in affectibus*), see Quint. *Inst.* 6.1.1.

53. Cf. Wyke 114.

54. E.g., *Rosc. Am.* 23, 113; *Mil.* 104; *Phil.* 1.13; etc.

55. Cf. Tibullus' hope that the retinue who accompanies Messalla on his journey across the Aegean will, like Messalla himself, remember him (Tib. 1.3.2): *o utinam memores ipse cohorsque mihi* (oh, would that you and your cohort may remember me). Propertius' *iace verba* (77) in fact suggests unguarded speech of the kind that may be reported elsewhere. Cf. Cic. *Cat.* 4.14: *iaciuntur . . . voces quae perveniunt ad auris meas* (remarks are being thrown about that reach my ears).

56. As James Zetzel points out, "The fact that poetry is immortal and can share that immortality with its subject is itself a reversal of the traditional Roman roles of patron and client" (Zetzel 1982: 101).

57. Kierdorf 111.

58. Thus my account of the poems accords well with recent critics' varying interpretations of Book 4's relation to the earlier books. For Miller, "the elegiac subject has become definitively displaced [in Book 4], no longer speaking as if it were the poet. . . . Instead, we have a figure that sometimes represents Propertius . . . but who has no discernible location and seems oddly separate from the first-person speaker of books 1–3" (2004: 187). For DeBrohun, conversely, "Propertius does not ultimately present a complete about-face in Book 4; to do so would have required a complete exposure and destruction of his former *ego,* an aspect of his elegiac identity the poet was not prepared to abandon altogether. . . . Propertius' final book is aetiological in two competing senses, as the elegist simultaneously explores the present and past both of Rome and of his own elegiac poetry" (23).

59. Heiden (161–62) documents many of the interpretive questions the poem has raised for scholars and goes on to propose a new scenario possibly arising from the undefined relationship between Gallus, his addressee, and the "sister" of line 6. Goold (97) interprets Gallus as already dead when he speaks in Prop. 1.21.

60. Heiden 166–67. On the similarities between Prop. 1.21 and the language of epitaphic inscriptions, see Williams 1968: 177–81; Hodge and Buttimore 210–14: Fedeli 485–95.

61. Putnam 1976 remains an excellent introduction to this feature of Prop. 1.22. Cf., more recently, Stahl 1985: 99–129; Janan 50–52. The poem's status as Book 1's *sphragis* (seal) suggests to the reader that Prop. 1.22 is especially indicative of Propertius' general concerns.

62. For a different perspective on images of death in Propertius and Tibullus, see Müller. I am grateful to Rachel Sternberg for allowing me to read her unpublished paper on a similar theme.

63. An image of death's barrenness also punctuates Tib.1.10 (33–38).

64. The six surviving poems of Lygdamus (included in the spurious Book 3 of Tibullus) include one that looks forward to private commemoration of the dead poet by his wife and her mother ([Tib.] 3.2). It concludes with an epitaph that the poet hopes will be *in celebri fronte* (on the face [of a stone] viewed by many) (28). This suggests Propertius' concerns to some extent, but commemoration hardly receives the same emphasis here as in Prop. 2.1. In [Tib.] 3.5, Lygdamus, sick, expresses his hope that his friends will remember him, but goes no further. The poems of Sulpicia ([Tib.] 3.13–18) offer no significant points of comparison with Propertius' in this regard.

65. More typical of Ovid are self-confident assertions that his fame will live on through his work (*Am.* 1.3.25–26; 1.15; etc.)

66. The lines are perhaps a parody of Propertius in particular. For the concluding epigram as a Propertian device, see Richardson 218.

67. See Dufallo 2005.

Chapter Five

1. Propertius himself may have been inspired by the Vergilian precedent. For the *Aeneid* as a subtext to Elegy 4.11, which postdates it, see Wyke 113; Williams 1968: 395–400.

2. For the idea of cultural "alternatives" I employ here, I am particularly indebted to Andrew Feldherr's discussion of Livy's *History* as an "alternative of drama" that "differentiates the 'spectacles' his own text offers from other, less beneficial, forms of visual display" (1998: 165). To the extent it also recuperates past performance traditions from an Augustan perspective, Livy's text can be seen as the *Aeneid*'s great prose counterpart in the terms I develop.

3. While all ancient poetry was written to be read aloud (cf. the previous chapter), we possess a series of testimonia pertaining to special performances of Vergil's work. For a compilation of the evidence, see Quinn. The *vita Donati* relates that Vergil recited *Aeneid* 2, 4, and 6 for Augustus (32). This is the source of the famous story that Octavia fainted when she heard Vergil name her recently dead son, Marcellus, among the spirits of Roman heroes. Servius, too, mentions Vergil's reading of Book 4 before Augustus and a small group, and we hear of still other performances before different audiences as well (Serv. *A.* 4.323; cf. *vita Donati* 33). During Vergil's lifetime, his works were adapted for performance in the theater and became a feature of recitations in school curricula (Suet. *Gram.* 16; Serv. *Ecl.* 6.11; *vita Donati* 26; cf. Quinn 151–54). See Markus on important differences between these kinds of performance. For the "oral mindset" and "rich oral residue" of the *Aeneid* as a text, see Campbell.

4. For a similar emphasis in recent criticism, see Bell, who, examining the *Aeneid*'s "popular poetics and politics," argues that the poem casts the figure of the leader in a popular image as preeminent at public spectacles; Feldherr 1995 considers *Aeneid* 5 and Augustan circus spectacle; see further Pomathios. On the popular audience of the *Aeneid* in antiquity, see also Horsfall 1995: 251–52.

5. Williams 1967: 35; cf., e.g, Williams 1983: 105.

6. Ovid seems to have remarked on the affinities between the Remus story and Vergil's Hector in modeling his account of Remus' ghost (*Fast.* 5.457–76) on the Vergilian passage (Hinds 146 n46; Bömer 1958 *ad* Ov. *Fast.* 5.460). In Nicoll's view, Vergil reworks the story of Remus' death again in the death of Palinurus at the close of *Aeneid* 5 (Nicoll 466–70).

7. Aeneas' dream has clear antecedents in the Greco-Roman epic tradition reaching back to Homer, but such scenes are less than fully adequate as explanatory models. The main precedents are Ennius' dream of Homer at the beginning of the *Annales* and Achilles' dream of Patroclus at *Iliad* 23.65–101 (e.g., Clark 833–34; Wigodsky 73–74). Hector, however, is not easily assimilable either to a Greek poet or to the unburied ghost of Achilles' close companion. Remus, it should be noted, was not alone among mythical figures whose actions and deaths were said to have contributed to ongoing Roman suffering. Vergil himself points to another such tradition in his recollection of the curse of Hector's own grandfather, Laomedon, at the end of *Georgics* 1 (501–502).

8. On Apollo in Augustan ideology, see Galinsky 188–89, 215–19, 297–99, 314.

9. Aeneas' wife Creusa was one of Hector's sisters. In Latin terms, Aeneas would be Hector's *sororius*. Aeneas calls attention to the relationship between Hector and himself at *A.* 12.439–40: *te animo repetentem exempla tuorum / et pater Aeneas et avunculus excitet Hector* (both your father Aeneas and your uncle Hector will inspire you as you recall models among your family), and the same connection is made by Andromache at 3.342–43. Aeneas' closeness with Hector is all the more noteworthy since stories of archaic Roman families tended to stress the opposition between a harsh father and an indulgent or protective *avunculus* (uncle [lit. "little grandfather"]). See Bettini 1991: 39–66.

10. In a brilliant revisionist argument, Wiseman 1995 associates the creation of the Remus story with plebeian aspirations in the fourth century BCE and links the death of Remus to foundation-sacrifice in 296 BCE, when Rome was threatened by alliance of Etruscans, Samnites, and Gauls (Wiseman 1995: 117–25). (The conventional date for the emergence of Latin literature is 240 BCE, when Livius Andronicus produced his first play.) Other scholars would make the Remus legend even older. See Wiseman 1995: 18–42, 89–102 with bibliography.

11. Cf. DuQuesnay 20–21. For the dating of Horace's *Epodes* and their association with the historical context of the late 30s BCE, see Mankin 10–12. The collection may have been published as a whole in 30 BCE. On Horace's response to civil war in the *Epodes,* see further Oliensis 64–101.

12. See chapter 2, n42.

13. DuQuesnay 38–39 suggests that the poem reflects the propaganda of Octavian against Sex. Pompeius, associated, though Nigidius Figulus, with the Pythagoreans, to whom arcane practices including necromancy were often attributed. Cf. Anderson; Oliensis 68–77; Welch 2001; Cic. *Vat.* 14; Plin. *Nat.* 7.52.178–79.

14. On the potential ambiguity of the passage, see the conclusion, p. 125.

15. Many other passages in Augustan poetry express distress over Rome's history of

civil war without referring directly to Remus. See Gurval 1995, esp. chapters 3–6 on Horace, Propertius, and Vergil.

16. Bacon 312–14; Feeney 1986: 9; cf. O'Hara 151–55 and 155–63 on the debate over the identity of the Caesar (Julius or Augustus) referred to in lines 286–96.

17. The Trojans are of Italian descent through their ancestor Dardanus (cf. *A.* 3.94–96, 163–68, 7.240–42, etc.).

18. As Mackie points out, moreover, Dido and Turnus are distant cousins through their common Argive descent; the conflict between the Greeks and the Trojans thus repeats itself, to some extent, in Aeneas' encounters with them. For further implications of this connection, see Hannah.

19. For the "exorcism" of the Carthaginian component of Dido's curse, see Williams 1972: 513.

20. On the problem of the *parva Troia,* see Grimm; Bright; Quint 53–65; Bettini 1997.

21. Serv. auct. *A.* 3.306; cf. Grimm 155; Bright 43; Quint 59; Bettini 1997: 13–14.

22. Egan 39.

23. Quint 53–65. Serv. *ad A.* 3.46 explains that Vergil drew the idea for the growing spears that transfix Polydorus from the tradition that Romulus, after the augury confirming him as ruler of Rome, scaled the Palatine and there planted his spear, which took leaf and became a tree. H. P. Stahl, too, thinks that the episode helps identify Aeneas as "king" of the Trojans: "If [Aeneas] acquired his position by default, it is highly desirable that the death of Priam's last surviving son is confirmed, of the son whom the king of Troy has spirited away when the city's situation began to turn hopeless." But, like Quint, Stahl detects a reference to the context of civil war. Aeneas' situation, for Stahl, mirrors that of Octavian faced with Antonius' claim to guardianship of Julius Caesar's son, Caesarion, whom Octavian was quick to have assassinated after the fall of Alexandria. Aeneas, for Stahl, "is placed in a more humane position: he only has to take care of a decent burial" (Stahl 1998b: 43–44).

24. Vergil's debt to Euripides' *Hecuba* in the Polydorus episode of *Aeneid* 3 has been evident to scholars at least since Heinze (1957: 105 n1) remarked a series of verbal echoes between Vergil's text and two passages in Euripides' play: the prologue spoken by Polydorus' ghost and the trial of Polymestor near the drama's conclusion.

25. See chapter 1, n72.

26. Ennius' Latin adaptation of Euripides' play assures familiarity among the *Aeneid*'s original audiences with the great trial scene that concludes the *Hecuba* (E. *Hec.* 1109–292). Cf. Enn. *scen.* 194–212 Vahlen. Accius, too, composed a *Hecuba,* whose one surviving fragment (Acc. *trag.* 481 Ribbeck) echoes E. *Hec.* 584.

27. In the course of the play, Hecuba has also lost her daughter Polyxena, who has become a human sacrifice to the ghost of Achilles.

28. Polymestor's prophecy (1259ff.) further undermines Hecuba's judicial success in looking forward to her renewed suffering when, transformed into a bitch, she will fall from a ship's mast at sea.

29. It is perhaps worth recalling that Thrace, a troublesome region for Augustus, did not become a Roman province until 46 CE.

30. Cf. Putnam 1980: 3 on Aeneas as "the symbolic cannibal who wrenches the body beneath the ground and as such becomes himself a form of corrupter." But *contra* Putnam, see Stahl 1998b: 43 n18. On Aeneas' action as a religious violation, see also Dyson 35–38.

31. Putnam 1980: 3.

32. For the debate over remembrance and forgetting as attitudes toward the past advocated in the *Aeneid,* see Bleisch.

33. D.C. 49.43.5; cf. 52.36.1–3. See Dickie 155, 192, and, for more on constraints against magicians in Rome, 142–61.

34. See above, n12.

35. Khan emphasizes the tradition of curse-literature, including the poetry of Horace, for its capacity to illuminate a pattern of curses and dreams at the end of *Aeneid* 4; but Vergil's engagement with the traditions illustrated by Horace includes not only curses per se, but also the larger stigmatization of the magical practices (necromancy, love spells, etc.) of which such curses formed a part. For more on magic in *Aeneid* 4, see Eitrem; Tupet 232–66; Dickie 138–39.

36. For parallels between the Massylian priestess of *Aeneid* 4.483ff. and Apollonius Rhodius' Medea, see Pease *ad loc;* for Homeric precedents, see Kaiser 197–208; cf. Hexter. For the influence of the Roman elegists, see Cairns 144–46. The stigmatization of magic from a political perspective was engrained, before Vergil and Horace, in invective oratory. Cf. Cic. *Vat.* 14; *Pis.* 16. Imperial declamation continues to handle charges of magic as a theme (e.g., at [Quint.] *Decl.* 10.2, 6–8, 16, 18).

37. See Welch 2001: 184–89. As she suggests, Horace here identifies the witches Canidia and Sagana with the marginal space of Rome (the Esquiline cemetery before Maecenas' restoration of it) only to expel them from this space as he relates its recuperation as a pleasant and accessible part of the city. For Welch, however, this makes the gardens an uncomfortable place for satire, since Horace, through the witches, to some degree identifies himself with the Lucilian tradition of invective even as he claims to transform it. Other scholars, as Welch notes (187), have read the poem as posing "a contrast between present and past" and exposing "the fissures in the new order." Cf., e.g., Anderson, who finds optimism in Horace's outlook, and Zetzel (1980: 71), who emphasizes the embarrassment to Maecenas the poem must have caused.

38. On Horace's witches as a cultural other, see further Oliensis 68–90.

39. On the episode as *parentatio,* see Scheid 1993, who summarizes and reconsiders the earlier views of Bailey 291–93; Bömer 1943: 12–14; Bayet, and Boyancé 146–51. Among the central questions to which interpreters of the passage have sought answers is the identity of Vergil's serpent (see below) and the extent to which the ritual represents an amalgam of the traditional Roman rite with elements of other traditions, especially Greek hero cult (cf., e.g., Bayet's conclusions at 381). Scheid (1993: 192ff.) de-emphasizes both questions in favor of interpreting the passage with the "official" Augustan version of *parentatio* performed for the dead L. Caesar and recounted on the first *decretum* of Pisa (*ILS* 139).

40. Cf. Serv. *A.* 5.45.

41. See Scheid 1993, esp. 190–200.

42. Views summarized at Scheid 1993: 190–92.

43. See Boyce; Bayet 374–77; Dumézil 60–61, 305, 367, 443, 502–3.

44. The parallel was recognized already by Macrobius. The basic modern study is Norden 47–48; cf. Lamacchia. In what follows, I have also benefited from Hardie 69–83.

45. Similarly, Plato's Er overhears other souls' discussions of conditions in the heavens and on earth (Pl. *R.* 614e–615a), although he does not engage in dialogue himself. Further Roman instances of the tradition include Ennius' dream of Homer at the beginning of the *Annales* as well as his *Epicharmus,* where the poet relates a dream in which, having died, he learns the truth of nature and the elements, probably from Epicharmus himself.

The Greek author Heraclides Ponticus' well-known *Vision of Empedotimus* belongs in the same genre (Hardie 81), which can also be said to have precedents in the inspired visions of the Presocratic philosophers and, ultimately, in the Homeric *nekuia*. Plato's "Myth of Er" and Cicero's "*Somnium Scipionis*," we may note, are easily grouped as performances alongside the more obviously performance-based works of Vergil and Ennius, since in both Plato and Cicero, the revelation takes the form of a story told (complete with audience reactions) by one of the dialogue's participants. Habinek 1989 encourages us to interpret the formal qualities of *Aeneid* 6 as a key to its adaptation of cultural patterns expressed in philosophy by illuminating Vergil's reproduction of the twofold emphasis within Roman moral discourse on the scientific and the hortatory (present also in Cicero and Seneca).

46. For a summation of topics and bibliography pertaining to the "political" interpretation of Cicero's *De re publica*, see Zetzel 1995: 27–28.

47. On the doubtfulness of Vergil's underworld, with special reference to a number of the details on which I concentrate in this chapter, see the sensitive treatment in Reed 2001: 165–67 and 2007. The latter promises to revise substantially our perspective on Vergil's handling of Augustan ideology as it relates to Roman identity both in Book 6 and in the *Aeneid* as a whole. Cf., e.g., Tarrant; West 1987; Zetzel 1989: 272–76; O'Hara 170–72.

48. For the scene as *pompa funebris*, see Skard; Burke; Novara; Bettini 1991: 144–50; Flower 1996: 109–14. The funeral procession, of course, does not exhaust the passage's cultural resonance, which also extends to commemorative statuary, inscriptions, and coinage (see Horsfall 1976: 84). For literary precedents and influence, see Grebe.

49. See Flower 1996: 223–55.

50. On the darker aspects of the "Review of Heroes," see esp. Feeney 1986.

51. Ibid., 10–11.

52. Ibid., 11–14.

53. Similarly, the physical distance between the figures in the procession becomes a sign of Vergil's cultural gesture in bringing together disparate elements: note *procul* at 808 and 824.

54. See esp. Reed 2001 and 2007; cf. Glei. For the Marcellus passage's links to the traditional funeral oration and epigram, see Norden 338–46; Brenk 218–28.

55. Feeney 1998: 55–56.

Conclusion

1. For an illuminating discussion of ancestral curses in imperial literature, see Bernstein 2003.

2. Cf. Gowing.

3. For the claim that Remus' very presence in a supposedly celebratory poem is suspect, see Hinds 143; cf. Newlands 119–21. In Barchiesi's view (251–56), Ovid, as a poet, is necessarily implicated here both in the promotion of Augustan ideology and in a certain resistance to it. On Romulus' ambiguity in the *Fasti*, see further Harries; Stok; Boyd. For the case that Augustus' own associations with Romulus would not have been felt strongly enough by the time of the later regime to make the negative connotations of Remus' murder significant as a political critique, see Herbert-Brown 60–62 and *passim;* cf. Littlewood.

4. For a recent discussion of the motif in Ovid's exile poems, see Miller 2004: 210–36,

who notes its familiarity from ancient philosophy (Miller 2004: 223 citing Claassen 20, etc.).

5. Miller 2004: 2224–25; cf. Habinek 1998: 151.

6. For the passage as a reminiscence of the Roman ritual, see Miedel 51–52; Fortgens 133; Vessey 211.

7. For perspectives on the politics of the *Thebaid* (a topic of much recent debate), see Coleman with bibliography.

WORKS CITED

Alexander, M. C. 2002. *The Case for the Prosecution in the Ciceronian Era.* Ann Arbor.

Alföldi, A. 1973. "La divinisation de César dans la politique D'Antoine et d'Octavien entre 44 et 40 avant J.-C." *RevNum,* 6th ser., 15: 99–128, Pl. IV–XIII.

———. 1985. *Caesar in 44 v. Chr.* Vol. 1. Ed. H. Wolff, E. Alföldi-Rosenbaum, G. Stumpf. Bonn.

Anderson, W. S. 1972. "The Form, Purpose, and Position of Horace's *Satire* I, 8." *AJP* 93: 4–13. Rpt. in *Essays on Roman Satire,* 74–83. Princeton, 1982.

Austin, R. G., ed. 1960. *M. Tulli Ciceronis pro M. Caelio oratio.* 3rd ed. Oxford.

Bacon, H. H. 1986. "The *Aeneid* as a Drama of Election." *TAPA* 116: 305–34.

Baehr, P. R. 1998. *Caesar and the Fading of the Roman World: A Study in Republicanism and Caesarism.* New Brunswick, NJ.

Bailey, C. 1935. *Religion in Virgil.* Oxford. Rpt. New York, 1969.

Ballaira, G. 1968. "Una sentenza di Appio Claudio Cieco." *SIFC* 40: 190–99.

Barchiesi, A. 1997. *The Poet and the Prince: Ovid and Augustan Discourse.* Berkeley.

Bayet, J. 1971. "Les cendres d'Anchise: dieu, héros, ombre ou serpent?" In *Croyances et rites dans la Rome antique,* 366–81. Paris.

Beard, M. 1993. "Looking (Harder) for Roman Myth: Dumézil, Declamation and the Problem of Definition." In F. Graf, ed., *Mythos in mythenloser Gesellschaft: Das Paradigma Roms,* 44–64. Stuttgart.

Bell, A. J. E. 1999. "The Popular Poetics and Politics of the *Aeneid.*" *TAPA* 129: 263–79.

Bennett. A. W. 1967. "Sententia and Catalogue in Propertius (3,9,1–20)." *Hermes* 95: 222–43.

Bergmann, J. R. 1993. *Discreet Indiscretions: The Social Organization of Gossip.* Tr. J. Bednarz Jr. New York.

Bernstein, N. W. 2003. "Ancestors, Status, and Self-Presentation in Statius' *Thebaid.*" *TAPA* 133: 353–79.

———. 2004. "*Auferte oculos:* Modes of Spectatorship in Statius *Thebaid* 11." *Phoenix* 58: 62–85.

———. 2005. "Mourning the *puer delicatus:* Status Inconsistency and the Ethical Value of Fostering in Statius, *Silvae* 2.1." *AJP* 126: 257–280.

Bettini, M. 1991. *Anthropology and Roman Culture: Kinship, Time, Images of the Soul.* Tr. J. Van Sickle. Baltimore.

————. 1997. "Ghosts of Exile: Doubles and Nostalgia in Vergil's *parva Troia* (*Aeneid* 3.294ff.)." *CA* 16: 8–33.

Berry, D. H., ed. 1996. *Cicero: Pro P. Sulla oratio.* Cambridge.

Blänsdorf, J. 1995. *Fragmenta poetarum Latinorum epicorum et lyricorum praeter Ennium et Lucilium.* 3rd ed. Leipzig.

Bleisch, P. 1999. "The Empty Tomb at Rhoeteum: Deiphobus and the Problem of the Past in *Aeneid* 6.494–547." *CA* 18: 187–226.

Bloomer, W. M. 1992. "A Preface to the History of Declamation: Whose Speech? Whose History?" In Habinek and Schiesaro, 199–215.

Bömer, F. 1943. *Ahnenkult und Ahnenglaube im alten Rom.* Beihefte zum Archiv für Religionswissenschaft 1. Leipzig.

————. 1958. *P. Ovidius Naso, Die Fasten.* Vol. 2. Heidelberg.

————. 1964. "Claudia Quinta." *MDAI(R)* 71: 146–51.

Bourdieu, P. 1977. *Outline of a Theory of Practice.* Tr. R. Nice. Cambridge.

————. 1990. *The Logic of Practice.* Tr. R. Nice. Cambridge.

Boyancé, P. 1963. *La religion de Virgile.* Paris.

Boyd, B. W. 2000. "*Celabitur auctor:* The Crisis of Authority and Narrative Patterning in Ovid *Fasti* 5." *Phoenix* 54: 64–98.

Boyce, G. K. 1942. "Significance of the Serpents on Pompeian House Shrines." *AJA* 46: 13–22.

Boyle, A. J. 1997. *Tragic Seneca: An Essay in the Theatrical Tradition.* London.

Braden, G. 1985. *Renaissance Tragedy and the Senecan Tradition: Anger's Privilege.* New Haven.

Brenk, F. 1986. "*Auorum spes et purpurei flores:* The Eulogy for Marcellus in *Aeneid* VI." *AJP* 107: 218–28.

Bright, D. F. 1981. "Aeneas' Other Nekyia." *Vergilius* 27: 40–47.

Brunt, P. A. 1988. *The Fall of the Roman Republic and Related Essays.* Oxford.

Bruun, C. 1997. "Water for the Roman Brothels: Cicero *Cael.* 34." *Phoenix* 51: 364–73.

Buchheit, V. 1975a. "Chrysogonus als Tyrann in Ciceros Rede für Roscius aus Ameria." *Chiron* 5: 193–211.

————. 1975b. "Ciceros Kritik an Sulla in der Rede für Roscius aus Ameria." *Historia* 24: 570–91.

Burke, P. F. 1979. "Roman Rites for the Dead and *Aeneid* 6." *CJ* 74: 220–28.

Butler, S. 2002. *The Hand of Cicero.* London.

Butrica, J. L. 1999. "Using Water 'Unchastely': Cicero *Pro Caelio* 34 Again." *Phoenix* 53: 136–39.

Cairns, F. 1989. *Virgil's Augustan Epic.* Cambridge.

Campbell, B. G. 2001. *Performing and Processing* The Aeneid. New York.

Camps, W. A., ed. and comm. 1965. *Propertius: Elegies, Book IV.* Cambridge.

Cerutti, S. M. 1996. *Cicero's Accretive Style: Rhetorical Strategies in the* Exordia *of the Judicial Speeches.* Lanham.

Claassen, J.-M. 1999. *Displaced Persons: The Literature of Exile from Cicero to Boethius.* London.

Clark, M. E., and J. S. Ruebel, 1985. "Philosophy and Rhetoric in Cicero's *Pro Milone.*" *RhM* 128: 57–72.

Clark, R. J. 1998. "The Reality of Hector's Ghost in Aeneas' Dream." *Latomus* 57: 832–41.

Classen, C. J. 1973. "Ciceros Rede für Caelius." *ANRW* I.3: 60–94.

————. 1985. *Recht–Rhetorik–Politik. Untersuchungen zu Ciceros rhetorischer Strategie.* Darmstadt.

Code, L. 1994. "Gossip, or In Praise of Chaos." In R. F. Goodman and A. Ben-Ze'ev, eds., *Good Gossip,* 100–105. Lawrence, KS.

Coffey, M. 1986. "Notes on the History of Augustan and Early Imperial Tragedy." In J. H. Betts et al., eds., *Studies in Honour of T. B. L. Webster.* Vol. 1: 46–52. Bristol.

Coleman, K. M. 2003. "Recent Scholarship on the *Thebaid* and *Achilleid:* An Overview." In D. R. Shackleton Bailey, ed. *Statius,* Thebaid, *Books 1–7.* 9–37. Cambridge, MA.

Conte, G. B. 1994. *Latin Literature: A History.* Tr. J. B. Solodow. Rev. D. Fowler and G. W. Most. Baltimore.

Corbeill, A. 1996. *Controlling Laughter: Political Humor in the Late Roman Republic.* Princeton.

Covino, W. A. 1994. *Magic, Rhetoric, and Literacy : An Eccentric History of the Composing Imagination.* Albany.

Craig, C. P. 1993. *Form as Argument in Cicero's Speeches: A Study of Dilemma.* Atlanta.

Crawford, J. 1984. *M. Tullius Cicero: The Lost and Unpublished Orations.* Göttingen.

————. 1994. *M. Tullius Cicero, The Fragmentary Speeches: An Edition with Commentary.* 2nd ed. Atlanta.

DeBrohun, J. B. 2003. *Roman Propertius and the Reinvention of Elegy.* Ann Arbor.

Deutsch, M. E. 1926–1929. "Antony's Funeral Speech." *University of California Publications in Classical Philology* 9: 127–48.

Dickie, M. W. 2001. *Magic and Magicians in the Greco-Roman World.* London.

Dimundo, R. 1990. *Properzio 4.7: Dalla variante di un modello letterario alla costante di una unità tematica.* Bari.

Dobesch, G. 1966. *Caesars Apotheose zu Lebzeiten und sein Ringen um den Königstitel: Untersuchungen über Caesars Alleinherrschaft.* Baden bei Wien.

Drerup, H. 1980. "Totenmaske und Ahnenbild bei den Römern." *MDAI(R)* 87: 81–129.

Drexler, H. 1944. "Zu Ciceros Rede *pro Caelio.*" *NAWG:* 1–32.

Dufallo, B. 2005. "The Roman Elegist's Dead Lover *or* The Drama of the Desiring Subject." *Phoenix* 59: 112–20.

Dugan, J. 2005. *Making a New Man: Ciceronian Self-Fashioning in the Rhetorical Works.* Oxford.

Dumézil, G. 1974. *La religion romaine archaïque, avec un appendice sur la religion des Étrusques.* 2nd ed. Paris.

Dupont, F. 1985. *L'Acteur-roi ou le théâtre dans la Rome antique.* Paris.

————. 1987. "Les Morts et la mémoire: le masque funèbre." In F. Hinard, ed. 1985. *La Mort, les morts et l'au-delà dans le monde romain,* 176–92. Actes du colloque de Caen, 20–22 nov. 1985. Caen.

————. 1997. "*Recitatio* and the Reorganization of the Space of Public Discourse." In Habinek and Schiesaro, 44–59.

DuQuesnay, I. M. Le M. 1984. "Horace and Maecenas: The Propaganda Value of *Sermones* I." In T. Woodman and D. West, eds., *Poetry and Politics in the Age of Augustus,* 19–58. Cambridge.

Durry, M. 1950. *Éloge funèbre d'une matrone romaine (éloge dit de Turia).* Paris.

Dyck, A. R. 1998. "Narrative Obfuscation, Philosophical *Topoi,* and Tragic Patterning in Cicero's *Pro Milone.*" *HSCP* 98: 219–41.

————. 2001. "Dressing to Kill: Attire as a Proof and Means of Characterization in Cicero's Speeches." *Arethusa* 34: 119–30.

————. 2002. "The 'Other' *Pro Milone* Reconsidered." *Philologus* 146: 182–85.

————. 2003. "Evidence and Rhetoric in Cicero's *Pro Roscio Amerino:* The Case against Sex. Roscius." *CQ* 53: 235–46.

Dyson, J. T. 2001. *The King of the Wood: The Sacrificial Victor in Virgil's* Aeneid. Norman, OK.

Edmonds, L. 2005. "Critical Divergences: New Directions in the Study and Teaching of Roman Literature." *TAPA* 135: 1–13.

Egan, R. 1974. "Aeneas at Aineia and Vergil's *Aeneid.*" *Pacific Coast Philology* 9: 37–47.

Eitrem, S. 1933. "Das Ende Didos in Vergils Aeneis." In *Festskrift til Halvdan Koht*, 29–41. Oslo.

Erskine, A. 1997. "Cicero and the Expression of Grief." In S. M. Braund and C. Gill, eds., *The Passions in Roman Thought and Literature*, 36–47. Cambridge.

Faraone, C. A. 1999. *Ancient Greek Love Magic.* Cambridge, MA.

Faraone, C. A., and D. Obbink, eds. 1991. *Magika Hiera: Ancient Greek Magic and Religion.* New York.

Fear, T. 2000. "The Poet as Pimp: Elegiac Seduction in the Time of Augustus." *Arethusa* 33: 217–40.

Fedeli, P. 1980. *Sesto Properzio: Il primo libro delle elegie.* Florence.

Feeney, D. C. 1986. "History and Revelation in Vergil's Underworld." *PCPS* 32: 1–24.

————. 1998. *Literature and Religion at Rome: Contexts, Cultures, and Beliefs.* Cambridge.

Feldherr, A. 1995. "Ships of State: *Aeneid* 5 and Augustan Circus Spectacle." *CA* 14: 245–65.

————. 1998. *Spectacle and Society in Livy's* History. Berkeley.

————. 2000. "*Non inter nota sepulcra:* Catullus 101 and Roman Funerary Ritual." *CA* 19: 209–31.

Flaschenriem, B. L. 1998. "Speaking of Women: 'Female Voice' in Propertius." *Helios* 25: 49–64.

Fliegelman, J. 1993. *Declaring Independence: Jefferson, Natural Language, and the Culture of Performance.* Stanford.

Flower, H. I. 1995. "*Fabulae praetextae* in Context: When were Plays on Contemporary Subjects Performed in Republican Rome?" *CQ* 45: 170–90.

————. 1996. *Ancestor Masks and Aristocratic Power in Roman Culture.* Oxford.

Fortgens, H. W. 1934. *P. Papinii Statii de Opheltis funere carmen epicum, Thebaidos liber VI 1–295.* Zutphen.

Gaffney, C. E. 1995. "*Severitati respondere:* Character Drawing in *Pro Caelio* and Catullus' *Carmina.*" *CJ* 90: 423–31.

Gagarin, M., ed. and comm. 1997. *Antiphon: The Speeches.* Cambridge.

Gager, J. G. 1992. *Curse Tablets and Binding Spells from the Ancient World.* New York.

Galinsky, K. 1996. *Augustan Culture: An Interpretive Introduction.* Princeton.

Gamel, M.-K. 1998. "Reading as a Man: Performance and Gender in Roman Elegy." *Helios* 25: 79–95.

Gazich, R. 1995. *Exemplum ed esemplarità in Properzio.* Milan.

Geffcken, K. A. 1973. *Comedy in the* Pro Caelio *(With an Appendix on the* In Clodium et Curionem*).* Leiden.

Gesche, H. 1968. *Die Vergottung Caesars.* Frankfurter Althistorische Studien 1. Kallmünz.

Giardina, G. C. 1974. "Sui frammenti di Appio Claudio Cieco." In misc. ed., *Poesia Latina in frammenti*, 257–61. Genoa.

Glei, R. F. 1998. "The Show Must Go on: The Death of Marcellus and the Future of the Augustan Principate (*Aeneid* 6.860–86)." In Stahl 1998a, 119–34.

Gold, B. K. 1993a. "'But Ariadne Was Never There in the First Place': Finding the Female in Roman Poetry." In N. S. Rabinowitz and A. Richlin, eds., *Feminist Theory and the Classics*, 75–101. New York.

———. 1993b. "The Master Mistress of My Passion: The Lady as Patron in Ancient and Renaissance Literature." In M. DeForest, ed., *Woman's Power, Man's Game: Essays on Classical Antiquity in Honor of Joy King*, 279–304. Wauconda, IL.

———. 1998. "'The House I Live in is Not My Own': Women's Bodies in Juvenal's *Satires*." *Arethusa* 31: 369–86.

Goldberg, S. M. 1996. "The Fall and Rise of Roman Tragedy." *TAPA* 126: 265–86.

Goold, G. P., ed. and trans. 1999. *Propertius: Elegies*. Rev. ed. Cambridge, MA.

Gotoff, H. C. 1986. "Cicero's Analysis of the Prosecution Speeches in the *Pro Caelio*: An Exercise in Practical Criticism." *CP* 8: 122–32.

Gowing, A. M. 2005. *Empire and Memory: The Representation of the Roman Republic in Imperial Culture*. Cambridge.

Graf, F. 1997. *Magic in the Ancient World*. Tr. F. Philip. Cambridge, MA.

Grebe, S. 1989. *Die vergilische Heldenschau: Tradition und Fortwirken*. Frankfurt am Main.

Greenidge, A. H. J. 1901. *The Legal Procedure of Cicero's Time*. Oxford.

Grimm, R. E. 1967. "Aeneas and Andromache in *Aeneid* III." *AJP* 88: 151–62.

Gruen, E. S. 1968. *Roman Politics and the Criminal Courts, 149–78 B.C.* Cambridge, MA.

———. 1974. *The Last Generation of the Roman Republic*. Berkeley.

———. 1992. *Culture and National Identity in Republican Rome*. Ithaca.

Guillemin, A. 1950. "Properce, de Cynthie aux poèmes romains." *REL* 28:182–93.

Gunderson, E. 2003. *Declamation, Paternity, and Roman Identity: Authority and the Rhetorical Self*. Cambridge.

Gurval, R. 1995. *Actium and Augustus: The Politics and Emotions of Civil War*. Ann Arbor.

———. 1997. "Caesar's Comet: The Politics and Poetics of an Augustan Myth." *MAAR* 42: 39–71.

Habinek, T. N. 1989. "Science and Tradition in *Aeneid* 6." *HSCP* 92: 223–55.

———. 1998. *The Politics of Latin Literature: Writing, Identity, and Empire in Ancient Rome*. Princeton.

———. 2005a. "Latin Literature between Text and Practice." *TAPA* 135: 83–89.

———. 2005b. *The World of Roman Song: From Ritualized Speech to Social Order*. Baltimore.

Habinek, T. N., and A. Schiesaro, eds. 1997. *The Roman Cultural Revolution*. Cambridge.

Halkin, L. 1953. *La supplication d'action de graces chez les romains*. Paris.

Hallett, J. P. 1973. "The Role of Women in Roman Elegy: Counter-Cultural Feminism." *Arethusa* 6: 103–24. Rpt. in J. Peradotto and J. P. Sullivan, eds., *Women in the Ancient World: The Arethusa Papers*, 241–62. Albany, 1984.

———. 1985. "Queens, Princeps and Women of the Augustan Elite: Propertius' Cornelia-Elegy and the *Res Gestae Divi Augusti*." In R. Winkes, ed., *The Age of Augustus: Interdisciplinary Conference Held at Brown University, April 30–May 2, 1982*, 73–88. Louvain-la-Neuve.

———. 1989. "Women as *Same* and *Other* in Classical Roman Elite." *Helios* 16: 59–78.

Hannah, B. 2004. "Manufacturing Descent: Virgil's Genealogical Engineering." *Arethusa* 37: 141–64.

Hardie, P. R. 1986. *Virgil's Aeneid:* Cosmos *and* Imperium. Oxford.

Harries, B. 1989. "Causation and the Authority of the Poet in Ovid's *Fasti.*" *CQ* n.s. 39: 164–85.

Haviland, J. B. 1977. *Gossip, Reputation, and Knowledge in Zinacantan.* Chicago.

Heiden, B. 1995. "*Sic te servato:* An Interpretation of Propertius 1.21." *CP* 90: 161–67.

Heinze, R. 1925. "Cicero's Rede *Pro Caelio.*" *Hermes* 60: 193–258.

———. 1957. *Virgils epische Technik.* 4th ed. Darmstadt.

Herbert-Brown, G. 1994. *Ovid and the* Fasti: *An Historical Study.* Oxford.

Hexter, R. 1992. "Sidonian Dido." In R. Hexter and D. Selden, eds., *Innovations of Antiquity,* 332–84. New York.

Highet, G. 1957. *Poets in a Landscape.* New York.

Hinds, S. 1992. "*Arma* in Ovid's *Fasti*—Part 2: Genre, Romulean Rome, and Augustan Ideology." *Arethusa* 25: 113–53.

Hodge, R. I. V., and R. A. Buttimore. 1977. *The "Monobiblos" of Propertius.* Cambridge.

Horsfall, N. M. 1976. "Virgil, History and the Roman Tradition." *Prudentia* 8: 73–89.

———. 1983. "Some Problems in the 'Laudatio Turiae.'" *BICS* 30: 85–98.

———. 1995. "Virgil's Impact at Rome: The Non-Literary Evidence." In N. Horsfall, ed., *A Companion to the Study of Virgil,* 249–55. Leiden.

Hubbard, M. 1974. *Propertius.* London.

Humbert, J. 1925. *Les plaidoyers écrits et les plaidoiries réelles de Cicéron.* Paris.

Hunter, V. J. 1994. *Policing Athens: Social Control in the Attic Lawsuits, 420–320 B.C.* Princeton.

James, C. L. R. 1989. *The Black Jacobins: Toussaint L'Overture and the San Domingo Revolution.* 2nd ed. New York.

Janan, M. 2001. *The Politics of Desire: Propertius IV.* Berkeley.

Johnson, W. R. 1997. "Final Exit: Propertius 4.11." In D. H. Roberts, F. M. Dunn, and D. Fowler, eds., *Classical Closure: Reading the End in Greek and Latin Literature,* 163–80. Princeton.

Johnston, S. I. 1999. *Restless Dead: Encounters between the Living and the Dead in Ancient Greece.* Berkeley.

Jost, K. 1935. *Das Beispiel und Vorbild der Vorfahren bei den attischen Rednern und Geschichtschreibern bis Demosthenes.* Diss. Basel. Kallmünz bei Regensburg.

Kaiser, E. 1964. "Odyssee-Szenen als Topoi." *MH* 21: 109–36, 197–224.

Kaster, R. A. 1998. "Becoming 'CICERO.'" In P. Knox and C. Foss, eds., *Style and Tradition: Studies in Honor of Wendell Clausen,* 248–63. Stuttgart.

Kennedy, D. F. 1993. *The Arts of Love: Five Studies in the Discourse of Roman Love Elegy.* Cambridge.

Kennedy, G. A. 1968. "Antony's Speech at Caesar's Funeral." *The Quarterly Journal of Speech* 54: 99–106.

———. 1972. *The Art of Rhetoric in the Roman World, 300 B.C.–A.D. 300.* Princeton.

Ker, W. C. A. 1926. *Cicero: Philippics.* Cambridge, MA.

Khan, A. H. 1994. "Demonizing Dido: A Rebounding Sequence of Curses and Dreams in *Aeneid* 4." In A. H. Sommerstein, ed., *Religion and Superstition in Latin Literature,* 1–28. Bari.

Kierdorf, W. 1980. *Laudatio Funebris: Interpretationen und Untersuchungen zur Entwicklung der römischen Leichenrede.* Beiträge zur klassischen Philologie 106. Meisenheim am Glan.

Kinsey, T. E. 1975. "Cicero's Speech for Roscius of Ameria." *SO* 50: 91–104.

———. 1980. "Cicero's Case against Magnus, Capito and Chrysogonus in the *Pro Sex. Roscio Amerino* and Its Use for the Historian." *AC* 49: 173–90.

———. 1982. "The Political Insignificance of Cicero's *pro Roscio.*" *LCM* 7: 39–40.

———. 1985. "The Case against Sextus Roscius of Ameria." *AC* 54: 188–96.

Knoche, U. 1934. "Der römische Ruhmesgedanke." *Philologus* 89: 102–24.

Krokowski, G. 1926. "*De Propertio ludibundo II.*" *Eos* 29: 81–100.

Kröner, H. O. 1986. "Ciceros 9. Philippica: Cicero und Servius Sulpicius Rufus. Zugleich ein Beitrag zu: Cicero und der römische Staat." *Der altsprachliche Unterricht* 29: 69–82.

Kubiak, D. P. 1989. "Piso's Madness (Cic. *In. Pis.* 21 and 47)." *AJP* 110: 237–45.

Kyle, D. G. 1998. *Spectacles of Death in Ancient Rome.* London.

Lacey, W. K., ed. and trans. 1986. *Cicero: Second Philippic Oration.* Warminster.

Lahusen, G. 1985. "Zur Funktion und Rezeption des römischen Ahnenbildes." *MDAI(R)* 92: 261–89.

Lamacchia, R. 1964. "Cicero's Somnium Scipionis und das sechste Buch der *Aeneis.*" *RhM* n.s. 107: 261–78.

Lange, D. K. 1979. "Cynthia and Cornelia: Two Voices from the Grave." In C. Deroux, ed., *Studies in Roman Literature and Roman History.* Collection Latomus 1: 335–42. Brussels.

La Penna, A. 1951. *Properzio.* Florence.

———. 1977. *L'integrazione difficile: Un profilo di Properzio.* Turin.

Laurence, R. 1994. "Rumour and Communication in Roman Politics." *Greece & Rome* 41: 62–74.

Lausberg, H. 1998. *Handbook of Literary Rhetoric: A Foundation for Literary Study.* Tr. M. T. Bliss, A. Jansen, and D. E. Orton. Leiden.

Leach, E. W. 2001. "Gendering Clodius." *CW* 94: 335–59.

Leeman, A. D. 1949. *Gloria; Cicero's Waardering van de Roem en haar Achtergrond in de hellenistische Wijsbegeerte en de romeinse Samenleving.* Rotterdam.

Lefkowitz, M. R. 1981. *Heroines and Hysterics.* London.

Leigh, M. 2004. "The *Pro Caelio* and Comedy." *CP* 99: 300–35.

Lenaghan, J. O., ed. and comm. 1969. *A Commentary on Cicero's Oration* De haruspicum responso. The Hague.

Lintott, A. W. 1999. *Violence in Republican Rome.* 2nd ed. Oxford.

———. 1974. "Cicero and Milo." *JRS* 64: 62–78.

Littlewood, R. J. 2001. "Ovid among the Family Dead: the Roman Founder Legend and Augustan Iconography in Ovid's *Feralia* and *Lemuria.*" *Latomus* 60: 916–35.

Loraux, N. 1986. *The Invention of Athens: The Funeral Oration in the Classical City.* Tr. A. Sheridan. Cambridge, MA.

Loutsch, C. 1994. *L'exorde dans les discours de Cicéron.* Collection Latomus 224. Brussels.

Lucrezi, F. 1986. "Ius imaginum, nova nobilitas." *Labeo* 32: 131–79.

Luck, G. 1959. *The Latin Love Elegy.* London.

MacBain, B. 1980. "Appius Claudius Caecus and the Via Appia." *CQ* 30: 356–72.

Mackie, C. J. 1993. "A Note on Dido's Ancestry in the *Aeneid.*" *CJ* 88: 231–33.

Mankin, D., ed. and comm. 1995. *Horace, Epodes.* Cambridge.

Manuwald, G. 2001. *Fabulae praetextae: Spuren einer literarischen Gattung der Römer.* Zetemata 108. Munich.

Marini, M. 1985. "Osservazioni sui frammenti di Appio Claudio." *RCCM* 27: 3–11.

Markus, D. D. 2000. "Performing the Book: The Recital of Epic in First-Century C.E. Rome." *CA* 19: 138–79.

Marshall, B. A. 1987. "*Excepta Oratio,* the Other *Pro Milone* and the Question of Short-hand." *Latomus* 46: 730–36.

May, J. 1988. *Trials of Character: The Eloquence of Ciceronian Ethos.* Chapel Hill.

Meijer, F. J. 1986. "Marius' Grandson." *Mnemosyne* 39: 112–21.

Miedel, J. 1891. *De Anachronismo qui est in P. Papinii Statii Thebaide et Achilleide.* Passau.

Millar, F. 1998. *The Crowd in Rome in the Late Republic.* Ann Arbor.

Miller, P. A. 1999. "The Tibullan Dream Text." *TAPA* 129: 181–224.

———. 2004. *Subjecting Verses: Latin Love Elegy and the Emergence of the Real.* Princeton.

Mitchell, T. N. 1991. *Cicero, the Senior Statesman.* New Haven and London.

Moreau, A. 1985. *Eschyle: La violence et le chaos.* Paris.

Müller, C. W. 1995. "Imaginationen des Todes in den Elegien des Tibull und Properz." *Antike und Abenland* 41: 132–40.

Narducci, E. 1997. *Cicerone e l'eloquenza romana: Retorica e progetto culturale.* Rome.

Newlands, C. E. 1995. *Playing with Time: Ovid and the Fasti.* Ithaca.

Ngugi wa Thiong'o. 1984. Interview with Bettye J. Parker. In G. D. Killam, ed., *Critical Perspectives on Ngugi wa Thiong'o,* 58–66. Washington, D. C.

Nicolet, C. 1980. *The World of the Citizen in Republican Rome.* Tr. P. S. Falla. Berkeley.

Nicoll, W. S. M. 1988. 'The Sacrifice of Palinurus." *CQ* n.s. 38: 459–72.

Nisbet, R. G. M. 1965. "The Speeches." In T. A. Dorey, ed., *Cicero,* 47–79. London.

Norden, E. 1995. *P. Vergilius Maro, Aeneis Buch VI.* 9th ed. Stuttgart.

North, J. A. 1975. "Praesens Divus." *JRS* 65: 171–77.

Novara, A. 1987. "Les *Imagines* de l'Élysée virgilien." In F. Hinard, ed. 1985. *La mort, les morts et l'au-delà dans le monde romain,* 321–49. Actes du colloque de Caen, 20–22 Nov. 1985, Caen.

Ogden, D. 2001. *Greek and Roman Necromancy.* Princeton.

O'Hara, J. J. 1990. *Death and the Optimistic Prophecy in Vergil's Aeneid.* Princeton.

Oliensis, E. 1998. *Horace and the Rhetoric of Authority.* Cambridge.

Pacitti, G. 1961. "Cicerone al processo di M. Celio Rufo." In *Atti del Congresso internazionale di studi Ciceroniani.* Vol. 2: 67–79. Rome.

Pease, A. S. 1935. *Publi Vergili Maronis Aeneidos liber quartus.* Cambridge, MA.

Pennacini, A. 1989. "L'arte della parola." *Lo spazio letterario di Roma antica* 2: 215–67.

Pomathios, J.-L. 1987. *Le pouvoir politique et sa représentation dans l'Énéide de Virgile.* Collection *Latomus* 199. Brussels.

Powell, A. 1998. "The Peopling of the Underworld (*Aeneid* 6.608–27)." In Stahl 1998, 85–100.

Powell, J., and J. Paterson, eds. 2004. *Cicero the Advocate.* Oxford.

Putnam, M. C. J. 1976. "Propertius 1.22: A Poet's Self-Definition." *QUCC* 23: 93–123.

———. 1980. "The Third Book of the *Aeneid:* From Homer to Rome." *Ramus* 9: 1–21. Rpt. in *Virgil's* Aeneid: *Interpretation and Influence,* 50–72. Chapel Hill, 1995.

Quinn, K. 1982. "The Poet and his Audience in the Augustan Age." *ANRW* II.30.1: 75–180.

Quint, D. 1993. *Epic and Empire: Politics and Generic Form from Virgil to Milton.* Princeton.

Ramsey, J. T., ed. 2003. *Cicero, Philippics I-II.* Cambridge.

Ramsey, J. T., and A. L. Licht. 1997. *The Comet of 44 B.C. and Caesar's Funeral Games.* Atlanta.

Reckford, K. J. 1998. "Reading the Sick Body: Decomposition and Morality in Persius'

Third Satire." *Arethusa* 31: 337–54.

Reed, J. 2001. "Anchises Reading Aeneas Reading Marcellus." *SC* 12: 146–68.

———. 2007. *Vergil's Gaze: Nation and Poetry in the Aeneid.* Princeton.

Reitzenstein, E. 1969. "Die Cornelia-Elegie des Properz (IV 11)." *RhM* 112: 126–45.

Reitzenstein, R. 1925. "Cicero's Rede für Caelius." *NAWG:* 25–32.

Reumaux, F. 1994. *Toute la ville en parle: Esquisse d'une théorie des rumeurs.* Paris.

Ribbeck, O., ed. 1897–1898. *Scaenicae Romanorum poesis fragmenta.* 3rd ed. 2 vols. Leipzig.

Richardson, L., Jr., ed. and comm. 1977. *Propertius. Elegies I–IV.* Norman, OK.

Richlin, A. 1992. *The Garden of Priapus: Sexuality and Agression in Roman Humor.* Rev. ed. New York.

Riencourt, A. de. 1957. *The Coming Caesars.* New York.

Riggsby, A. 1999. *Crime and Community in Ciceronian Rome.* Austin.

Roach, J. 1996. *Cities of the Dead: Circum-Atlantic Performance.* New York.

Romilly, J., de. 1975. *Magic and Rhetoric in Ancient Greece.* Cambridge, MA.

Rosnow, R. L., and G. A. Fine. 1976. *Rumor and Gossip: The Social Psychology of Hearsay.* New York.

Ruebel, J. S. 1979. "The Trial of Milo in 52 B. C.: A Chronological Study." *TAPA* 109: 231–49.

Salzman, M. R. 1982. "Cicero, the *Megalenses,* and the Defense of Caelius." *AJP* 103: 299–304.

Schäublin, C. 1988. "Cicero's demosthenische Redezyklen: Ein Nachtrag." *MH* 45: 60–61.

Schechner, R. 1985. *Between Theater and Anthropology.* Philadelphia.

———. 1986. "Victor Turner's Last Adventure." Preface to V. Turner, *The Anthropology of Performance,* 7–20. New York.

———. 1990. "Magnitudes of Performance." In R. Schechner and W. Appel, eds., *By Means of Performance: Intercultural Studies of Theatre and Ritual,* 19–49. Cambridge.

Scheid, J. 1993. "Die Parentalien für die verstorbenen Caesaren als Modell für den römischen Totenkult." *Klio* 75: 188–201.

———. 2001. "Claudia the Vestal Virgin." In A. Fraschetti, ed., *Roman Women.* Tr. L. Lappin, 23–33. Chicago.

Schotter, J. 1989. "Rhetoric and the Recovery of Civil Society." *Economy and Society* 18: 149–66.

Seager, R. J. 1982. "The Political Significance of Cicero's pro Roscio." *LCM* 7: 10–12.

Settle, J. N. 1963. "The Trial of Milo and the Other *Pro Milone.*" *TAPA* 94: 268–80.

Shackleton Bailey, D. R. 1967. *Propertiana.* Amsterdam.

———, ed. and trans. 1986. *Cicero, Philippics.* Chapel Hill.

Skard, E. 1965. "Die Heldenschau in Vergils Aeneis." *SO* 40: 53–65.

Skinner, M. B. 1983. "Clodia Metelli." *TAPA* 113: 273–87.

———. 1993. "Catullus in Performance." *CJ* 89: 61–68.

Skutsch, O. 1985. *The Annals of Q. Ennius.* Oxford.

Sordi, M. 1990. "Cicerone e il primo epitafio romano." In M. Sordi, ed., *"Dulce et decorum est pro patria mori": La morte in combattimento nell'antichità,* 171–79. Milan.

Spacks, P. M. 1985. *Gossip.* New York.

Spengler, O. 1926–1928. *The Decline of the West.* Tr. C. F. Atkinson. 2 vols. New York.

Stahl, H.-P. 1985. *Propertius: "Love" and "War"—Individual and State under Augustus.* Berkeley.

————, ed. 1998a. *Vergil's* Aeneid: *Augustan Epic and Political Context.* London.

————. 1998b. "Political Stop-overs on a Mythological Travel Route: from Battling Harpies to the Battle of Actium (*Aen.* 3.268–93)." In Stahl 1998, 37–84.

Steel, C. E. W. 2001. *Cicero, Rhetoric, and Empire.* Oxford.

Stoessl, F. 1979. "Die Sententiae des Appius Claudius Caecus." *RhM* 122: 18–23.

Stone, A. M. 1980. "*Pro Milone:* Cicero's Second Thoughts." *Antichthon* 14: 88–111.

Stok, F. 1991. "L'ambiguo Romolo dei *Fasti.*" In I. Gallo and L. Nicastri, eds., *Cultura poesia ideologia nell'opera di Ovidio,* 183–212. Naples.

Strachan-Davidson, J. L. 1912. *Problems of the Roman Criminal Law.* Vol. 2. Oxford.

Stroh, W. 1975. *Taxis und Taktik. Die advokatische Dispositionskunst in Ciceros Gerichtsreden.* Stuttgart.

————. 1982. "Die Nachahmung des Demosthenes in Ciceros Philippiken." In W. Ludwig, ed., *Éloquence et rhétorique chez Cicéron.* Entretiens Fondation Hardt 28, 1–31. Vandoeuvres-Geneva.

————. 1983. "Ciceros demosthenische Redezyklen." *MH* 40: 35–50.

Sullivan, J. P. 1976. *Propertius: A Critical Introduction.* Cambridge.

Syme, R. 1939. *The Roman Revolution.* Oxford.

Tar, I. 1975. *Über die Anfänge der römischen Lyrik.* Szeged.

Tarrant, R. J. 1982. "Aeneas and the Gates of Sleep." *CP* 77: 51–55.

Taylor, L. R. 1931. *The Divinity of the Roman Emperor.* Middletown, CT.

Tupet, A.-M. 1976. *La Magie dans la poésie latine.* Diss. Paris. Lille.

Vahlen, J. 1928. *Ennianiae poesis reliquiae.* 3rd ed. Leipzig. Rpt. Amsterdam, 1967.

Valette-Cagnac, E. 1997. *La Lecture à Rome: rites et pratiques.* Paris.

Vasaly, A. 1993. *Representations: Images of the World in Ciceronian Oratory.* Berkeley.

Vessey, D. 1973. *Statius and the Thebaid.* Cambridge.

Vollmer, F. 1892. "Laudationum funebrium Romanorum historia et reliquiarum editio." *Jahrbücher für classische Philologie.* Suppl. 18: 445–528.

Wachter, R. 1998. "'Oral Poetry' in ungewohntem Kontext: Hinweise auf mündliche Dichtungstechnik in den pompejanischen Wandinschriften." *ZPE* 121: 73–89.

Wallace-Hadrill, A. 1997. "*Mutatio morum:* The Idea of a Cultural Revolution." In Habinek and Schiesaro, 3–22.

Walter, U. 2004. *Memoria und res publica: Zur Geschichtskultur im republikansichen Rom.* Frankfurt am Main.

Walters, J. 1998. "Making a Spectacle: Deviant Men, Invective, and Pleasure." *Arethusa* 31: 355–67.

Warden, L. 1980. *Fallax Opus: Poet and Reader in the Elegies of Propertius. Phoenix.* Suppl. Vol. 14. Toronto.

Weinstock, S. 1971. *Divus Julius.* Oxford.

Weische, A. 1972. *Cicero's Nachahmung den Attischen Redner.* Heidelberg.

Welch, T. S. 2001. "*Est locus uni cuique suus:* City and Status in Horace's *Satires* 1.8 and 1.9." *CA* 20: 165–92.

————. 2005. *The Elegiac Cityscape: Propertius and the Meaning of Roman Monuments.* Columbus.

West, M. L. 1973. "Indo-European Meter." *Glotta* 51: 161–87.

Wigodsky, M. 1972. *Vergil and Early Latin Poetry. Hermes* Einzelschrift 24. Wiesbaden.

Williams, G. 1968. *Tradition and Originality in Roman Poetry.* Oxford.

————. 1983. *Technique and Ideas in the* Aeneid. New Haven.

Williams, R. D. 1967. "The Purpose of the *Aeneid.*" *Antichthon* 1: 29–41.

————. 1972. *The Aeneid of Virgil, Books 1–6.* Basingstoke.

Winterbottom, M. 2004. "Perorations." In Powell and Paterson, 215–30.

Wiseman, T. P. 1985. *Catullus and his World: A Reappraisal.* Cambridge.

————. 1995. *Remus: A Roman Myth.* Cambridge.

————. 1998. *Roman Drama and Roman History.* Exeter.

Wooten, C. W. 1983. *Cicero's* Philippics *and Their Demosthenic Model: The Rhetoric of Crisis.* Chapel Hill.

Wyke, M. 2002. *The Roman Mistress: Ancient and Modern Representations.* Oxford.

Yardley, J. C. 1977. "Cynthia's Ghost: Propertius 4.7 Again." *BICS* 24: 83–87.

Zanker, P. 1988. *The Power of Images in the Age of Augustus.* Tr. A. Shapiro. Ann Arbor.

Zehnacker, H. 1981. "Tragédie prétexte et spectacle romain." In *Théâtre et spectacles dans l'antiquité.* Actes du colloque de Strasbourg, 5–7 nov. 1981, 31–48. Leiden.

Zetzel, J. E. G. 1980. "Horace's *Liber Sermonum 1:* The Structure of Ambiguity." *Arethusa* 13: 59–77.

————. 1982. "The Poetics of Patronage in the Late First Century B.C." In B. K. Gold, ed., *Literary and Artistic Patronage in Ancient Rome,* 87–102. Austin.

————. 1989. "*Romane memento:* Justice and Judgment in *Aeneid* 6." *TAPA* 119: 263–84.

————, ed. and comm. 1995. *Cicero, De re publica: Selections.* Cambridge.

Zumpt, A. W. 1871. *Der Kriminalprozess der römischen Republik. Ein Hilfsbuch für die Erklärung der Klassiker und Rechtsquellen.* Leipzig.

GENERAL INDEX

Achilles, 78, 85, 94, 150n7, 151n27
Aemilius Paullus Lepidus, L., 74, 85–86,
    147n34
Aemilius Scaurus, M., 114, 142n10
Aeneas, 11, 51, 99–102, 104–6, 109–20, 124,
    150nn7, 9, 151nn18, 23, 30
Aeschylus, 5, 23, 45, 50, 139n21
Allecto, 51, 120, 140n36
Amatius. *See* Pseudo-Marius
ancestor worship. *See Feralia, parentatio,*
    Parentalia, Lemuria
Anchises, 99, 104, 111–18
Andocides, 130n1
Annius Milo, T., 15, 30–34, 47–48, 135n54,
    136nn56–57, 62, 139n28, 140n32
Antiphon, 130n1, 137n2
Antonius, M., 5–6, 9, 28, 53–56, 58–64, 66–
    70, 76, 141nn5–6, 142n12, 142–43n20,
    143nn22–23, 144n32, 145n4, 151n23
apotheosis, 112
Athamas, 45–46, 50
Auden, W. H., 1
Augustus, 4, 6, 9–10, 35, 51, 55, 57–59,
    68–73, 75–76, 78, 85–90, 93, 95–96, 99,
    102–3, 106–9, 111–12, 115, 117–21,
    124–25, 140n41, 142n12, 142–43n21,
    144n31, 146n28, 147n22, 149n3,
    150n13, 151n23

Bacon, H., 104
Baehr, P., 71
Bourdieu, P., 56, 66–67, 142n8, 144nn27–
    29

Boyle, A., 49

Caecilius Metellus Celer, Q., 20, 22, 28
Caecilius Metellus, L., 55, 63, 133n27
Caelius Rufus, M., 10, 15–25, 27, 29, 78,
    86, 90, 92, 131nn7–8, 133n18, 134n28,
    135nn47, 52
Callimachus, 11, 90–91
Calpurnius Piso Caesoninus, L., 37, 45–46,
    49–50, 141n5
carmina, 8, 15, 26, 134nn38–39, 41
Cassius Longinus, C., 61, 142n12
Catalinarian conspiracy, 37, 44–46
Catullus, 10, 77, 89, 96
Chloris, 79
Cicero: assessment of Julius Caesar, 54–55,
    60, 66, 141n3; characterization of exile,
    46–47; condemnation of Catiline, 17,
    44, 133n17; condemnation of P. Clo-
    dius Pulcher, 29–34, 45–46, 48, 133n16,
    138n14; death of, 38, 69; grief over
    death of daughter, 65–66; *In Pisonem,*
    38, 44, 45, 50, 140n40, 141n5; *In Ver-*
    rem, 14, 38, 49, 50, 56, 133n16, 140n38;
    on magic and superstition, 30, 34;
    mourning for the *res publica,* 64–65; on
    murder of C. Trebonius, 57, 67; perfor-
    mance as Ap. Claudius Caecus, 8, 10,
    13, 15–17, 19–30, 76–78, 80, 82, 85, 87,
    90–92, 134n35, 147n45; philosophical
    views, 15, 30, 33–34, 48, 65, 115, 117;
    Philippics, 9, 14, 53–57, 59–73, 141nn3,
    6, 142n7, 142–43n20; praise for Mar-